A

'Alan Hansen c                                              t is
much more than      . .       , the BBC pundit and *Express*
columnist has more than enough tales to tell from
fourteen seasons at Liverpool. But *A Matter of Opinion* is
precisely that. Hansen shares his thoughts on a variety of
aspects of the game but the spotlight is never more
illuminating than when cast upon himself . . . Now, nine
years after hanging up his boots, the analytical style that
takes a back seat often enough to allow the dry humour to
come through, makes this one of the more readable
football books . . . The thoughts of Hansen are a hit'
*Express on Sunday*

'This new autobiography from the celebrated *Match of the
Day* pundit covers far more ground than his previous
attempt . . . He offers his uncompromising views on the
game today as well as his playing days . . . All in all it is an
enjoyable and frank account of a glorious career'
*Independent* (Read of the Week)

'This book is a great read. Not only does Hansen give an
insight into the Liverpool side which won eight
championships, but in print he combines his trademark
bluntness with a degree of tact few of us ever suspected he
could achieve'
*Glasgow Sunday Herald*

# A
# MATTER OF
# OPINION

## ALAN HANSEN
*with Jason Tomas*

**BANTAM BOOKS**

LONDON • NEW YORK • TORONTO • SYDNEY • AUCKLAND

**A MATTER OF OPINION**
**A BANTAM BOOK : 0553812106**
**9780553812107**

Originally published in Great Britain by Partridge Press,
a division of Transworld Publishers

PRINTING HISTORY
Partridge edition published 1999
Bantam Books edition published 2000

7 9 10 8 6

Set in 11/12½pt Granjon by
Falcon Oast Graphic Art.

Bantam Books are published by Transworld Publishers,
61–63 Uxbridge Road, London W5 5SA,
a division of The Random House Group Ltd,
in Australia by Random House Australia (Pty) Ltd,
20 Alfred Street, Milsons Point, Sydney, NSW 2061, Australia,
and in New Zealand by Random House New Zealand Ltd,
18 Poland Road, Glenfield, Auckland 10, New Zealand
and in South Africa by Random House (Pty) Ltd,
Isle of Houghton, Corner of Boundary Road & Carse O'Gowrie,
Houghton 2198, South Africa.

The Random House Group Limited supports The Forest Stewardship
Council (FSC®), the leading international forest certification organisation.
Our books carrying the FSC label are printed on FSC® certified paper.
FSC is the only forest certification scheme endorsed by the leading
environmental organisations, including Greenpeace. Our
paper procurement policy can be found at
www.randomhouse.co.uk/environment

Printed and bound in Great Britain by Clays Ltd, St Ives PLC

To Janet, Adam and Lucy

# Contents

# A MATTER OF OPINION

# 1 So You Think You Know Me . . . ?

There are two sides to every story. Mine starts with a centre-forward by the name of Billy Whitehurst.

He played for Oxford United in the 1980s and he was no more than a run-of-the-mill striker compared to a lot of men I played against during my 14 years with Liverpool. But Whitehurst, a Yorkshireman who also had spells with Hull City, Newcastle, Sunderland and Sheffield United, was exceptionally strong – he was six feet tall and weighed more than thirteen stone – and he knew how to exploit this. Indeed, because of his power in the air, aggression and courage, he was one of the opposing strikers who frightened me most – and I do mean 'frightened'.

When the fixtures were published before the season, I would usually look at who Liverpool were playing in the first and last matches, and the dates for our matches against Everton and Manchester United, our major northern rivals. When Whitehurst was with Oxford there was only one fixture I was looking for!

I became particularly neurotic about him when we played at Oxford on Boxing Day 1987. We had beaten Oxford 6–0 at Anfield, and it seemed certain that he would not play in the return game because of a facial injury. I couldn't believe it when I saw his name on their team-sheet before the kick-off, and when the teams came out, I was horrified to see the stitches in his face augmented by what appeared to be staples. You didn't need to be a genius to appreciate that Whitehurst might have felt he had some scores to settle. So, this was one occasion when my penchant for settling on the ball went out of the window. Every time I got it, a voice in my brain screamed, 'Get rid of it!' When Whitehurst was in the general area of the ball, it shrieked, 'Don't go near him!'

With Liverpool having established a 2–0 lead, Whitehurst seemed to be getting more and more agitated, which was not good news for anyone in a red shirt, let alone the people with the responsibility for picking him up. However, I thought I'd seen the back of him fifteen minutes from the end, following a collision with a Liverpool player, he went down with a head injury. It caused his wound to open – there was blood everywhere – and the physio who had come on to attend to him said: 'Sorry, Billy, it looks as if we are going to have to take you off.'

Whitehurst just looked up at him and snarled, 'Take me off, and I'll break your ******* neck.'

Without doubt that was among the longest fifteen-minute spells I have ever had on a football field.

Yet no-one would have expected a player with my record to lose sleep over a centre-forward like

Whitehurst. My career at Anfield, from April 1977 to February 1991, spanned the period when Liverpool were the best team in Britain if not Europe. In those fourteen years, there was only one season when Liverpool finished lower than second in the table, and only two seasons in which we failed to land a trophy. Despite being hampered by knee problems, I made 621 appearances and ended up with 17 major club honours to my name. Almost everything we touched seemed to turn to gold – especially in 1984, when we achieved the treble of Championship, European Cup and League Cup, and in 1986 when we achieved the Championship–FA Cup double, with me as captain.

Liverpool's trophy-capturing record in the other seasons I was there was: 1977/78; European Cup. 1978/79; Championship. 1979/80; Championship. 1980/81; League Cup and European Cup. 1981/82; Championship and League Cup. 1982/83; Championship and League Cup. 1987/88; Championship. 1988/89; FA Cup. 1989/90; Championship.

I gained three European Cup-winners' medals, and the only player ever to match my total of eight Championship medals was my Liverpool colleague Phil Neal.

But I *always* had panic attacks against men like Billy Whitehurst because they had the qualities I knew I lacked. My skill might have been greater but they were fearless. It makes me laugh when people talk about how confident I seemed on a football field because the reality is quite different. I suffered badly from pre-match nerves, and found it increasingly difficult to cope with the pressures of playing for a club like Liverpool. I have never been assertive. All my life I have been so scared of failure it isn't true. I've inhabited a world of negatives! 'Conservative' is my middle name.

I could never imagine living anywhere else during the first 22 years of my life in the old Scottish mining village of Sauchie, near Alloa. Even when Liverpool signed me, I found it a tremendous wrench to leave. Now I would have the same feeling if I had to terminate my 22-year residency in Southport.

I must have been one of the easiest players the Liverpool board ever had to deal with. Nobody can say I struck a hard bargain in my contractual negotiations – I accepted what was offered and I never seriously considered going anywhere else. It worked out well for me, through the honours I achieved, and the fact that when I retired Liverpool treated me exceptionally well. However, if anyone were to suggest that I lacked ambition, I would have to say that they had a point.

In my TV career, I could have branched out in a number of ways with programmes people have thought potentially exciting opportunities for me, but my temperament has made it difficult for me to take them up. In my first season of *Match of the Day*, it was suggested I might eventually take over from Des Lynam as presenter. 'I don't think I will,' I said. 'I'll never have the confidence.' As a lad in Sauchie, I found it difficult to have conversations with people I didn't know really well. I even crossed the road to avoid having to talk to someone walking towards me. It was not that I disliked the person, just that I didn't know what to say.

This shyness has also been apparent throughout my

adult life. At Liverpool, I hardly opened my mouth for the first six months. Of course, I was no shrinking violet after that but even then I dreaded the thought of having a change of room-mate for away trips. The problem of mixing with players I didn't know was even more acute when I was in the Scotland squad, and a number of people interpreted this as aloofness. That I have become more outgoing has been down to the influence of my wife, Janet, a more communicative and expansive person than I could ever be.

My relative success in TV has probably come as less of a surprise to her than it has to me because she would be among the first to confirm that I have always been opinionated. Though I was never comfortable with airing my thoughts publicly, I was the opposite when surrounded by my family, close friends and colleagues. With them, I have never been afraid to express strong views. It is something I inherited from my father, John – the most opinionated person I have ever come across outside football!

My father, now 72, was also a central defender and played in amateur football in Scotland. Like me, he can argue about the game until the cows come home. It makes for a lot of fun – if that's the right word – when we're together. I've tried to mellow as I've got older. Whenever I become involved in a conversation about football, I give myself a little warning about the need to keep my cool and take on board what the other person has to say – but before long I find myself trying to force my opinion down people's throats. I can get quite het up at times. This is obviously a big plus for my employers at the BBC – being prepared to say what you think and occasionally crossing swords with people like Des Lynam and other pundits is 'good television', as they say. But the irony of my *Match of the Day* role in analysing the performances of teams and players – and particularly my views on where they might have shot themselves in the feet – is that *I* never took criticism at all well when I was a player!

I hesitate to use the word 'paranoia', but when it came to football pundits putting me under the microscope, I was nothing if not hypersensitive. This is not unusual among successful footballers. Generally, the more accomplished a player becomes, the more touchy he is likely to be about people finding fault with him. In my case, even a comment that might have been deemed totally innocuous by most people would touch a raw nerve. And my photographic memory has proved a mixed blessing: while I can vividly remember all the great moments that came my way, equally clear in my mind are the times when it was suggested I had erred.

It is indicative of the extent to which players care about what is said and written about them – and especially my own need to be given plenty of recognition – that I still wonder if I was given as much credit for my ability as I deserved!

Among the experiences that caused me to feel like that was the general reaction – or lack of it – to my performance in Liverpool's 1–1 draw at Manchester United in the 1984/85 season. It was the last season in which I was able to get forward whenever I wished, before my knee problems forced me to curtail this aspect of my game – and it was one of my best seasons for Liverpool. I played as well in that match at Old Trafford as I've ever played. After the match the Liverpool chairman, John Smith, came into the dressing room. While he was there, with Joe Fagan and the coach, Roy Evans, Joe turned to me and said, 'Alan, that was the finest performance I have ever seen from a Liverpool defender, and I have seen a few.'

I went home elated, told Janet what Joe had said, and we couldn't wait to get the newspapers the following day to see what they had made of my performance. We bought them all, and not one mentioned it. My central-defensive partner, Mark Lawrenson, attracted a lot of praise, and I could hardly begrudge him that because he was a fantastic player and we had combined well together. But I had played out of my skin too. The Monday papers didn't mention it either. I thought, Well, that's newspaper pundits for you. It sums up how little they really understand what goes on during a match.

When I got to Anfield, I bumped into Roy Evans in the treatment room, and he said, 'I bet you got every paper, didn't you?'

'Too right I did,' I said, 'and I won't be getting them again!'

Although I produced the best form of my career that season – Joe Fagan described it as 'awesome' – I did not win the Professional Footballers' Association or Football Writers' Association Footballer of the Year award, which went to Everton's Peter Reid and Neville Southall respectively. Not only that but another Everton player, Kevin Ratcliffe, pipped me for a place in the all-star First Division team of the year – the only time I failed to get the necessary votes for inclusion in the side. I even got into it in 1982/83, my worst Liverpool season.

I would be fibbing if I said I don't regret never getting my hands on one of those Footballer of the Year awards, but I do feel that such awards can be misleading: they usually go to players in the teams who get the most media coverage. In those days, there was nowhere near as much football on TV as there is now, so opinions about a player were often shaped by what people read.

Kevin Ratcliffe was a tremendous player, and in that 1984/85 season Everton – having spent years in Liverpool's shadow – won the Championship and European Cup-winners Cup double. We didn't win anything, but I still found it difficult to accept that Kevin had performed better than me. Obviously, I wouldn't have dreamed of saying so publicly, but at the risk of being considered a bad loser, I have to concede now that I thought it.

It was the same when I came runner-up in the Football Writers' Association Player of the Year poll, in 1986 and 1990. The 1989/90 season – my last – was very special for me. To be captain of another Liverpool Championship-winning team was a massive end-of-career bonus, given that I was 35 and had been out of action the previous season for nine months due to injury. I felt I had an exceptional season.

However, it was another Liverpool player, John Barnes, who won the FWA's Player of the Year award, even though he had played better in previous seasons than he did in 1989/90. I just felt – and still do – that many of the southern reporters who had voted for him based their view largely on what they had seen of Liverpool in their away matches, on grounds where my ability to involve myself creatively in the play – the most impressive aspect of my game – was inevitably less pronounced.

Football is a game of opinions, and as I have got older and have been able to take a more detached view of my career, my opinions about myself have tended to change. In some ways my self-esteem has increased. When I was playing for Liverpool, I knew I was good, but I never thought I was the best. It was only when I stopped playing and compared myself with other central defenders in Britain that I started to see myself in a different light. I wish I had rated myself more highly during my career because, leaving aside the obvious dangers of putting oneself too much on a pedestal, I think that that confidence would have made me an even better player.

Even now, though, my appraisal of myself can tend to be quite negative. Although I have tapes of all the big tele-vised matches I played in, I have never sat down and watched more than a handful of them: I hate the way I look when I run. While I was often described as 'elegant' when I was running with the ball, I always felt that when I didn't have it my running style was the exact opposite. I am not too keen on the way I speak either. When I started on *Match of the Day* Clive Tyldesley advised me, 'You should tape the programme, and study your performance every week.' But every time I did it, I cringed. As I said to Clive, 'If I watched myself every week, I might never do the programme again!'

## 2 'Do I Not Like That'

If Alan Hansen the television pundit had observed Alan Hansen the Liverpool player, he would have drawn your attention to the following faults.

For a start I couldn't tackle. That might seem an exaggeration, but it wasn't too far off the mark if you compared this aspect of my game with that of other defenders. When it came to winning the ball in a direct challenge with someone, I wasn't even in the top half of the table – and if I had to get my body into a position to block the ball, I was even lower. Moreover, despite my height (I'm six foot two), I was no more than average in the air, especially when I faced a strong physical challenge. Indeed, in terms of my general approach to the game, my level of determination and aggression left a lot to be desired.

I often joke about my deficiencies. For example, when people ask why I was not as good in the air as they might have expected from someone of my height, I begin by recounting how I was badly concussed once while attempting to make a headed clearance in a testimonial match at Shrewsbury. The floodlights there were not the best and I accidentally made contact with the mud-covered ball with the back of my head instead of my forehead. What a state I was in. I was dazed for four or five days, which ultimately made me think about what it must have been like for players who were heading in the days when the balls were heavier. It also made me think of what some medical experts have to say about the dangers of heading – so to those who argue that I wasn't dominating enough in the air, my tongue-in-cheek defence is, 'I'm told that you lose 150 brain cells every time you head the ball so I tried to avoid it.'

While I talk a lot on television about the importance of qualities such as character and the will-to-win, I don't think I epitomized these attributes when I started at Liverpool. Even at the end of my career there, when I had become conditioned to the determination that has been central to the club's success, I don't think you could put me in the same class as my inspiring former Liverpool colleague Tommy Smith. I was once talking to Roy Evans about this, and I said to him, 'I never had a big heart.'

He didn't see it that way: 'Well, I think you did because you've had bad knees for as long as I can remember, and look how many games you played.'

Still, while accepting that there are more ways than one in which a player can show such characteristics, I never had any illusions about myself. Suffice it to say that the old motto 'When the going gets tough, the tough get going' is inclined to make me feel slightly embarrassed. Whenever I hear that, I think back to a bitterly cold night in Turin in 1984, when Liverpool, then the European Cup holders, were beaten 2–0 by Juventus, the European Cup-winners Cup holders, in the European Supercup final. Six inches of snow had fallen on the city when we arrived the night before, and parts of the pitch were frozen solid when I went out for my pre-match warm-up. After a couple of minutes, I'd had enough, so I returned to the dressing room and sat in the corner, shivering.

'You're going to love this match, aren't you?' joked Joe Fagan, the manager.

'Too right I am,' I said, playing along with the wind-up. 'This is the finest night of my life, this is.'

At that point, our right-back and captain Phil Neal came through the door. 'What a pitch – great!' he said. 'Some of those Italians won't fancy these conditions.'

Joe and his first-team coach, Ronnie Moran, just looked at me and smiled.

Nobody was more surprised than me when Kenny Dalglish, Joe Fagan's successor and a close personal friend, made me Liverpool captain the following season. Although I spent time with him socially, Kenny gave me no inkling of this: not once did he say, 'Do you fancy being captain?' or 'I'm going to make you captain.' He just sprang it on me, 10 minutes before we were due to take the field for a pre-season game at Brighton at the start of his reign as manager.

He turned to me and said, 'You take the ball,' and I said, 'I don't take the ball.' He thought it was a wind-up. 'You taking the mickey?' he asked. I explained that I never went out with a ball, and he said, 'I want you to go out with the ball as captain.'

If he had given me time to think about it, I might well

have said I didn't want the job. In terms of my idea of what a captain should be like, I was never one. The true captains are those who, when you're a goal down, will try to lift the team even if they're having a bad time themselves. I was a great captain when we were 3–0 up and I was playing well. In that situation, what a leader I could be!

As far as my technical ability was concerned, my pace and anticipation, two of the key points of my game, were not always enough to enable me to do my job properly. I remember our League Cup final against Arsenal in 1987, when the Gunners equalized as a result of my failure to deal with two crosses from Viv Anderson. With his first cross, the ball went through my legs as I ran towards him in an attempt to block it; I failed to block the ball a second time as it came back to him and he set up Charlie Nicholas for the finishing touch.

There were other central defenders who would have dealt with the situation more aggressively – and effect-ively – than I did. I am convinced Arsenal would not have scored that goal if Colin Hendry had been in my shoes because he was tremendous at getting in the way of crosses and shots. As it turned out, Nicholas went on to score again to give the Gunners a 2–1 victory.

Another challenge I remember – or would prefer to forget – came in a match at Watford, when I gave chase to a player who had burst through from the halfway line and gained about six yards on me. I knew I had the pace to catch up with him before he could manoeuvre himself into a shooting position. Instead, though, I attempted a sliding tackle, missed the ball and he went on to stick it in the net. In my defence, it was a period when I was having a bad time at Liverpool, and I had lost a lot of confidence. However, Bob Paisley gave me the most stinging rebuke I have had from any manager when he told me, 'That was a coward's tackle.'

It was quite rare for me to be on my backside. Defensively, my game was all about jockeying people, and nicking the ball from them rather than steaming into them. I felt I always had to keep on my feet. It became something of an in-joke in the Liverpool dressing room. After a match, the cleanest things among the pile of players' kit in the middle of the dressing room tended to be mine. Someone would pick up a spotless pair of shorts and say, 'These must be Al's.'

In view of this, there are no prizes for guessing that I was never sent off, and hardly ever booked – most managers would say that this is a ridiculous record for a central defender. Also, while a lot of centre-halves have almost as many facial scars as Henry Cooper, I am virtually blemish free. I do have one prominent scar on the forehead just above the bridge of my nose: it didn't come from any bruising encounter with a centre-forward but a collision with a plate-glass panel at the entrance to a youth club in Stirling when I was 17. I was late for a volleyball match, and as I was running into the club, the light made it virtually impossible to see the glass. I smashed straight into it, and ended up needing 32 stitches in my head and a similar number for gashes in my left leg.

At the hospital shortly after the accident, a doctor spent something like two and a half hours trying to stop the bleeding. At one point, he went off for a coffee, and I got up to have a look at myself. I fainted. It was when they got me back on to the bed that I saw my brother John. He was a great help. His first words to me were 'Brain of Britain!'

I sued the local authority for damages, and received only £700. That was down to my honesty in saying yes when the Edinburgh specialist who examined me was sticking needles in me and asking whether I felt anything. I should have got more than £700, especially as the scar on my forehead becomes embarrassingly noticeable in harsh weather conditions.

I was careful to avoid similar physical damage at the hands of opponents on a football field. I was not a weakling – I had enough strength to get my body between an opponent and the ball and hold him off – but when it came to the really bruising bodily contact, my attitude to whoever I was playing against was 'You don't touch me, and I won't touch you.'

There were some players you could not intimidate even if you had wanted to do so. Rumbustious forwards like Joe Jordan at Leeds and Manchester United, Gary Thompson and Cyrille Regis at West Bromwich Albion (and, of course, Billy Whitehurst!) were so strong and single-minded they seemed to run straight through you. I have often thought I should have waved goodbye to such strikers and gone to play in a country in which the game was less physical than it was in England. However, I think I would have suffered from stress wherever I played.

Even in my present *Match of the Day* role, I get very tense sometimes. Janet says to me, 'Try to relax.' But I say, 'How? If I knew the secret to that, I wouldn't have suffered so much when I was a player.'

The stress of playing for Liverpool was immense. I loved being with the rest of the players for training sessions during the week, and I loved playing. Yet the build-up to matches – and especially the period of 45 minutes or so before the kick-off – were purgatory. The amazing thing was that when I stepped out of the dressing-room tunnel, all the anxiety evaporated. I thought, Where's it gone? It was bizarre. I wish I could have felt like that in the dressing room. I hid it well – the only real giveaway was the number of visits I made to the toilet. But when I was sitting in the dressing room, people would look at me and think I didn't have a care in the world. Billy Joel was one of my favourite singers, and I would be sitting humming one of his songs and reading a newspaper. But inside I was a bag of nerves, and the older I got, the worse I was affected. The high expectations of the club and the fans wore me down. By the time I was ready as a player to call it a day, I felt like a nervous wreck.

Managers have become increasingly switched on to this in recent years. Take Glenn Hoddle, and his decision to bring his faith-healer friend, Eileen Drewery, into the England set-up in the belief that her counselling skills could help to make his players more relaxed and confident, as well as improve their physical well-being. Hoddle was lambasted by the media over this policy and, indeed, it contributed to his eventual downfall. I felt that, providing Hoddle did not force his players to seek Ms Drewery's assistance or make them feel that they needed to do so to be favoured by him, there was nothing wrong with it. If players decided they might benefit from a consultation with her, I would have been the last person to knock the idea. When I was a player, the vast majority of us were sceptical of such outsiders. I remember being told about the assistance Tottenham tried to give their team through the noted sports psychologists John Syer and Chris Connelly. Just before they were due to take the field, players were apparently told, 'I want you to put all your doubts and fears into a box, lock it and throw away the key.' It was perhaps typical of the puerile mentality of professional footballers then that the idea was dismissed with derision among those with whom I discussed it.

However, I now appreciate why more and more current players are taking the 'mental' side of the game more seriously nowadays – it would certainly have been an advantage to me to have done so. All players suffer some degree of anxiety, and I can understand how some attempt to escape the pressures by turning to drink, gambling or drugs – or, like Paul Merson, all three. One of the problems is that because they are at work for just two or three hours each weekday, they have plenty of time to dwell on their troubles. Outside Liverpool FC, I was able to immerse myself in my family life. Each day it was a bonus for me to be at home when my children – Adam and Lucy – returned from school. I cherished seeing so much of them when they were growing up.

Yet the accumulative effect of those football pressures got to me. I was not only 'gone' physically (because of the wear and tear on my knees) but mentally. I think I knew I'd had enough of professional football during the summer break before my last season, when I started drinking more alcohol. I was alarmed to discover that instead of drinking my usual pot of tea at lunchtime I was having a couple of pints of lager. Most people would not think twice about something like that, but I felt that for someone like me, a creature of habit who thought nothing of having a few drinks on two or three nights of the week but never during the day, the change was significant.

I feel awkward using the word 'pressure' in relation to playing professional football. As a lot of people will point out, 'How can you be under pressure when you're being paid for enjoying yourself? A guy who is unemployed and has three kids – he's the one under pressure.' I can see that, obviously. But, because of the expectations, being with a club of Liverpool's stature was never an easy ride. To claim that players shouldn't allow this to affect them is a bit like saying that players should never fail to score in a penalty shoot-out.

Liverpool were used to winning trophies. They were elated when they had them in their hands but, at the same time, they were always conscious of the need to keep the players' feet on the ground. The first Championship I won with Liverpool was the 1978/79 title, when we scored 85 goals and conceded 16, and we lost only four matches. It was a fantastic record, but the manner in which it was celebrated was understated. You needed to have played in at least 13 matches to qualify for a Championship medal. When the title was clinched, and we were drinking champagne in the dressing room, Ronnie Moran came in holding a box. 'Right,' he said. 'Who's played thirteen games?' He delved into his box, took out the medals and tossed one to each player who put his hand up, as if he was just handing out sweets.

I just expected a greater measure of pomp and ceremony

than there was. Liverpool's message to the players seemed to be, There's no point getting carried away – it's your job to win trophies.

One of the Liverpool dressing-room sayings then – and I use it a lot on TV – was, 'First is first, and second's nowhere.' In other words, winning was everything. This was instilled into everybody at the club, and if you didn't have that attitude, you were quickly out of the door. That's where the pressure came in. You knew that your run of success was bound to end some time. You knew you couldn't go on for ever. I carried the additional burden of knowing that I was far from my best physically because of the wear and tear of playing in so many matches, which explains why, when the curtain came down on my playing career, I was not interested in becoming a football-club manager. I'd had enough of the pressurized existence that revolved around a Saturday football result.

I was never offered the Liverpool job, although everybody assumed that I would be. What happened was that when Kenny resigned, the local radio station announced that I was 6–4 on favourite to succeed him. Before long, people seemed to look upon it as a *fait accompli*. Even my family were arguing about whether I should accept the post. My father and brother felt I should – they were repeatedly on the phone urging me to have a crack at it – while Janet just said, 'You do what you think is right for you.'

I went to see Tom Saunders, the Liverpool chief scout, who was looked upon as something of a guru at Anfield because of his knowledge of every aspect of the club, and asked, 'Am I in the frame for this job?'

He confirmed that I was, and I said, 'Well, will you go and tell them [the Liverpool directors] that I don't want it?' He said it would be better if I told them myself, so I had a meeting with Peter Robinson, the most prominent member of the board, and told him exactly what I had told Tom. He said, 'Fair enough,' and it was left at that.

There is still an element of disappointment in my family over the decision, not least from my two children. Adam and Lucy are both Liverpool fans – especially Lucy who, like thousands of other teenage girls, is an avid Michael Owen fan. But I knew what I was doing. I knew that Liverpool could not dominate the game for ever, and it suited me to quit while I was ahead. When people ask if I 'bottled' it, I say, 'Too right I did.' I had seen what football management can do to people.

It is an incredibly tough job and even the calmest, most philosophical of men can be badly affected by the stress. When Arsene Wenger became manager of Arsenal, my colleagues at the BBC all remarked that he seemed different from a lot of British managers. He was university-educated, articulate and, above all, the epitome of calm. Nothing seemed to fluster him. However, when you saw him in the dug-out eighteen months down the line, you got a different picture of him. There was one match when I thought, The tension's got to him – he's gone.

Des Lynam summed it up when he observed, 'Well, he's got the British bug, hasn't he?'

The effects can be frightening. Perhaps the most salient example is Brian Clough, whose life in recent years has been beset by drink and health problems. Even when he appeared to be in peak condition, you could argue that he would have been well advised to stay clear of any manager's post. He did some strange things at times, as I found while I was walking down the players' tunnel at the City ground, for the half-time break in Liverpool's European Cup first-leg tie against Nottingham Forest in 1978. Cloughie, immediately behind me, tried to needle me by prodding the back of my leg. He did it two or three times, and each time I just turned around and glared at him. Neither of us said a word.

All of which leads me to suggest that if you're still sane after ten or twenty years in the job you've done well. So many things can go wrong – so many things that are out of your control – which would never appeal to me. Basically, I wanted to keep my hair relatively black. Also I had a lot of friends in that Liverpool dressing room and I'm not sure that I'd have been able to separate myself from them as their boss.

You have to be ruthless to be a manager. In his autobiography, Graeme Souness put it this way: 'I have come to the conclusion that nice men do not make good managers.'

Kenny Dalglish once told me, 'When you have to make a hard decision, one that is going to upset someone you like and respect, it makes it easier if you think that your family's well-being is depending on it.' It was great advice, but whether I could ever have applied it in managing a football club is another matter.

As a player, I was generally able to push aside my worries when I stepped through the front door of my home, but I think it becomes more difficult when you're a manager. I also think that Kenny, and a lot of other managers, is obsessed with the game in a way that I could never be. When I did my 1997 BBC television documentary about managers and their way of life – *The Sack Race* – it struck me that even when we were off camera all the managers I interviewed just wanted to talk about football.

Kenny's knowledge of teams and players is remarkable, which is not surprising considering the number of matches he watches. He has the most sophisticated of satellite TV systems at home, and he hardly misses a televised match in the world. He eats, drinks and sleeps football. One reminder of his insatiable appetite for it came when he was Newcastle's manager, and I stayed at his house in the North-east after accompanying him to Glasgow to watch the Celtic–Liverpool Uefa Cup tie in September 1997.

It was about 1 a.m. when we got back, and all I wanted was a quick cup of tea and then to go to bed. Kenny, though, switched on the TV, and clicked through the channels to find a game – any game – to watch. The more channels he flicked through without finding one, the more determined he became.

I learned a lot from my involvement in *The Sack Race*. In addition to Graeme Souness and Kenny, the other managers I interviewed and spent some time with included Jack Charlton and Bobby Robson – vastly experienced as club managers and as managers of the Irish Republic and England national teams, respectively – and Barry Fry, one at the 'have-nots' end of the scale. My overall impression of the lives they have led in the job was that they must be little short of masochists to do it.

Managers tend to be as competitive as they were as players and the buzz they get from competing is like an addictive drug. It is a dangerous buzz for managers because, unlike the players, their influence on performances and results is limited. I wasn't 'hooked' because I looked upon football as a job of work and distanced myself from the more extreme aspects of its competitiveness. But Bobby Robson needed his 'fix' of football, and football management. You would have thought that he had experienced more than enough stress in one lifetime as manager of the England team, a post which is fast becoming almost impossible to handle because of the criticism – not to mention personal abuse – from the tabloid media when things are not going well.

Bobby, like his successors, Graham Taylor and Glenn Hoddle, was put under enormous pressure and the strain showed. There were times when he appeared on the verge of breaking point. But after his spells as a coach abroad with Porto and Eindhoven Bobby jumped back into the high-pressure pot as manager of Barcelona – one of the biggest clubs in the world – at the age of 60! The stress level at Barcelona was no lower than it had been when he was in the England job. The Catalan club, renowned for making life difficult for its managers through its internal politics, were not doing as well as had been expected and there were numerous reports that Bobby would be sacked or moved into a different role. When I met him in his Barcelona office for *The Sack Race*, the thing that struck me most about him was how edgy he seemed. As we were discussing the questions I intended asking him, he got players' names wrong – which is characteristic of Bobby when he is stressed. Then, as he was about to pour the coffee, he knocked over the pot and the cups. I thought, He's a bag of nerves – we're never going to get any good material out of him.

As it happens, we did. The longer I spent with him the more relaxed he became. Finally, I asked him why such a battle-fatigued man as himself was managing Barcelona. Bobby smiled and more or less confirmed that he found the excitement impossible to resist. He made it all sound like a test of his courage. Referring to his decision to move to Barcelona, he told me, 'When I'm seventy-five, at least I'll be able to look back and say that I didn't "bottle" it.'

Little wonder that Bobby was even happy to become Newcastle's manager this season.

It is a similar story with Graeme Souness, who was in charge at Southampton when he appeared in my documentary. In his previous job as manager of Liverpool, Graeme had undergone a triple heart bypass operation, then suffered a relapse as a result of an infection caused by his attempting to exercise back to fitness too quickly. I visited him in hospital at that time and was stunned by how bad he looked. When I returned home, I said to Janet, 'There's no way he's going to go back into football,' which only goes to show the difference between Graeme and me in our attitudes to the game. I told Graeme he must be crazy to subject himself to the 'drug' of football management again, after what he had been through, and he didn't disagree.

I'm sure that he will have remembered our former Scotland team manager, Jock Stein, who collapsed and died of a heart attack at 62, at the end of the vital 1986

World Cup qualifying tie against Wales at Ninian Park, Cardiff, in September 1985. Neither Graeme nor I was in the squad for that incredibly tense match (a 1–1 draw that put Scotland into a play-off for a place in the Mexico finals with Australia) but it was no secret that Stein hadn't been in good health for some time. Doubts as to whether he could cope with the strain of football management had dated back some 10 years, to the day he almost lost his life in a head-on car crash. On top of this, it was common knowledge that he had heart problems. On the day of the Wales game, there had been much comment at the squad's base in Bristol that he looked unusually pale. In an interview Stein gave a week or two before his death, he was asked whether he had contemplated retirement. He replied that he could not imagine what he would do without the excitement of being involved in football: 'For me, there's no life after football,' he said. 'No life at all.'

When I pointed out to Graeme that the excitement of football management might eventually kill him, his reply was similarly poignant: 'But I need it.'

Barry Fry is another present-day manager with a history of heart trouble. We filmed him in the dug-out during a match, but to appreciate fully the extent of his emotional involvement in the game all you really needed to do was close your eyes and listen to the number of times he screamed and swore. I would place him right at the top of the expletives table with Peter Reid, who also turned the air a particularly deep shade of blue when he was featured in the TV documentary series about Sunderland's Premiership relegation plight a few seasons ago.

Not all managers lose control of themselves. Blackpool's Nigel Worthington is apparently one of the strong, silent types. However, when the local newspaper arranged for a doctor to assess his inner turmoil during a match against Preston – through a pulse monitor strapped to his wrist – the rise in his heart-rate whenever Preston scored was likened to that of 'someone suddenly confronted by a gunman while shopping in a supermarket'.

Even allowing for a degree of exaggeration in that opinion, my views on the manager's lot are best summed up by the immortal words of Graham Taylor: 'Do I not like that?'

I was very fortunate in that I was reasonably secure financially: unlike many other players, I was not forced to remain in the game for the money. As we have seen, several become managers or coaches for the enjoyment they get from the game, but for others it is a question of Hobson's choice.

In recent years the number of managerial responsibilities has been reduced as clubs have got bigger and more multifaceted. They are not so much football clubs now as business empires, and a manager who in the old days would have run the whole show has become just the head of a department. With transfer negotiations and players' contracts handled by the chairman or chief executive, the manager is free to concentrate on the football side. However, I still don't think the post is attractive.

The financial gap between the haves and have-nots of English football, between the likes of Manchester United, Arsenal and Liverpool and the rest, has become wider than ever. There are perhaps no more than a dozen clubs in the whole of English football in which the manager has what I would consider a reasonable chance of success at the top level. It is said that managers have to learn their trade in the Nationwide League lower divisions, or in non-league football, but I think that any former top-class player prepared to do that must be off his head.

If you fail to make an impact as manager of a club with massive financial resources, at least you know you've failed because you're not good enough. For me, that's much more acceptable than failing because of a lack of money. The methods needed to achieve success with the clubs in the lower divisions are different, and if I were in that position, I would not know where to begin. Even in the Premiership, it seems to me that a number of managers are knocking their heads against a wall.

One who clearly enjoys management is Dave Bassett, whose ability to make bricks without straw has led to a number of unlikely success stories, the most notable of which was his feat in steering Wimbledon from the old Fourth Division to the First in four seasons. As manager of Nottingham Forest, Bassett led the club to promotion to the Premiership in 1998, but had to cope with the loss of his top scorers – Pierre van Hooijdonk, who walked out, and Kevin Campbell, who was sold by the board (reportedly against Bassett's wishes and without his knowledge) while he was on holiday. Equally revealing about Bassett's struggle to ensure Forest's Premiership survival was that he had less money to spend in the transfer market than most of the other managers. However, none of this seemed to count for much in the eyes of his employers in January 1999 when, with Forest

at the bottom of the table – which most people had anticipated before the start of the season – he was sacked.

As an effect of a club's current expectations, I found
Bassett's fate frightening. He had built up an impressive
CV in management, so I can never visualize him
struggling to find another club. But what must it be like
for the men who are just starting a managerial career? As
Coventry's Gordon Strachan has said, 'The name of the
game is building up the right amount of knowledge and
expertise – it's all about survival. You just hope that your
inexperience, and the mistakes you make as a consequence, will not rebound on you too heavily.'

Strachan rightly singled out the experience of my
former Liverpool colleague Steve McMahon to illustrate
the problems that confront managers in the cash-strapped
lower echelons of professional football. Because of his
playing background, Steve was looked upon as one of the
most promising managers in the game when he joined
Swindon in November 1994, the season after their
relegation from the Premiership. But after four tough
years there – in which Swindon dropped into the
Second Division in 1995 before bouncing back to the First
Division in 1996 – the strain seemed to have worn him
down. Steve decided to leave Swindon, apparently
because of the effect his job had on his home life. The
club was £5 million in debt by that time, and Steve
had been taking so much flak from the fans that his
family had moved back to Southport. 'It saddens me that
it has come to this, but something had to give,' he said. I
take my hat off to him. He showed tremendous strength
of character as a player but it still amazes me that he lasted

there so long. I probably wouldn't have lasted five minutes.

I have had a couple of other opportunities to take the football-management plunge, with Manchester City and QPR. The approach by City, after the sacking of Brian Horton in 1995, came as a result of a conversation at a race-meeting between the club's then chairman, Francis Lee, and Kevin Keegan. They were discussing contenders for the job when Kevin, then Newcastle's manager, said, 'Why don't you go for Alan Hansen? He's said he doesn't want to go into football management but, then, I took that stance before the Newcastle post was offered to me, so you never know.'

When Francis spoke to me I told him: 'I'm flattered, but I'm not interested in going into management in the slightest.'

Strange as it might seem, managing a club like Manchester City would probably have appealed to me more than managing Liverpool, perhaps because a club in the state that City were in at that time could only improve! I remember making the point to my father-in-law the following day when we were discussing my decision. He must have thought I'd lost my marbles when I said, 'It's a dream job. If I were interested in being a manager, I'd have taken it like a shot.'

QPR, the smallest of the three clubs who showed an interest in me, made their approach via my BBC colleague Trevor Brooking after they had parted company with Ray Wilkins in 1996. During a visit to Loftus Road, Trevor, the former West Ham and England midfielder, was asked by a QPR official whether he would sound me out on their behalf. Here again I had no hesitation in saying, 'Thanks, but no thanks.'

What has happened to me since my retirement from the game has confirmed that my decision to steer clear of football management was the best I could have made.

Kenny has told me that one of the reasons why he chose me as Liverpool captain was that he has always considered me a lucky person. You only have to look at the breaks I've had to appreciate that his observation is spot on. In that light, I was interested to read a newspaper interview with Andy Gray, in which Andy, referring to his own switch to a television career, commented, 'My friends always say I'm the luckiest person they've ever met, and I wouldn't argue with that. How else do you explain the fact that at thirty-three years of age, you're sitting at home waiting for the phone to ring – and it isn't ringing – wondering where the next penny is coming from when suddenly the phone does ring? But it isn't a football club wanting to take you on as a player, it's a TV producer who wants you to front a new show.'

When I retired as a player, I didn't have a clue what I was going to do next. I was naïve enough to think that, because I was famous in the game, I would be inundated with offers. In fact, when Janet and I discussed the situation, I said, 'It's just a question of wait and see. For the next six months, this phone is not going to stop ringing.' I was wrong.

I started looking for work. Having already carried out one broadcasting assignment, as a match summarizer at a Liverpool game for Radio 5, I was alerted to the possibility of work with BSkyB when Andy Gray left to join Ron

Atkinson at Aston Villa as assistant manager. I thought, You have to do something – why not have a go at this and see what it's like? My new proactive stance paid off. I contacted Richard Keys, the BSkyB football presenter, and he approached the producer. The result was a six-month trial for me.

Even then, it never struck me that this could lead to the sort of TV career I have today, which to some extent I just fell into. But I also fell into my football career.

# 3 Addicted to Golf

The title of this book should really be *How to Become a Professional Footballer Without Really Trying*.

To play football for a living is a dream shared by millions of boys, and only a tiny percentage are able to bring the fantasy to reality. I was different. I never thought about becoming a professional footballer – if anything, I wanted to be a professional golfer.

That is not to say that I didn't get a lot of enjoyment from the game as a schoolboy. As a spectator, my favourite team was Rangers, while the England team I favoured was not Liverpool but Manchester United. As for the Scotland team, I was thirteen when I saw them play at Hampden for the first time, in a 2–1 win over Austria in a World Cup qualifying tie in 1968. But the biggest thrill I got was when I saw Bobby Moore playing for England against Scotland in the 1–1 draw at Hampden in the same year. That was a European Championship qualifying tie, and though Moore was not the most popular figure among Scottish crowds – with his blond hair and cool, composed style of play, they viewed him as the archetypal English poseur – I was captivated by him. No matter how much pressure he was under at the back, he always seemed to have enough time and space to do whatever he wanted. To me, the way he played was what the game was all about. It was certainly the way I wanted to play, but I don't think I even got close.

Outside playing for my school and my local boys' side, Sauchie Athletic, I spent countless hours taking part in impromptu games with my friends – games where you used jackets as goalposts and nobody bothered about the number of players you had on either side – and when I came home from school at four o'clock, I would go out by myself with a ball and kick it against a wall.

It isn't like that now. Schoolboys have so many more distractions than I had when I was in my teens in the mid-1960s, which is surely one of the main reasons why the standard of players coming into the game appears to have dropped. You cannot teach a lad of 18 how to have a good right or left foot, how to control the ball and pass it: these attributes have to be learned well before then. In the past, youngsters acquired them by playing and practising.

A lot of coaches in their fifties and sixties will tell you that with virtually all of the great players of their generation, their success was founded in the hours they spent playing football in the streets. It was an important part of the culture of working-class lads. However, the increase in road traffic and the omnipresence of office and residential developments have made street football largely extinct. Still, although much is said about so-called 'gifted' teenagers who have been lost to the game, I believe that the really talented ones emerge eventually.

My own case bears this out. My parents, who keep all my football memorabilia at their Sauchie home, still have a letter I received from Liverpool after I had a week's trial when I was 15. It came from the chief scout, Geoff Twentyman, and said simply: 'It was decided after trials that you did not reach the standard required.' This wasn't Geoff's opinion. He hadn't seen me and was heeding the recommendations of the Liverpool coaches who had supervised those trial games. Ironically, Geoff kept closer tabs on me when I was with Partick, and if anybody was instrumental in bringing me to Liverpool in 1977 it was him.

Still, there's no way I can criticize those who prompted that thanks-but-no-thanks letter to me six years earlier.

Until I was 14, I was quite small and tubby, but then my growth pattern changed dramatically. I got much taller and ridiculously thin. I was like a wet lettuce – I remember my PE teacher putting me into the 400 metres at my school sports day, and me giving up at the halfway stage. Anyone watching me might easily have had the impression that I wasn't strong enough. At 20, I had reached my full height but weighed no more than eleven and a half stone. It was only when I was at Liverpool and got my weight up to thirteen stone that I began to look like a professional footballer.

On my first day on trial at Liverpool, I had found the training so hard that at the end of it I was 'gone'. I did not do myself justice at all. The worst moments came in a match against another club's A team, a side so combative and rugged that the only benefit in playing against them was that I developed a reasonable ability as a hurdler. No wonder the Liverpool coaches weren't impressed.

My lack of physical prowess might go some way towards explaining why I was never chosen for the Scotland under-15 and under-18 squads. I took part in trial matches but, as is so often the case at this level, skill on the ball was deemed less important than athleticism. From the age of 10, I had played regularly for my county side – but I feel duty-bound to point out that Clackmannanshire is the smallest county in the United Kingdom. I also have to concede that I was not committed to football. In fact, I had the wrong attitude to a lot of things.

My mother, Anne, who had a part-time job in the local Co-op, still laughs over some of the wheezes I got up to to avoid hard work. She liked making bramble jam, and when I was seven or eight, she offered me sixpence to pick a bucketful of blackberries for her from a field close to our home. I took the money, but the prospect of being scratched while ferreting around in the bushes did not appeal to me so I secretly filled up my bucket with the berries she had previously collected. I was a resourceful lad.

My mother wasn't the only person to find out that I didn't have the makings of a good employee. Between the ages of 10 and 16, I had a paper round, and needed to get up at seven to have enough time to do the job and catch the eight fifteen bus to school. It was a balancing act I rarely managed, and the paper round was a particular problem on a Sunday when I would think nothing of lying in bed until lunchtime. A number of people in Sauchie tended to receive their Sunday papers on Monday.

I can't say I worked very hard at school either. My reports from Lornshill Academy in Alloa tended to be punctuated with words like 'lackadaisical' and 'casual'. The general conclusion was that while I had the ability to do well academically, I needed to apply myself better. That summed it up, really, especially when I was in the fifth and sixth forms and treated the 'free' study periods as an opportunity to enjoy myself with my friends.

My 18-year-old son, Adam, who is reading economics at Warwick University, is much more conscientious than I was. When he came home from school you never had to push him to do his homework. He doesn't get that from me.

From 16 to 18, I went through what can best be described as a rebellious phase. I was part of a small class group who took nothing seriously. To us, everything was a laugh. I have often thought that some of the things we got up to in class – taking the mickey out of people and generally fooling around – was the perfect rehearsal for being in a football dressing room.

I blame this on Lornshill Academy: they had great sports facilities, and made it very hard for me not to spend virtually all my free time using them.

When I reached the fifth form, my height led me into volleyball. I was a member of the school team, which reached the national championship finals two years in succession; I was selected for the East of Scotland team to face England at Meadowbank, and I was included in a training programme for the full Scotland squad. When I reached the sixth form, I was playing squash on the school court three or four times a day – before my first lesson in the morning, at lunchtime, and during periods set aside for revision. But I don't think I've set foot on a squash court more than half a dozen times since.

I emerged from my misspent youth with seven O levels and four A levels – in history (my favourite subject), English, maths and Latin – but this was principally because of my photographic memory. At Liverpool, my recall of past players and matches prompted team-mates to refer to me as 'The Memory Man', and it was a great advantage at school. In the build-up to exams, my ability to memorize things after reading them just once or twice got me out of all kinds of difficulties. It came in particularly handy for A-level Latin. In the section where you had to translate Latin into English, I did it by having memorized *en bloc* all the relevant chapters in the set textbook.

Things came easy to me out of the classroom, too, and that includes sport. I enjoyed playing football but my number-one sport was golf. Outside my family, it is perhaps the only aspect of my life that could be truly described as a passion.

The only explanation I can give for this is that when it comes to sport I have always been very competitive, and golf – which is, arguably, the hardest sport of all to master – best stimulates this side of me. Golf constantly frustrates you and, for me, that is the beauty of it: you know that you may be very good one day and very bad the next. Even today, while I realize that I can never hope to be as good at golf as I was at football, I haven't stopped trying.

The encouragement to play football stemmed largely from my father, who earned his living as a long-distance lorry-driver and then as a haulage company transport manager. As he and my mother had both left school at 14, the thing they wanted most for me and my older brother and sister was a good education. They are immensely proud that Maureen gained an MA in English at Aberdeen University and that John and I, while not following in her footsteps, were academically bright, too.

My parents are a solid, working-class couple who lived for many years in a council house. As you would expect of two people who have devoted so much care and attention to their children, they derive enormous contentment from the happy families and professional lives that Maureen, John and I have created for ourselves. Maureen, who lives in Aberdeen, was an English teacher before she started a family, while John, who lives in Surrey, is a regional director with the Abbey National. Of course, for my father, John's and my footballing careers have been a bonus.

For some time, all my Liverpool medals were kept in an old box at my parents' house, and my mother was so proud that she showed them to everybody. I don't think there is a person in Sauchie who hasn't been invited to the house to see them. The medals would still be there but for the shock my father had when he discovered how much they might be worth, when Ray Kennedy's collection was auctioned and fetched more than £90,000. As my medals were not insured, my father insisted that they be put in a secure place – in the Liverpool FC museum. But much remains for my parents to show their guests: I should imagine that they have every newspaper or magazine article ever written about me, not to mention countless photographs.

My parents weren't the only family members to take an avid interest in John's and my football fortunes. The others were John McDonald, my father's uncle, and John Gillon, my mother's brother. Two larger-than-life characters who never believed in doing things by halves, they were prepared to go anywhere to watch me in action. They were my personal fan club.

John McDonald, whose ownership of a thriving dry-cleaning business in Alloa made him the most affluent member of our family, hated it when newspapers misspelt our names. The papers referred to my brother as 'Hanson', until they received a letter from Uncle John pointing out their error. If he showed that level of interest in John, whose football career was comparatively limited, imagine how much he showed in me: throughout my Liverpool career, he had a subscription to the *Liverpool Echo* – he actually received a copy every day.

In my early days at Liverpool, my father and John McDonald would come to see me in Saturday home matches. After a while, they would make a weekend of it, staying in Preston on the Friday, with me on the Saturday, and go back on Sunday. They probably got to know more people at Anfield than I did. Even when I go back there now, people ask, 'How's your dad and uncle John?'

Both uncles saw no reason why everyone else shouldn't share their enthusiasm for their nephew – and at times went over the top. John Gillon, a miner with a wonderful singing voice, must have bored people to death talking about me and showing them pictures. If ever I was in his company, I would say to him, 'Look, I don't want you telling anybody who I am, right?' He didn't take any notice. You could bet on him disappearing after five minutes then bringing someone back with him and saying, 'I want you to meet Alan Hansen, my nephew.' John McDonald, who died a few years ago, was just as bad. My brother is fond of recalling the 'fan club's' train journey to London for the 1978 Liverpool–Bruges European Cup final at Wembley, when he told him, 'You stay with us all the time – don't talk to anybody.' But he let him go off to get a sandwich, and when Brother John went looking for him, half an hour later, he found our uncle holding court about me with a large group of supporters. Later, at the club's post-match reception, when he was reminded to keep a low profile and stay with the group, he went missing again. This time, though, he came back of his own accord – arm in arm with Bill Shankly.

While it was a boon to have such loyal support from people whose hearts were in the right place, I was not comfortable with it. I probably felt a little embarrassed for my brother's sake about the attention I got. He has said that, compared to me, he was 'just a runner'. But if anyone deserved recognition it was him. Arguably, I went further in the game than I deserved; for John it was the other way round.

In the early days, my attitude must have caused no end of frustration to my father. While John was bursting to play, and go as far as he could, I was ambivalent. If it could have been possible to combine the two of us – John's determination with my talent – the result would have been a footballing dream ticket. My father felt that the standard of football in which I was playing was too low for me and that if he could get me up to a higher level I might become as fired up as John. Needless to say, it was a pretty tough struggle for Dad.

My father once played at non-league level – 'junior' football, it's called in Scotland – as a centre-half. He jokes that he could have got a lot further in the game than he did, except that he lost his hair when he was in his early twenties, on National Service overseas, and looked older than he was. However, as a player, he had one claim to fame: in 1952, aged 27, he was a member of the Falkirk team, Camelon Juniors, who reached the final of the Scottish Junior Cup for the first time. They played against a team in which the goalkeeper was the father of Gordon McQueen, the former Manchester United, Leeds and Scotland centre-half, and they lost 1–0. You can understand why the experience is embedded in my father's memory: the match was played at Hampden Park and attracted an attendance of 72,000.

In one of his favourite anecdotes about the occasion, he tells us that he and the other players were expecting a crowd of just a few hundred, and in the dressing room before the game, he and the other members of his half-back line were playing dominoes. 'How naïve we were,' he says. 'We just didn't realize how big an occasion it was. Someone looked at his watch and said, "Shouldn't we start to get changed?" Just imagine what we felt like when we went out for the pre-match warm-up and saw the packed terracing.'

When I had my first game at Hampden, for Scotland, he reminded me, 'All I got at the end for playing there was twenty-five pounds and a meat pie!'

In both football and golf, my brother John, five years older than me, blazed a trail for me. His path to the professional game, which also began with Sauchie Athletic's under-16 and under-18 teams, was big news in the village. The only previous player of note to have been born and raised there was Willie Morgan, the former Burnley, Manchester United and Scotland winger. John seemed set for a similarly successful career.

He joined Partick at 17, largely because the club was prepared to accommodate his academic ambitions. He had previously had a successful trial with Aberdeen, but turned down the chance to start his career there because he could not find a course at Aberdeen University that would have allowed him to continue with his football. At Partick he could carry on with his studies at Alloa Academy, especially as it was anticipated that it would be a couple of seasons before he was ready for a regular first-team place.

John was a striker then and initially played up front in Partick's reserve team. However, he made his début for them – at 17 – at centre-half, and it was at right-back that he achieved the most success. To my father's delight, I not only followed John to Partick – aged 18 in 1973 – but played with him in the same Partick team for four years.

One of the main differences between us is that John is more placid than I am – playing alongside me, he needed to be. We still joke about an incident in a Scottish Cup match against St Mirren, when I gave him the shock of his life by playing the ball back to him when he was standing on our goal-line, with two opposing players on him. Not surprisingly, he took an almighty swipe at the ball and hoofed it down the park. Then I said, 'Why didn't you just bring it down and play it?' He wasn't amused, especially when I added, 'You'll have to learn how to play this game.'

I know I'm prejudiced, but having watched him in action for Partick since I was 15 or 16, I thought he was an excellent player. Not for nothing did Partick appoint him captain when he was only 22. While he might be the first to concede that he was not the most skilful right-back in the world, I cannot think of many defenders who were quicker than him, and it is even harder to recall those who were fitter. Indeed, his fitness was something of an obsession with him and he was prepared to try anything to keep it up. When he was about 18, he was influenced by a book in which the former Motherwell, Rangers and Crystal Palace centre-half Roger Hynd explained that he had become 'hard' by sleeping on the floor and eating three raw eggs for breakfast each morning. For a year, John did the same.

John also preceded me in the Scotland Under-23 and senior teams, of course. He made the first of his two senior international appearances under the management of Tommy Docherty in a European Championship qualifying tie against Belgium at Aberdeen in February 1971 – the match in which Kenny Dalglish also made his Scotland début. He was drafted into the pool because of an injury to David Hay, and with Scotland needing to protect a 1–0 lead, he was brought on for the Celtic winger Jimmy Johnstone for the last ten minutes.

That was probably John's best-ever season because his other highlight was that Partick, then newly promoted to

53

the old First Division, produced one of the greatest achievements in their history by beating Celtic 4–1 in the League Cup final. I was sitting just above the players' tunnel at Hampden, and John says that his most vivid memory of the events after the final whistle is the beam on my face as the team went up to collect the trophy and their medals. He still says that he has never seen me so excited about anything before or since.

The irrepressible Docherty loved him. Whenever I run into him now, the first question he asks is, 'How's John?' The feeling was mutual. The Doc has been one of the most controversial figures in the game but John has always felt that, in his honesty with the players and his motivational ability, Docherty was the best manager he ever worked with. He would have relished being with Docherty at club level – and probably would have made it but for injuries.

Shortly after John played in his second international (again as a substitute) against Yugoslavia in the 'mini World Cup' competition in Brazil in the summer of 1972, Docherty left the Scotland job to become manager of Manchester United. There was speculation that he might sign John, but he bought Alex Forsyth, the other Partick full-back in the Scotland squad. Many believe the decision came from doubts over John's recovery from a cartilage operation. He had had it just two months before the Scotland squad were due to leave for Brazil and, perhaps typically, caused further knee damage by trying to get back too quickly. Instead of going ahead with a second operation immediately, he elected to remain in the squad and take whatever playing opportunity was offered. He was nowhere near 100 per cent fit when he was brought on as a sub against Yugoslavia, and inevitably did not do himself justice.

Though John continued as a key player for Partick, things went from bad to worse for him injury-wise. He underwent five operations, three in two years, and with his knees in even worse shape than mine – he had lost all his cartilages and had had surgery on his cruciate ligaments – he was forced to retire at 29. He spent eight years as Partick's financial director, and his present position with the Abbey National involves the supervision of staff in almost 150 branches. However, as might be expected of someone whose football career was cut short prematurely, John still misses the game – and I think he finds it disconcerting to hear me say that, apart from the camaraderie of the dressing room, I don't. Having achieved at Liverpool almost everything it was possible for me to do, my attitude is, 'That's past – finished, I have a new life now.' For John, the sense of unfulfilment might have faded, but I don't think it will ever be driven out of his system completely.

I also followed in John's footsteps on the golf course, the course in question being Schawpark, which is little more than a stone's throw from my parents' house and is flanked by the Sauchie Athletic football pitch. If there was the equivalent of Alcoholics Anonymous for people addicted to golf, then I would be in it. My introduction to golf came at the age of eight. My brother, too, had become interested in the game at that age, and I used to follow him around the Schawpark course, pestering him. Usually, he was patient with me, although once I nagged him so much that even he cracked. He whacked me over the head and an elderly gentleman came over to remonstrate. John said, 'It's OK. He's my brother.'

John and I both had a lot of help from a friend of Dad's, Andy Garvey. A keen golfer himself, he lived across the road and took John and me under his wing. Before long, I was spending almost all of my spare time on the golf course – I was hardly ever off it in my school holidays. Even when I was studying for my A levels, I would come back from school at lunchtime and play golf for the rest of the afternoon.

Junior members of Schawpark were not allowed to play there on Saturday, so until I became a full member at 16, I played football instead – for my school on Saturday morning and for Sauchie Athletic in the afternoon. The school team was run by Jim Cousins, a former Falkirk player who knew the game inside out. Another enjoyable aspect of being involved with the football in Sauchie was that it brought me into contact with Hamish Mitchell and Jimmy Miller. They ran the two football clubs in the village – Sauchie Athletic and Sauchie Juniors – and, like so many with enthusiasm to burn for the game at grass-roots level, they were great characters. My closest boyhood friend, George Ramage, also played in their teams, and whenever we get together now, we can amuse ourselves for hours with anecdotes about the pair.

Jimmy was the archetypal old-school football supporter: he loved to see the ball being whacked up the park and players chasing it Charge-of-the-Light-Brigade fashion. His attitude to my style of play was: 'You've been watching too much TV, son.' He was also great at dressing-room one-liners.

One player had been given a lecture by Jimmy on how he could do better and asked the old man, 'Jimmy, have you ever played the game of football?'

Quick as a flash, Jimmy retorted, 'Aye, son, and I was like you . . . I wasn't any good at it either.'

Jimmy, who was also a Partick scout – hence my arrival there at the start of my professional career – could keep you entertained for hours with his reminiscences and his views on politics, life, everything. Yet I don't think he has been outside Scotland more than twice in his entire life, once when he came to Liverpool in my benefit year to appear in a mock *This Is Your Life* show set up by my testimonial committee. With Kenny Dalglish also taking part, Jimmy walked up to the  microphone and said, 'There are two people here tonight who have managed Alan Hansen – and the jury is still out on who did it better!'

Hamish was cast in a similar mould. Like Jimmy, he was a straightforward guy who loved his football to the point where if his team were beaten it was as if his whole world had collapsed. He had no great tactical or coaching knowledge; for him, it was all about effort. 'Come on, son, give us a bit extra,' he would shout.

When I was old enough to play golf on Saturday, something had to give – and it was usually Sauchie Athletic. I decided to pack in football twice, when I was 15 and again at 17, and only played if my arm was twisted. It was handy that the Sauchie Athletic pitch was right next to the golf course when it came to playing both sports on the same day. It was not unusual for me to finish my round of golf, get changed into my soccer kit and be brought on for Sauchie as a substitute. John used to refer to me as 'Roy of the Rovers', because of the number of times I came on and had an influence on the pattern and outcome of the game. I know it wasn't right to be given such preferential treatment – it even happened once in a Cup final – and I would have been seething had I been the player who was replaced.

Even when I was a part-time professional at Partick, golf was probably the most important part of my life – so much so that I had no compunction about playing even on a match day. For one end-of-the-season game, with Partick in a safe mid-table position, the players were told that they could be at the ground later than usual, at two fifteen instead of eleven o'clock. I used the extra time to play in a competition at Schawpark. Absolutely crazy.

In my defence, I like to think that my addiction had a positive effect on me as a person. Notwithstanding that John and I were brought up with good values by our parents, I'm sure that our interest in golf was another key factor in helping to keep us on the straight and narrow as boys. A golf course is a controlled environment, and the strict etiquette of the game means that if a youngster steps out of line, there is no shortage of people prepared to pull them up.

I won a number of trophies in local competitions, and I played for the Clackmannanshire men's team at 15. I was the same age when I shot my best-ever Schawpark score – a three-under-par 69. The next year, when I had a handicap of two, I reached the last 16 of the Scottish Boys' Championship and came seventh in the Scottish Stroke-play Championship. On the strength of those achievements, I was selected as first reserve for the

Scotland team in a boys' international against England at Moortown, Leeds. It was around this time that the idea that I might be able to earn a living from playing golf took root.

However, it coincided with another opportunity to forge a career in football, this time with Hibernian. Eddie Turnbull, the manager and one of the most respected figures in the Scottish game, invited me to train with them for three or four weeks in the close season. Most lads would have snatched his hand off, but I said, 'I'll train for the first week but then I'm playing in the Scottish Stroke-play Championship.'

The training was nothing if not gruelling: on the second day, I was so tired that on my way home I fell asleep on the train, and eventually got off not at Stirling – the mainline station closest to my home – but some 40 miles further down the line at Perth. On the Friday, though, Turnbull offered me a contract. 'I don't want to be a footballer, I want to be a golfer,' I told him. 'If the worst comes to the worst, I can always play junior football.'

He told me it would be a big mistake for someone of my potential to play in part-time professional football. 'Be sensible,' he said. But my mind was made up.

The next time I came across Turnbull I was playing at right-back for Partick in a reserve match against Hibernian the following year. The amusing thing was that, during the game, the guys on the Hibs bench kept shouting to the player I was marking, 'He's a lazy so-and-so. Take him on! You'll murder him!'

Nobody could accuse me of being lazy on the golf

course, but after the trial with Hibs, I was forced to accept some harsh truths. From 16 to 18, I felt it essential to get my handicap down to scratch, but no matter how much I practised it remained at two. Also, instead of going further in top competitions, I seemed to be slipping back. The crunch came in the next Scottish Boys' Championship, when I was knocked out in the second round. I badly wanted another chance at this level, but my eighteenth birthday came before the Stroke-play event so that was the end of the road for me in boys' golf. I knew then that golf did not come as naturally to me as football. It was time, therefore, to switch my attention to football. And even then, other options still got in the way.

My first idea had been to take a degree in history at Aberdeen University. I had passed the necessary exams and was offered a place on the course. However, because of my interest in sport, friends persuaded me that I might be better off doing a PE course at Jordanhill College. It was a great idea, except that Jordanhill took only one pupil from each school and I was one of five applying from Lornshill Academy.

To be accepted at Jordanhill, you undergo a physical test and two interviews. The first part of the physical involved getting from one end of the gym to the other by stepping into hoops. It looked so easy. I can't go wrong here, I thought, but it was more difficult than it looked and I knocked the hoops all over the place. I failed even more miserably on the tasks that followed. In one section of the test you could choose particular skills to demonstrate. Each carried a certain number of marks, depending on its level of difficulty – for example, you could get a maximum of 10 marks for a back-flip off a beam, three for a wrestler's bridge and one for a forward roll. I felt confident about doing the latter two, and plumped for the wrestler's bridge because it carried the higher number of marks – but I was hopeless at that too.

Things looked up when I attended my first interview. The guy looked down my list of sporting achievements, and said, 'You'll have no problem getting in here whatsoever.' Unfortunately for me, however, the next interview focused on my academic achievements, and had to be backed by a report from my headmaster and PE teacher. I knew the headmaster would not go overboard in his praise, but neither did the PE teacher; he was in charge of the school volleyball team and maybe had taken a bit of the needle with me when I stopped playing for his side on a Sunday in favour of golf.

So there I was, out of school and looking for a job.

Within a few weeks of my getting the brush-off from Jordanhill, a friend who was then at the start of a successful career in the building trade – Billy Fullerton – found me some work on a building site. I was part of a gang converting and restoring council houses which introduced me to such duties as sweeping up after the bricklayers and joiners, and burning off old floor tiles. That it wasn't quite the life I had in mind was emphasized one day when I took a break from scorching tiles off the wall and fell asleep. I would probably have got away with it – but the blow torch was on the floor and I had forgotten to switch it off. I was awoken by the smell of smouldering wood and promptly sacked.

Enter Partick Thistle FC. Their manager, Davie

McParland, had been interested in me for a while and it was my good fortune that, shortly after the rejection by Jordanhill, I played for Sauchie Juniors in a friendly match against Partick. It was quite a big occasion for me because John had just gained his first Scottish cap with Partick. It was also my first game for ages and I had not even been training. But although Sauchie were beaten 5–1, I did well enough for Partick to offer me a part-time professional contract. Even then, I wasn't sure that this was what I wanted to do or what I should do, but with nothing else in the offing, my father was becoming exasperated. I had promised McParland that I would let him have a decision by the time of the May bank holiday weekend, and my father, who was planning to take Mum away for a break, told me, 'When I get back, I want to hear that you have accepted Mr McParland's offer.'

In fact, when they returned, the first thing my father asked was, 'Have you signed for Partick?'

When I said yes, the next question was, 'How much will they be paying you?' I couldn't answer that – typically, I had forgotten to ask.

My wages were actually £12 a week, which forced me to keep looking for a daytime job. But the one I found – with General Accident at £28 a week – turned out to be as unsatisfactory for me and my employers as the building work had been. There were only a couple of other lads in the office, and with all the mickey-taking that went on, it was not unlike being back at school. I knew nothing about motor insurance and the lads who did would disappear at lunchtime, leaving me to deal with enquiries on my own.

It was a nightmare. People who telephoned for quotes

were rarely prepared to ring back later, so I virtually had to make them up. The trick was to avoid giving them figures that were too low, which would have landed me in trouble when they were about to sign on the dotted line. I was on safer ground by giving them quotes high enough to ensure that they would not be in contact with us again.

I can't think of anything in that place I took seriously. One way in which I amused myself was to hide the office girls' lunchboxes. They had the last laugh, though: one day before I was due to play for Partick, they tricked me into eating a laxative chocolate bar, with the inevitable consequences.

Apart from all the laughs, I hated the job with a vengeance. Amazingly, though, despite my being little short of a liability in that office, General Accident did not sack me. Instead I resigned after about six weeks and never bothered to look for anything else. I vowed never to set foot in another office.

# 4 The Fun Game

Professional footballers are a laddish breed and in the dressing room of a football club they can – and do – become kids again. It's a bit like belonging to a social club, and when your membership has expired, it's as if a big hole has appeared in your life. You tend to miss it even more than playing.

Dressing-room humour is based on mickey-taking, and though generally it is all given and taken in a good spirit, you learn quickly that if you're not on your toes all the time, you're liable to be verbally destroyed. It is difficult to go into details about this aspect of professional football life without making it sound too infantile. Janet shakes her head in despair when I reminisce about it – she thinks it's just too childish. But some of my happiest moments as a professional footballer came in the laughs I shared with my colleagues off the field, and I found this one of the major attractions in playing for Partick Thistle. In fact, I would have been content to stay with Partick for the rest of my career, had they been able to match the money that Liverpool or another big club could offer me.

I am not saying that Firhill Park was some kind of holiday camp – it was far from that – but while they are located in the so-called football hotbed that is Glasgow, Partick Thistle's status as one of the small clubs preserves them from much of the hysteria that surrounds Rangers and Celtic. Partick is a homely little club without an enemy in the world. In some ways, their image is similar to Chelsea's in the decades before their emergence as one of the Premiership's super clubs.

You can understand why Chelsea's chairman, Ken Bates, once bought a controlling interest in Partick. Like Chelsea, Partick are a 'West End' club. Like Chelsea when they were the butt of comedians' jokes in the 1950s because of their unpredictability, Partick have a reputation for having had players who were great 'characters'. In the old days it was often said that if you wanted to see something different you went to Partick. The best way I can sum them up is that, like me, they did not take themselves too seriously.

Although my brother John, one of my Partick teammates, was nothing if not intense about his football, even he got caught up in the dressing-room fun. Instead of protecting his kid brother from the wind-ups, he took the view, 'It's every man for himself.'

One player who tended to be ribbed more than most was Bobby Houston, a right-back or right-side midfielder. He was so neurotic about his performances that after every match the first words he uttered in the dressing room were, 'How did I play? Give me marks out of ten.' Anyone who knows what cruel pranksters team-mates can be will understand why the other players rarely gave him more than five, and sometimes it was only one or two. You could see it bothered him – 'Was I that bad?' he would ask earnestly – but he carried on setting himself up for this.

Every newcomer to Partick was subjected to some April Fool-type initiation ceremonies. The most common involved one player stretching out his hands and another – the new boy – attempting with his eyes closed to bring his own hands up and down between them without touching them. The new lad would be told, 'This is the way they assess your sense of balance in America. The world record is two hundred and forty strokes. See how many you can manage.' We would let him get to, say, 30, cheering every successful stroke he had made, then everyone would slip out of the room and leave him making those strange chopping motions on his own. Another favourite ruse was to tell the new player a joke, in the company of all the others, which had no punch-line. The new guy, mystified that everybody was laughing, would ask for the joke to be repeated. This time, he would laugh too, for fear of being made to look foolish. Pathetic it might have been, but it's amazing how many players fell for it, and strange the extent to which you can miss such silly things when you are no longer in the game.

In those days, I was very headstrong. Nobody could tell me anything – I thought I knew it all. Of course, I listened to the senior professionals at the club, but if they drew my attention to anything they thought I had done wrong during a match, I would be inclined to dispute it. It was a similar story in my relationship with Bertie Auld, who was the manager for most of my time there.

Bertie succeeded Davie McParland at the start of my second season at Partick. As a player himself – an astute midfield play-maker noted for being combative – he had been one of the stars of Celtic's 1967 European Cup-winning team under Jock Stein. You might say that his blend of skill and steel made him the Graeme Souness of his day. As a manager, Bertie, like Graeme, was not a man to mess with. However, being the stubborn nonconformist that I was in those days, I was prepared to take the risk of incurring his wrath.

In fairness, I was not the only one who rubbed him up the wrong way. Another was Alan Rough, the Partick goalkeeper who also became my team-mate in the Scotland Under-21 and Under-23 sides, and in the senior Scotland team. In maintaining the reputation of Scottish keepers for eccentricity and fallibility as effectively as anyone, Alan epitomized the notion that you need to be crazy to fill the position. He was a born comedian and always had a group of players sitting with him, listening to his stories. The jokes he told were chronic but, as Frank Carson would say, the way he told them was hilarious. Some of the things he got up to were mind-boggling. Among his favourite acts was to stop people in the street and ask them, with a stutter, for directions. As for his foot-balling ability, he had superb reflexes, but was awful on crosses: when the ball was played quickly into the middle, he was in trouble. That was why he never played for one of the bigger British clubs, although he played 53 times for Scotland, which was then a record for a keeper. His temperament was both his strength and his weakness. He never took things too seriously. Even if he was having a bad time, he seemed not to have a care in the world. There's a lot to be said for being like that in professional football, although Bertie Auld did not think so. Alan drove him up the wall.

Bertie thought I was lackadaisical, but compared to Alan, I was as uptight as they came. However, while I think Bertie admired my talent, there is little doubt that my rather casual style irritated him. Bertie had no time for pranks: he was too concerned with the business of football. When Sheffield Wednesday's manager, Danny Wilson, contemptuously labelled some of his foreign stars 'Fancy Dans', after Wednesday's Worthington Cup defeat by Third Division Cambridge in September 1998, I remember thinking, That's how Bertie Auld looked on me.

The fans loved to see me going forward and dribbling past opponents – there were games in which I was like a deep-lying forward working through the middle – and that was the way I most wanted to play. In common with other observers, Bertie didn't think I was aggressive enough, and seemed to take it as a personal slight that I continued to play the game my way not his. In fact, the only time I showed the 'fire in the belly' he was looking for from me was when I accidentally kicked a winger called Arthur Duncan in a match against Hibernian at Easter Road.

The other reason why that game stands out in my memory is that I scored possibly one of the greatest own-goals of all time to give Hibs a 2–2 draw! Duncan cut the ball back superbly from the left and, with our defence wide open, I elected to play it safe by side-footing it past the post. I hit the ball beautifully, exactly as I wanted to hit it — but I got my bearings slightly wrong and it went inside the post. For the next five minutes, I was engulfed in a red mist. It wasn't just anger, I was seriously confused. I couldn't understand how I'd made a mistake like that. I'd lost it completely, which is how I came to batter Duncan. I tried to make a tackle as he burst through, but completely mistimed the challenge and nearly broke his leg. In view of the force with which my studs caught him in the shin, it was a miracle that he was able to get to his feet after treatment and continue. I was fortunate that I was only booked.

Not surprisingly, I was immediately surrounded by Hibernian players threatening to rearrange my features. However, on reflection, I think everybody appreciated that this sort of tackle was out of character, as Hibernian's Scottish international defender John Blackley later acknowledged when he gave me a friendly wink, as if to say, 'I never thought you had it in you.'

There weren't many friendly winks from Bertie Auld, who apparently believed that the best way to manage a football team was to be tough and uncompromising. We had a lot of set-tos, the biggest of which came during the last of my four seasons at Partick, the 1976/77 campaign. It arose partly because he gave me a long run of matches in midfield, a position I hated. This was something of a U-turn for me, as I had happily played most of my matches for Sauchie Athletic in midfield, and when David McParland told me that he saw me more as a central defender, I had thought he was wrong. 'A central defender has to tackle, and I can't do that,' I said.

However, once I settled into the position, I realized that I was the one who had been wrong. During the periods when I was deployed in midfield at Scottish League level, I found I did not have the physical power for the amount of running necessary in that area of the field, and that when I was on the ball in tight areas, my height also counted against me. Unlike smaller players, I was inclined to appear slow or lazy or both. Also, instead of putting me in an anchor midfield role, just in front of the defence, Bertie used me as an attacking midfielder, in a sort of inside-right role.

I can see where he got that idea from. I made useful forward runs as a central defender, and Bertie reasoned that if I played up the field, I could capitalize on the diagonal passes of John Craig from the left side of midfield. The brother of the former Sheffield Wednesday and Newcastle player Tommy Craig, John was an excellent passer. But midfielders have to do much more running off the ball than central defenders, and when it came to getting on the end of John's passes, I was no Bryan Robson. After making two or three of those runs, I was on my knees.

Bertie and I also clashed over his assertion that I had not been aggressive enough in a match against Kilmarnock in October 1976. Although we won 2–1, Bertie told me that instead of training on Monday night – the first of the three evenings I had to spend at the club each week – I would have to turn up on Monday morning. I refused on the pretence that I had a job interview then. When I arrived on Monday night, he told me he was going to fine me £10 and that I would have to train with the reserves. From that point, we both dug our heels in and all reason went out of the window. When I came in the following evening, instead of in the morning, I was again informed that I would be fined, and banished to the reserves. This was followed by the Hansen drama-queen act: I walked out of the club and told Bertie that I wouldn't play for him again.

It became a matter of principle: I felt that Partick wanted things too much their own way. When I had joined the club, I had been persuaded by David McParland to sign a part-time professional contract on the understanding that if I failed to make the grade, I would have my job to fall back on. In those days, around a quarter of the Partick playing staff were part-timers, and while the full-timers trained four or five mornings a week, the part-timers did so on Monday, Tuesday and Thursday evenings. The club only went full-time at the start of my second season there but, oddly, reverted to part-time for my fourth, even though they had gained promotion to the Premier Division. By then, the number of part-time players had risen to around three-quarters of the staff.

I was not complaining about the money I was getting – a basic wage of £50 a week plus a £20 win bonus. Though this could not compare with what I earned at Liverpool from 1977 – initially a basic salary of £7,500 – it was probably more than the average wage in Britain at the time. However, I was becoming increasingly aware that I needed more, and what Partick paid me did not adequately reflect what they were beginning to demand from me.

However, my departure from the club was short-lived.

We were due to play Rangers at home that Saturday, and at lunch-time on Friday I received a telephone call from Partick's general manager Scot Symon – the legendary former Rangers manager – asking me to attend a meeting with Bertie and himself the following morning to sort out the dispute. And that's what we did. Bertie and I both conceded that the rift had been six of one, half a dozen of the other. We beat Rangers 2–1, and later Bertie could not resist the temptation to say, 'You see, you *can* play in midfield.'

Nor could I resist the temptation to have the last word. 'That's not the point,' I replied.

Playing for a club of Partick's modest stature and limited financial resources had its drawbacks. Clubs at this end of the scale inevitably put the emphasis on saving money, and while there is nothing wrong with that in principle, it is taken occasionally to the extreme. Partick's determination to cut costs when I was there extended to insisting that anyone who wanted steak for the pre-match meal the club organized on away trips would have to pay for it themselves, and they took liberties with the allocation of players' match tickets. John and I were en- titled to two tickets each, but, because we were brothers, Partick – or, rather, Bertie Auld – argued that for the most popular fixtures our combined total should be reduced to three. The majority of the players accepted stunts like that because, as part-timers, the money they earned from Partick represented a nice bonus on top of what they pulled in from their jobs. Although they all moaned about Partick's 'penny-pinching' and Bertie's abrasiveness, no one rocked the boat. But I did not have a job.

Despite all this I have never lost sight of what I owe to Partick — and to Bertie, even though I thought some of his training and coaching methods were quite bizarre. Whenever I come across my former Partick team-mates, the subject invariably gets around to the ways in which Bertie tried to get the best out of us. For instance, he decided that we would play a pre-match practice game — without any opposition. We had lost four games on the trot, and when the players arrived at the ground at eleven o'clock on the Saturday morning, Bertie said, 'I've been thinking about our pre-match training, and I've devised a new plan.' He went on to explain that he would pick the team for the match in the afternoon, and that the side should work together — in a 4–4–2 formation — on some basic attacking moves. It started with a move from the kick-off, with Bertie laying down instructions for the ball to be played back to one of the central midfielders, then to one of the full-backs, who had to drive it down the line for the midfielder on his side of the field to take it to the crossing stage. 'It's simple,' Bertie added.

Simple? What Bertie overlooked was that a straight pass down the touchline — in this case a pass of some 40 yards — is much more difficult than it seems because the player making it has such small margin for error. Also, if he screws it up the first time, it tends to get worse and worse. Needless to say, that manoeuvre was a farce — we would probably not have got it right if we'd been trying it all day. It was followed by something even more astounding. The three or four players who had struggled most in the 'game' were dropped from the side. Just imagine the conversations they might have had with their friends and families on Saturday night.

'Why didn't you play today?'

'I was dropped.'

'Why?'

'I played badly in the practice game.'

'Who were you playing against?'

'Nobody.'

This is even more pertinent in the case of Bob Paisley, who gave me my first-team chance at Liverpool at 22.

Being able to establish myself in the Partick and Liverpool teams so early was a major factor in my development. Because of the high number of foreign players who have come into British football in recent years, I think it would have been a different story for me if I had been at the start of my career today. It is difficult to dispute the view that the foreigners are stifling the progress of the home players, and that this is bound to have an adverse effect on the standard of our national teams. At the last count, some two hundred players from outside Britain were with Premiership clubs – around half the total – and that is surely far too many.

There were no foreigners in Scottish football when I started my career with Partick and, of course, I was also fortunate that the club had a comparatively small first-team squad.

When Partick's central defender and captain, Jackie Campbell, was unable to play due to injury, I was given my first-team début in a League Cup tie against Dundee. I was 18 and it was a couple of months after I had signed for the club. It was a personal disaster because we were beaten 4–0 and their fourth goal stemmed from me dwelling too long on a short goal-kick from Alan Rough and being dispossessed. The error was typical of someone as inexperienced as I was, and with my background of doing exactly as I pleased with Sauchie Athletic. But these are the things you learn from as a youngster in first-team professional football: the more you play at that level, the quicker you develop.

My only other first-team match that season was in October, when I came on as a sub in a 3–1 defeat by Clyde. Over the next three seasons, though, I was in the side most of the time. Partick were in the old First Division when I arrived and our failure to finish in the top 10 in the 1974/75 season (when we were thirteenth) meant that we missed out on being included in the inaugural Premier Division. Yet we won the First Division title in the 1975/76 season, finished a creditable fifth in the Premier Division the next season, when I played in every match, and by the time I moved to Liverpool, I had Scotland Under-21 and Under-23 caps to my name.

I made my Under-23 appearance in my second season at Partick, in the win over Sweden at Gothenburg – when Alan Rough was also in the side – and played for the Under-21s in a win over Romania in Bucharest shortly afterwards. On that occasion, in addition to Rough and myself, our Partick colleague Joe Craig was also in the team.

Some time later, immediately after I signed for Liverpool, I was a member of the Scotland Under-21 team for an eight-nation tournament in Toulon. We didn't do very well, losing three of our four matches and finishing sixth, but I emerged with the plaudit of the competition's most 'elegant' player. There are no prizes for guessing what Bertie Auld made of that!

In fact, it might have surprised a lot of people, bearing in mind that 'elegance' is the last characteristic you might expect to find in Scottish football, even in the Premier League. The game north of the border is possibly the quickest and most physical in Europe, so I'm quite proud that my talent – and especially my control and passing – shone through. Jackie Campbell, who played at Partick for many years, paid me one of the greatest compliments I have ever had when he said that in these aspects of the game I was far in front of anybody he had ever worked with.

People claim that the Premier League, in which teams play each other four times in a season and therefore get to know much about each other's strengths and weaknesses, militates against players developing their skills. While this format was badly needed to make the game there more competitive, it is argued that it has become too competitive.

I do not go along with that. For me, the most skilful players will stand out in any environment, although I have to agree that the extent to which they are able to do so in Scotland depends more on their fitness and strength than it might in other countries. Even when Partick were a part-time club, the training to which Bertie subjected us was probably harder than that at a lot of full-time clubs. It was definitely harder than the training at Liverpool, especially in the close season. At Liverpool, players had greater licence to do the work that suited them. The management's attitude was almost, 'You train as hard as you want to train. You know how fit you need to be.'

Under Bertie's management at Partick, the set-up was much stricter and more regimented. If he was not satisfied with what we were doing in a training session, he was quite capable of stopping it halfway through and making us start all over again. This often happened with a routine that involved placing 10 cones around the pitch, with the players having to sprint to the first, jog to the next, and gradually increase the number of sprints until they were sprinting all the time. Bertie brought us back to the start of the programme so many times that at the end of it you would be blowing bubbles. In fact, it was self-defeating because the possibility of having to do twice or three times as much work as had been initially set meant that some players deliberately held back to conserve their energy.

For home matches, we even trained on Saturday morning, a few hours before the kick-off – and I don't mean light training like loosening-up exercises but flat-out running. All the players hated it and – as you might expect of someone with my attitude to the physical side of the game – I hated it more than most. However, let me be fair to Bertie: when I joined Liverpool, the coaching and training staff there could not believe how fit I was. The only problem for me was that I did not have the necessary physical strength. At eleven and a half stone, I was a stone and a half underweight. Most people's weight problems are to do with putting on too much, but mine has always been the opposite. So much so, that Liverpool put me on a body-building regime based on Guinness and a 'seefood' diet – whenever I saw food, I had to eat it.

At Partick, my lack of strength worked against me in my attempts to attract interest from bigger clubs. Jimmy Armfield has said that, as manager of Leeds, he was disappointed when he watched me in a couple of games in that midfield role: he felt I was too easily knocked off the ball. In addition to Liverpool, other clubs who showed interest in me – or were reported to have done so – were Celtic, Rangers, Newcastle and Bolton.

I was alerted to the possibility of Celtic signing me by my old Sauchie Juniors friend Jimmy Miller. Midway through my third season at Firhill, Jimmy, by then a member of Celtic's scouting staff, rang me one day and asked to see me. When we met, he said, 'Celtic want to sign you. Would you go there?' He felt he needed to ask that question because of the sectarian division that exists between Celtic and Rangers. I was a Rangers supporter, and had been brought up a Protestant. However, the prospect of joining forces with the 'other side' did not disturb me in the slightest, especially as it was raised at a time when I was becoming increasingly conscious of the need to build a career. I said, 'I would go there in two minutes flat.' Almost as an afterthought, Jimmy mentioned that Celtic also wanted to sign Joe Craig, and asked if I thought Joe would fancy it, too. 'Well, I can't speak for Joe,' I said, 'but I'm sure he'll be as delighted as I am.' Joe lived in the same area as me, and at Jimmy's request I contacted him and asked him to ring the scout.

I did not hear any more about it until two weeks later when I was rushing home from training to watch something on TV. As I was walking through the village, someone shouted, 'Al, have you heard the news?'

'What news?' I asked.

'Joe Craig has signed for Celtic.'

I thought, Oh, thanks. That's wonderful!

I had to stay where I was. I still don't know for sure why Celtic did not follow up their interest in me. The only explanation I have been given came from Davie McParland. He told me that Jock Stein, who had just returned to the manager's job at Parkhead after a car accident, had disagreed with caretaker manager Sean Fallon's assessment of me.

It was a similar story with Newcastle. I'm sure I would have ended up there if Joe Harvey had continued as manager for a little longer. I gather that he started negotiations with Partick for me before he stepped into the position of general manager, but that his successor, Gordon Lee, said, 'No.' Harvey liked players with flair, but Lee seemed to prefer the more pragmatic types. However, the main reason – according to Lee – was that he had never seen me play and wanted to give his existing players the chance to show what they could do.

Rangers were rumoured to be on the point of signing me before the start of my last season at Partick, when I played against them in a four-team tournament that also included Manchester City and Southampton. Rangers beat us 2–1, and as we were coming off the pitch their captain, John Greig, remarked to me, 'Congratulations! I'll see you in a fortnight.'

'What do you mean?' I asked.

'Well, you'll be here – you'll be at our club,' he said. But that was the last I heard of it.

It was an even bigger disappointment to me than the

Celtic episode had been, so I felt an extra degree of satisfaction when Partick beat Rangers 4–3 at home towards the end of the season and I scored two goals in the last 10 minutes. The first, which made the score 3–3, came with a left-footed half-volley into the top corner. Then I converted a penalty for the winner. It was the first time in my Partick career that I scored twice in one game.

It was in the pre-season competition that I played against Manchester City's centre-forward, Joe Royle, an experience that did much to make me believe that I could more than hold my own in a higher standard of football. Partick were lucky to lose just 1–0: the difference between the two teams in control and movement was like night and day. However, I thought I did quite well, and some years later, Joe told me that when he and the manager, Tony Book, were discussing the clubs rumoured to be watching me, he advised Book to sign me.

As far as I know, Book never tried to follow the advice, but Bolton did. In my testimonial brochure, their then manager, Ian Greaves, wrote that he had been poised to buy me in the week of the Football League transfer deadline in March 1977, when Bolton were pushing for promotion from the Second Division. He added,

> I was not the only English manager interested in signing him. There was a whole gang of us who used to travel up to Partick to watch him, but nobody had actually made a bid.
>
> One or two managers felt he was a little bit short of pace. I never got involved in that particular discussion because I had my own theory on the subject.

I felt his long-striding action made him look a little slower than he was, but if I was right (and I was) I did not see the point in telling the others. So I kept the full extent of my interest under my hat and the day before the deadline, I made my bid – £85,000. It was the first concrete offer Partick had received, and they accepted it in principle, subject to a board meeting.

The following day, Greaves received a call from Partick telling him that, because the club was not safe from relegation, they had decided to hang on to me until the end of the season. But Bolton could not wait so Greaves switched his attention to another player, Sunderland's Ray Train.

Waiting for me to become available was no problem at all to a club like Liverpool, who had more than enough top-class players to get on with. Liverpool were then poised to win the Championship and the European Cup, as well as reach the FA Cup final, and in any event they generally preferred to give newcomers like me a lengthy apprenticeship in the reserves before putting them into the first team.

I often joke that the main reason Liverpool bought me was that I was tax-deductible. In those days Liverpool's tax year ended on the first Friday in May – in 1977, it was 6 May – and any transfer fees paid before that date could be offset against their corporation tax. A number of players who, like me, weren't viewed as immediate Liverpool first-team players, were bought before this deadline. I'm quite sure that, had Liverpool missed the boat with me, they would have spent the money on some-one else.

I do not know the exact point at which Liverpool made their initial approach to Partick, but I do know that the manager, Bob Paisley, agreed to sign me on the recommendation of the club's scouting staff, without having seen me play; and that Partick, no doubt anxious that I kept my mind on the job of helping to maintain their Premier Division place, kept it hidden from me for some time. My first official indication about Liverpool wanting me came on 3 May, two days before the deal was done. It was amazing how I was brought into it. Scot Symon telephoned me at home and asked, 'Do you still want to move?'

'Yeah,' I said, without any idea that I was about to get my wish.

The next question was, 'Would you sign for Liverpool?'

Before you start laughing over the apparent absurdity of the question, I should add that, in my case, it was not as daft as it seemed.

# 5 Finding My Feet

To most players, getting the opportunity to play for Liverpool is tantamount to making them feel as if they're in heaven. It wasn't like that for me. Believe it or not, the closer I got to finalizing the move, the more I wished that something would happen to scupper the deal and keep me in Scotland. While I badly wanted to better myself, this seemed almost too big a forward step. When I learned of Liverpool's interest in me, I remember thinking how great it was going to be to tell all my friends in Sauchie about it. But the downside was the thought that, after the applause, I would have to go to Liverpool and play for them.

It is no exaggeration to say that, while the prospect excited me, it also frightened the life out of me. Having heard so much about the high professional standards Liverpool set, I think I would have felt a lot happier if the club who wanted to sign me had been Tottenham, or any other middle-of-the-range First Division set-up that would not demand too much.

I wasn't too ill-at-ease on the train journey to Liverpool

to discuss my personal terms. Scot Symon accompanied me and we were met at Lime Street Station by Bob Paisley. During the drive to the ground in Bob's car, with Bob and Scot making small-talk in the front and me sitting in the back not saying a word, the conversation turned to golf. 'Oh, Alan's a golfer, you know,' Scot remarked. 'He plays off a two handicap.'

Bob was not impressed. 'We don't encourage golf at Liverpool,' he muttered, referring to the age-old view that it causes players to become heavy-legged.

I thought, Here we go, a black mark against me and I haven't even signed for the club yet! From then on, I was even more jumpy.

When we arrived at the ground and drove through the main gates, the vastness of Anfield was the first psychological hurdle for me to overcome. The next was the throng of reporters and photographers waiting outside the main entrance to record the transfer for their papers. The final one concerned the nonchalance with which Liverpool concluded the deal. The meeting to tie up all the loose ends, which was in Liverpool's imposing boardroom and involved Scot, myself, Liverpool's chairman, John Smith, and the club secretary, Peter Robinson, could not have taken more than 10 minutes. The only minor hiccup came when, after accepting Liverpool's offer of £150 a week, I brought up the subject of a signing fee. I had earlier discussed this with Scot, and he told me, 'I wouldn't do anything to scupper this deal if I were you.' In other words, 'Don't expect us to give you a signing fee from the £100,000 transfer fee we will be getting from Liverpool.' Peter, though, hardly gave it a moment's thought. 'Oh, yes,' he said, 'you're entitled to one,' adding that the money for which I was eligible – 5 per cent of the transfer fee – would be incorporated in my contract. This meant that Liverpool had to produce a revised contract, but to save time I agreed to sign a blank form and leave it to them to put in the financial details that we had discussed and agreed upon.

The only remaining item on the agenda concerned the way in which Liverpool were going to pay Partick the £100,000 transfer fee. Scot was under the impression that they would want to pay it in instalments, but Peter Robinson turned to John Smith and said, 'Will you sign a cheque?' He nodded and handed over the full payment as if he was paying for a pint of milk at his local corner shop.

Then I was taken down to the dressing-room area to meet the Liverpool players, among them Kevin Keegan who welcomed me to the club. I was with Kevin for some time, but much of what he said went over my head. It was the same when he and Liverpool's captain, Emlyn Hughes, Player of the Year, had a laugh with me as I was having my picture taken with them for the newspapers.

One of the things I remember most about the journey back to Scotland was that Scot Symon kept taking the cheque out of his pocket to look at it. I also remember my naïvety in wondering whether the £150 a week that Liverpool were going to pay me also applied to the summer months. Partick paid their players less in the close season and it never occurred to me that bigger clubs would not make the same distinction. Fortunately, the question of whether I would have to make do on less for two or three months was one I kept forgetting to ask.

When I arrived at Glasgow Central Station, my father and John were there to whisk me straight off for a celebration drink. I had suddenly gone from a small club who were going nowhere to one of the greatest clubs in the world. I felt like a million dollars – my ego was soaring somewhere in the skies. However, the feeling that I had made a mistake, that Liverpool were too big and powerful for me, persisted. Indeed, for some time after I moved, that feeling of wishing I was back in Sauchie got progressively worse.

My father took me to Liverpool, and on my first night in the city I was almost in tears. For my first twelve months there, I was a regular traveller on the five fifty Saturday-night train to Glasgow. I was so keen to spend my weekends at home that I even made the journey when I was in the first team.

My homesickness would have been unbearable but for the warmth and support of the Welsh woman who looked after me at my digs. She could talk for Britain but she was great company, as was the Irish lad who also lodged with her. They were like a second mother and brother to me. Also, I became close friends with a lad from Kilmarnock, who lived around the corner and who has remained one of my local pals to this day.

The other stroke of good fortune for me concerned the way I was treated by my fellow players. During my first week at the club, two of the senior professionals, Phil Thompson and Terry McDermott, made a point of offering whatever help I needed to settle in. Not once was I made to feel an outsider. That dressing room was filled with big-name players, who had seen and done it all in professional football. Yet I found it easy to make friends there, and after about six months of sitting in a corner and hardly opening my mouth, I got into the swing of the Liverpool dressing-room culture.

This, I was relieved to find, was no less infantile than it had been at Partick Thistle. Not all players relish the verbal cut and thrust that goes on, and I suppose that if there was one player at Liverpool who did not like it, it was Ian Rush. He was quite shy when he joined Liverpool from Chester, and Graeme Souness and Kenny Dalglish used to wind him up about his slicked-back hairstyle. They reckoned he was trying to model himself on the film star Omar Sharif and nicknamed him Omar. I sat next to Ian in the dressing room, and it was clear to me that he was quite sensitive about it. But as he became more integrated, he was able to take the mickey-taking in his stride.

No newcomer was sacred, no matter how big a star he was. And even the brightest of players could fall for the silliest practical jokes. I remember having a lot of fun with Ronny Rosenthal. When the Israeli international striker came to Anfield, I convinced him that any player who managed to sit on the ball on the goal-line during a practice match would be awarded three goals. Ronnie Moran was in charge of the session and his face was an absolute picture when Rosenthal did it. 'You've been talking to the wrong people,' he told him.

In all my time at Liverpool, the player who probably had to cope with more wind-ups than anyone was Steve Nicol. He must have been the most unstreetwise professional footballer in Britain when Liverpool signed him from Ayr United. It took him ages to stop falling for the traps that the rest of us laid for him. But he was a tremendously funny person anyway, and he laughed at the jokes against him as much as the rest of us did.

During Steve's first few weeks at the club, Bob Paisley came into the dressing room and handed every player – except Steve – a brown envelope containing an Inland Revenue tax demand for the previous financial year. 'How come you haven't got one, Steve?' we asked, not telling him what was in the envelope. 'I don't know,' he replied. We told him that the envelopes contained payments for being in the photograph of the Liverpool first-team squad, and suggested that as he had appeared in the photo, he should go to Paisley and tell him he wanted a brown envelope too.

And that's what he did. I'm told that Bob just laughed and said, 'Well, Steve, if you want a letter from the Inland Revenue, I'm sure we can arrange it.'

On another occasion, when Steve signed a boot contract with Puma, we left him a bogus message to meet the company's representative at a service station some 23 miles from Liverpool – on a Sunday morning. The following Monday, he said to me, 'You were never going to catch me on that one – I'm too sharp for that.' About three weeks later, though, when we were having a night out and he'd had a couple of drinks, he admitted that he'd waited at that service station for two hours – and had his wife with him.

During his most gullible days at Liverpool, hardly a week went by without Steve being tripped up. I don't know how he managed to shrug it off. More to the point is that later, when it came to putting egg on other players' faces, he was one of the ringleaders.

After all the fun I'd had at Partick, the Liverpool dressing room became a home from home. Liverpool also proved the perfect place for me to develop my talents.

My strengths were that I had two good feet – I could use my left foot as well as I could use my right – a lot of pace and the ability to read the game. But my number-one attribute was my ability to involve myself in the attacking play. Some defenders have to rely on anticipating situations because they lack pace, and vice versa, but I was fortunate in being able to base my approach to the game on both. My pace is possibly the only one of these qualities that some people would question. Even the curator of the Liverpool museum at Anfield seems to have doubts about me on that score. All my Liverpool medals are on display there, along with a card giving some details about my career. The last time I read it, when I took a friend to the museum, it said something like, 'The one weakness in Hansen's game was his lack of pace.' I thought, *What*? I even confronted the curator about it. 'Who wrote that?' I asked. He shrugged and explained that he'd read it in a book. I, too, have read that observation, but it was particularly galling to have it down in black and white at Anfield.

The truth is that my pace was deceptive. My height and long stride might have made it appear that I was not running fast, but I felt I was as quick as anyone. Throughout my time at Liverpool some players could beat me over 20 yards, but I am hard pressed to recall teammates who could do so over 50 or 60 yards.

Having been an attacking midfielder before I stepped

into professional football with Partick, I saw no reason why I should not continue to play like one. For me, it was all about getting the ball and 'playing' – making constructive passes and pushing forward to get the ball back, or taking the ball past opponents.

An aspect of the game I particularly enjoyed was 'playing with the eyes', the professionals' term for the art of looking in one direction and playing the ball in another. The late Billy Bremner, the former Leeds and Scotland midfielder, was renowned for this. The way he could shape to play the ball to his right then suddenly cut it across his body to the opposite flank was remarkable. Bremner was largely a right-footed player, and I seem to remember his Leeds manager, Don Revie, remarking, 'It's a wonder that he hasn't messed up his cartilages and knee joints.' Of the present-day stars, Manchester United's David Beckham shows a similar ability with his crosses, often delivered while running flat-out to the dead-ball line.

In my own case, outside the Liverpool players I came up against each day in training matches, I cannot think of any team who could counter this aspect of my play. In one game against Ipswich, when I was confronted by Arnold Muhren whenever I burst forward with the ball and was looking to make a pass, I must have deceived him 'with the eyes' half a dozen times. Towards the end, I was playing almost every pass like that. In my last season at Liverpool, it actually caused me pain because of my knee problems, but those passes had become a habit I couldn't break.

Liverpool were the ideal club for someone with my

style of play because their whole approach to the game was based on the principle of sound passing. In training and matches, the most common instructions or words of advice were, 'Pass and move.' This applied to defenders almost as much as it did to midfielders and strikers.

None of the managers and coaches there attempted to destroy my creative instincts. Nobody ever said to me, 'Don't try and play.' It was the exact opposite. I remember that whenever a new player arrived at Liverpool – especially a defender – the coach Ronnie Moran would point to me and say, 'Don't watch big Al play – don't try to do what he does because he's a one-off.'

It was not the only area in which Liverpool gave me the licence to be myself. I trained hard enough – after a fashion, because I was naturally fit – but I was the worst player in the world when it came to stretching and loosening-up exercises. I looked upon the pre-match warm-up just as something to counteract my anxiety. As for exercises, I was nothing short of embarrassing – I couldn't do them. This hardly made me a great example to younger players. However, as long as I didn't suffer from muscle strains – which, miraculously, I didn't – Liverpool were happy to leave me alone.

Among the pre-match exercises that represented a particular no-go area for me was the one in which the players had to lie on their backs and keep opening and shutting their legs while they were six inches off the ground. My feet were permanently on the ground. On one occasion when Ronnie Moran was having a go at a youngster who was not doing it properly, the lad pointed at me and said, 'Look at him – he's not doing it at all.'

'Don't worry about him,' Ronnie replied. 'When you've won as many Championship medals as him, you can do what you like as well. In the meantime, just get your own legs in the air!'

I probably gave the Liverpool management more grey hairs than anyone, especially when I tried drag-backs – where you invite an opponent to commit himself then roll the ball back, out of his reach, with the sole of the boot – inside my own box. The trick always appealed to me. As a youngster, a recording of the 1953 broadcast of Hungary's 6–3 thrashing of England at Wembley made a big impression on me, not because of England's humiliation but because of the famous drag-back by Ferenc Puskas that brought the 'Galloping Major' one of his three goals. You can imagine how I felt when I produced a successful one of my own against Liam Brady in Liverpool's 3–1 thumping of Arsenal in the 1979 Charity Shield at Wembley. The area I had to work in was not as tight as Puskas'. But, against that, I was a central defender, and I actually tried it on the edge of our six-yard box.

Really, when the ball came to me, I know I should have 'launched' it, as I now advise defenders on TV. 'If in doubt, launch it,' I say – it's one of my new maxims. But in that match against Arsenal, we were about 25 minutes into the game, a goal up, dominating the play, and I honestly couldn't see any danger. Like all good players, Liam had taken up a position to force me to take the ball forward, through the middle. But as he stuck out a foot to make contact with the ball, I dragged it back, and went past him the other way. I could have been doing laps of honour all week on the strength of that moment.

It was the same with my 'wonder' goal – a description I feel quite at liberty to make, given that the goal was never seen on television – in Liverpool's 2–0 home win over Manchester United on Boxing Day 1979. At that time, the rivalry between Liverpool and Manchester United was not as intense as it is now. However, as they were only a point ahead of us in the Championship, and we had a match in hand, this was an important game by any criterion. We were the reigning Champions, and had started that season on a roll. By the time of the game against United, we were unbeaten in 13 matches. Right from the outset, I was doing what I most wanted to do: getting the ball and playing it. I just had the feeling that this was going to be my day. After about 20 minutes, Graeme Souness got a pass from Phil Thompson and as I moved up beside him, just inside our half, he laid it off to me. Then I burst between two United players, played a one-two with Ray Kennedy on the edge of the United box, and stuck the return pass into the far corner of the United net.

In the dressing room afterwards, Phil Thompson said, 'You were like Franz Beckenbauer at his best.' Joe Fagan did not say much; he was already worrying about the next day's match at West Bromwich Albion. Before the kick-off, Joe said to me, 'Remember, this is a muddy pitch. You can't play like you did against Manchester United.' On that occasion, I kept it simple and straightforward, just did my basic job. 'That's the way to do it, son,' Joe remarked afterwards, tongue-in-cheek. 'That's how central defenders play.'

I laughed. But there were some aspects of Liverpool

that were definitely no laughing matter. Liverpool did what Partick couldn't do. They forced me to acquire a more professional attitude. They turned me into a winner.

# 6 Through the Pain Barrier

Even though I never played under the management of the late Bill Shankly, and met him only a couple of times, I have a lot to thank him for. After all, it was Shankly who took the club out of the Second Division and lifted them to the Championship and FA Cup in the space of five years. It was Shankly, Liverpool's manager from 1959 to 1974, and the most legendary figure in the history of the club, who sowed the seeds of their remarkable run of success when I was there.

One of my principal sources of information about him is the ex-Scotland centre-half Ron Yeats, who was signed by Shankly for Liverpool, from Dundee, and who is now the club's chief scout. Ron says that when he was initially approached by Shankly, he asked where Liverpool was situated geographically. 'We are in the First Division of the English League,' he was told.

'Oh, I thought you were in the Second Division, Mr Shankly,' Ron replied.

'Yeah, but we'll be in the First Division when we

sign you, son,' Shankly told him.

'At that moment,' Ron said, 'I knew there was only one man I wanted to play for. He made me feel like a million dollars.'

Another Shankly anecdote that says a lot about him concerns his eagerness to play in five-a-side matches – and always to finish on the winning side. Those matches took place after the first-team training session each day, and Shankly's team – comprising himself and his backroom coaching staff – would usually play the club's apprentice professionals. Shankly treated these occasions like cup finals.

One day, with only 10 players available, Shankly asked the club's milkman if he would make up the numbers. 'I'd like to, Mr Shankly,' he replied, 'but I haven't played football for years. I'd hate to let your team down.'

'Don't worry about that, son,' Shankly told him. 'You'll be playing for the other side.'

Shankly, indeed, had an obsession with winning. It's the same with most professional players and managers, but I think it was particularly true of Shankly. I say that because the methods of his successors stemmed from many of the principles that he established at the club, and the most striking common characteristic between all the Liverpool managers I played for – Bob Paisley, Joe Fagan and Kenny Dalglish – was that their attitude to defeat could never have been described as philosophical.

Bob, who took over from Shankly when he was 55, after many years as his right-hand man, and who signed me for Liverpool, came across publicly as a shy, retiring figure. His appearance and down-to-earth manner – not to mention his gentle Geordie accent – might have made it appear that Liverpool's players had their favourite uncle in charge of them. But Bob was no soft touch; neither did he fight shy of making difficult decisions. Indeed, you only have to look at his unsurpassed Liverpool managerial record of six Championships, three European Cups and three League Cups in nine years to appreciate that he was as tough as they came – and as ruthless too when he needed to be.

Although inevitably there were differences between Bob, Joe and Kenny – the main one being that Kenny was probably the most at ease in the manager's role – they all went about the job in what can best be described as an undemonstrative manner; they did not complicate the game and were exceptionally shrewd football judges.

Like everyone else, they had their red-mist moments, but generally, I think, they appreciated that the more animated a manager becomes, the more his message to the players can be lost. They also appreciated that players should be treated as adults, which meant that we were encouraged to voice our own opinions, without it being thought that we were trying to undermine the authority of the manager or coaches. Nor were we subjected to a lot of rigid disciplinary rules.

At Liverpool, they were not so much 'rules' as 'guidelines'. True, the management would clamp down on discipline when the team were going through a bad patch – just little things like players getting on the team bus to go to the training ground at ten fifteen instead of ten twenty or ten thirty, and the training sessions themselves would be more intense and closely supervised. But, generally, Liverpool felt it essential that players enjoyed coming in to work and tried to make their organizational framework as flexible as possible.

When Bob was manager, anyone present regularly at Liverpool training sessions might have had the impression that his contribution to the team during the week was nil. His coaches, Joe Fagan and Ronnie Moran, appeared to do everything. Bob would watch the training, and he hardly said anything – but you knew that he was the one who made all the decisions, that he did not miss a trick and that when he did speak to the players it meant something. Sometimes I had to laugh at Bob's use of words. During one team meeting, Bob was talking about a hard game we'd had at Aston Villa the previous Saturday, and said, 'If we had started off airy-fairy, we would have been right up the Swanee.'

However, it didn't matter that Bob wasn't the most articulate of people because his views on the game were so simple and straightforward. For instance, the way Liverpool played defensively, with a flat-back four pushing up to compress the play, meant that opposing players were often caught offside. We pushed up even more than Arsenal, another team noted for frustrating the opposition in this way, but while Arsenal's players immediately raised an arm as a signal to the officials when a player appeared to fall into the offside trap, Bob told us, 'Never raise your arm.' He pointed out the gesture could distract the defender and, if the offside decision wasn't given, make it easier for the opposition to score. He had lots of little rules like that, which were mostly about professional discipline. Among his favourites was one that concerned the importance of teams starting a match in a high tempo – 'It's easier to lower it than it is to raise it,' he would say – and also that players should anticipate situations rather than react to them. His attitude to the importance of pace was: 'For players at the highest level, the first two yards are in the head.' The greatest example of that was Kenny Dalglish. Most of his dialogue with the players took place in the dressing room before a match. He was a brilliant tactician and usually delivered what he had to say with the minimum fuss.

I still remember one of my earliest Liverpool matches – against Chelsea. I was sitting next to Kenny in the dressing room before the game, and as we were chatting Bob came across and said to Kenny, 'Watch out for John Phillips [Chelsea's keeper] straying too far off his line.'

Liverpool won that game 2–0, and there are no prizes for guessing that Kenny scored one of the goals – the first – with a long-range chip over Phillips's head.

Like Bob, Joe Fagan, Liverpool's manager from July 1983 to May 1985, and Kenny Dalglish, who filled the role up to February 1991, were also all promoted to the job from within. Joe was previously assistant manager to Bob – and Kenny had been Liverpool's most influential player. So all three were steeped in the culture of the club . . . a culture that meant those at the helm demanded and expected a successful team.

I think Shankly summed it up best with his famous response to someone who suggested that winning at football was not a matter of life or death. 'Aye,' Shankly said. 'It's more serious than that.'

The one thing that Bob, Joe and Kenny could not

accept was complacency: the mere mention of the word to them was like a clove of garlic to Count Dracula. Their attitude was: 'Once you start getting complacent, this game can kick you in the teeth. There is only one way to go from there and that's down.' And if anything was liable to send Bob off his head, it was players shouting their mouths off to the media about Liverpool's ability.

I've never known a player get the sort of half-time verbal rockets that Bob directed at our left-back Alan Kennedy over certain newspaper comments during our 1978/79 Championship-winning season. The day before Liverpool's Easter Monday match at Aston Villa, Alan was quoted as saying that Liverpool were already virtually assured of the title. It was not an unreasonable remark, considering we were well ahead at the time, having won 24 of our 34 matches and lost only two. But at the interval Villa were leading 3–1. When Alan came into the dressing room, Bob turned on him, and blamed him for the score-line on the grounds that his newspaper comments had wound Villa up. Although Alan had played well, Bob was so angry with him I almost thought he was going to have a heart attack. 'It's all your fault,' he shouted. 'Never, ever, say you've won something until you have the medal in your hand.'

I remembered this when Liverpool played Aberdeen – then managed by Alex Ferguson – in the second round of the European Cup in 1980. Before the first leg at Aberdeen, the local evening newspaper produced a big supplement about the tie, which was full of quotes from Aberdeen players and people connected with the club pro-claiming that the home team were going to beat us. After looking through that supplement, the Liverpool players were as wound up as any I have seen – and none more so than me. It meant a lot to me to ram those comments back down the throats of the people who made them, partly because of my rivalry at international level with Aberdeen's central defenders Alex McLeish and Willie Miller, and partly because of my desire to prove a point to those Scottish supporters critical of players like me earning their living in England. It showed, too – I never performed with as much fire and aggression as I did in that game, which Liverpool won 1–0. The other Liverpool players were amazed. It was the same in the second leg at Anfield, when we thrashed Aberdeen 4–0 and I scored one of the goals.

Those matches against Aberdeen emphasized Bob's shrewdness in 'using' the media. He was widely quoted as saying that Aberdeen's key midfielder, Gordon Strachan, was 'the best player in Britain' and worth 'at least £2 million' (a figure almost double the then record British transfer fee). I cannot say whether Gordon allowed this observation to go to his head, but he hardly got a kick of the ball over the two matches.

The one area in which Bob might have invited criticism from other managers was that when he was in charge at Liverpool technical coaching was virtually non-existent. Unlike most other teams, for example, we never practised free kicks and corners – our approach to corners was so haphazard that, whenever we were awarded one, I felt we might just as well have handed the ball straight back to the opposition. But to Bob, and the men who followed him in the job, it was more important to train the players' minds. After every season, no matter how much success we had achieved, the management line was, 'Enjoy it while you can because what you have won is going to count for nothing next time.'

There was nothing that Liverpool would not do to get the message across.

Even for someone as laid-back about the game as I was, this attitude, which permeated every corner of the club, was infectious. I became so hungry for medals that when asked at the start of each season what my biggest ambition was, my reply was, 'To play in at least thirteen Championship matches.' I managed to get medals for all eight of the Championships Liverpool won when I was there because in each season my number of appearances never dropped below 34. Equally telling was that after a while the prospect of defeat became so painful to me that I couldn't bear even to think about it.

I'm sure I would have had a good career with another leading club, but as far as personal development is concerned I don't think any club in England could have stretched me as far as Liverpool did. The nature of the club was an even greater development factor for me than that of being in such high-quality teams. One occasion that perfectly summed up the Anfield atmosphere was the FA Cup semi-final replay against Manchester United at Goodison Park in 1979, and the late Jimmy Greenhoff goal, which gave United a 1–0 victory. It was hard to take, given that in the first match at Maine Road, where I scored a late equalizer to give us a 2–2 draw, we'd had enough chances to have won fairly emphatically. The goal that sank us in the replay was a particular blow to Emlyn

Hughes: he was deemed the Liverpool player responsible for it.

By then, I had taken over from Emlyn at the heart of the Liverpool defence, alongside Phil Thompson, with Emlyn operating at left-back. During our team talk before the match, Emlyn was reminded about the importance of being 'tight' on United's outside-right Steve Coppell. Unfortunately, he took it a bit too literally. Greenhoff's goal came from a cross by Mickey Thomas from the opposite side of the field, and, to some extent, my impetuosity in moving out of the central area to cover a run into the box by Sammy McIlroy. It is possible that I might have stopped the goal had I remained where I was. When Bob Paisley and his coaching staff studied the video of the goal, they felt that in trying to stop McIlroy freeing himself to capitalize on the cross, I had been partly to blame for reacting too quickly.

They also noticed that Emlyn, who should have been in a position on the left to move infield and fill the gap left by me, was with Coppell some thirty yards up the field. He was seen as more culpable for the goal than me; and he paid a heavy price for it. Then in his thirties, he never played for Liverpool again, and was sold to Wolves in the summer. Emlyn was still a top-class player, but the standards Liverpool set were higher than at other clubs and when they decided that he was no longer capable of reaching them, his past record of success counted for nothing.

I found this chilling. It leads me to suggest that Liverpool players probably worried more when things were not going well for them than those at many other clubs.

Among the bad times for me as a senior player were when I was struggling with knee problems. Someone once said to me, 'Players should never play if they have fluid on the knees.' By that reckoning, I should have packed it in at Liverpool seven years before I did! The knee problems, which had started at Partick, grew worse as a result of my gangly build and the cumulative effect of playing so many matches. The worst injury I suffered was a left-knee dislocation in a pre-season friendly against Athletico Madrid in Spain in the summer of 1988, which came just a few months after a cartilage operation on the right knee and put me out of the side for nine months. The right knee hampered me most. The deterioration in the joint, which eventually forced me to cut down on my running in training and necessitated a small 'clean-up' operation at the end of each season, explains why my career at Liverpool can be divided into two periods in terms of my style of play.

Until the 1985/86 season, when I tore my right knee muscle midway through the campaign, I probably involved myself in attacking play as much as any central defender in the history of the game. Yet after the injury, which meant that my right knee was never the same again, I headed towards the other extreme of holding my position and concentrating on my defensive duties.

The big question, of course, is whether I would have lasted longer as a top-class player had I played less often. At times when I was struggling physically my view of whether I was fit enough to play for Liverpool did not always correspond with the club's. They tended to be as positive in these situations as I was negative. It would be an exaggeration to say that they forced me to play when I didn't think I was 'right' but they made me feel under pressure to do so. With the highly competitive nature of the club, it was difficult to say no without worrying that it might be held against you.

Deciding on a player's fitness is always tricky for managers, and at Liverpool I was fortunate that they did not put at risk my long-term well-being by repeatedly pumping pain-killing injections and tablets into me. I am sure some clubs do that. It was certainly rife in the days when knowledge of the effects of the treatment on players was more limited. As a player, you had to be very strong-minded to reject it, and several have suffered for having agreed to it, with chronic arthritis and other joint problems after their retirement from the game.

In the 1960s and 1970s some players had cortisone injections regularly throughout the season to get them through games. Liverpool, though, were opposed to this. I had two injections in the right knee in the 1980/81 season, and as I continued to be troubled by the injury, Bob Paisley asked Joe Fagan, 'Do you think we could give him another jab?'

'Oh, no,' Joe replied, emphatically. 'In any one year, you cannot give someone more than two cortisone injections in the same joint.'

That was great news for me – I objected to the injections because I couldn't stand pain at any price.

At one stage in my career, I was put on anti-inflammatory drugs, on the advice of a specialist. The tablets, which I started taking in the mid-1980s, worked well. On a Friday, if the pain in my knee was acute, I would take two tablets in the morning, and by the following day it was as if I had been given a new joint. However, my attitude to the pills changed one day when I happened to pick up a newspaper in the dressing room and saw a front-page story suggesting that one of their side-effects might be liver damage. Since my retirement, many companies have employed me for personal appearances and to make speeches at their sales conferences, including a German conglomerate that claimed to have produced the first anti-inflammatory drug without side-effects. I wish those tablets had been around when I was playing. I could certainly have done with them when the club twisted my arm to carry on after I hurt my right knee in a challenge on Garth Crooks at home to Tottenham in December 1980. In normal circumstances, I would have been given a rest, but Liverpool were experiencing other injury problems, and were not doing as well as expected in the league, so they pushed me back into action. I was given cortisone injections to relieve the swelling and pain before each of the next two matches, against Ipswich and Wolves, but in both games I was operating virtually on one leg.

Surprising as it might seem, Liverpool drew 1–1 in the first match and won the other 1–0. My handicap was so obvious that, during the Wolves game at Anfield, their manager, John Barnwell, and his training staff spent much of their time urging their players to 'get after number six'!

After the following game, a goalless draw at Manchester United (when I had to be substituted), I went into hospital for the removal of a growth on the side of the joint, which put me out of action for four matches. However, even when I went back to playing for the first team, against West Bromwich Albion in February, I felt I could have done with more time to recover.

Unable to rest the joint properly, I continued to have trouble with the knee right up to the end of the season. One game in which I had to play through the pain was the League Cup final replay against West Ham at Villa Park, where I actually scored one of the goals in our 2–1 win. The knee was so bad that, 20 minutes from the end, I signalled to the Liverpool bench to take me off. However, Ray Kennedy was also struggling and they felt that, from a tactical viewpoint, it would make more sense to take him off instead.

Once again Villa Park was the scene of me at my physical worst in 1988, when we beat Aston Villa there in the fourth round of the FA Cup. In the week before the game, my right knee swelled up like a balloon, and there was also a big injury doubt about Gary Gillespie, then my central-defensive partner. Apparently, when the Liverpool physio, Paul Chadwick, examined us on the eve of the tie, he told Kenny Dalglish, 'I don't think either will make it.' Kenny said, 'Don't worry about Al. I'm sure he'll be able to get through the game.'

In these situations, Kenny knew that I tended to adopt a negative stance and did not think it necessary to consult me. It was the same with Bob Paisley and Joe Fagan: they felt they could assess my capabilities better than me and, in retrospect, they were not bad judges.

I played in that match at Villa without being able to kick the ball or run properly. I had to try to fudge my way through the game, which I managed because of my experience, my positional sense, and because Liverpool dominated the game.

Of course, situations like this did nothing to ease my pre-match anxiety. But I appreciate now how Liverpool, in pushing me, helped improve my mental toughness.

My strength of character increased with my experiences of lost form. One such period came in the 1979/80 season, when for a run of matches I needed twenty minutes to get tuned in to a game. My slow starts led Joe Fagan to ask me if I was drinking, eating or socializing too much.

'Joe, I haven't had a drink for four weeks,' I replied. 'I'm watching what I eat, and the only time I go out during the week is when I visit Kenny on a Friday night to have a meal with him and his family.'

Joe – Mr Common Sense I call him – just looked at me in that deadpan way of his, and said, 'You're not enjoying yourself enough. You need a good night out – you're too uptight!' He was right – but he demanded such high standards I felt I had every right to get uptight about my job.

The fear of the axe being swung over my head was even greater towards the end of the 1982/83 season when I suffered the worst drop in form and confidence I ever experienced as a senior professional, in a team which took only one point from its last seven games. It could be that, with Liverpool so far ahead of second-placed Watford – we eventually finished 11 points in front of them – I allowed myself to relax. But it was not a conscious thing – it couldn't possibly have been at Liverpool where we were repeatedly reminded that less than 100 per cent would never be tolerated, even in matches where nothing was at stake.

I'd had two bad games on the trot before, but never six or seven. I became so demoralized that every time I had to make a decision during a match, I expected it to be the wrong one. I was hopeless, both on the deck and in the air. Liverpool kept me in the team because they felt I could play my way out of the bad spell. It was as if they were saying, 'You're a big boy now – get on with it,' but two or three matches before the end of the season I desperately wanted them to put me out of my misery by dropping me. Apart from the support of my family, it was an episode in which I was grateful for having friends in the dressing room like Graeme Souness and Kenny Dalglish. Both seemed to show a particular sense of responsibility towards me, if only because I was a fellow Scot. At the end of the season, Graeme came to me and said, 'I know you've had a nightmare but remember that you're a great player and that these things tend to even out.' It was shortly afterwards that I heard from Kenny, while we were playing golf together, that Liverpool were on the point of signing another Scottish central defender from Coventry.

'We're signing Gary Gillespie,' he said casually. Then, knowing how neurotic I could be about my first-team place, he added, 'It's only for cover, for you and Thommo [Phil Thompson].'

It was reassuring to hear that . . . but it didn't stop me worrying. It bothered me so much, in fact, that for the first time in my career I started running in the close season

– a major shock to those who had known me as a Sauchie Athletic and Partick Thistle player – and I even practised my heading in the garden.

When we reported back to Liverpool for pre-season training, Joe Fagan, in his first season as manager, noted my determination to get back on the right track and gave me as much encouragement as Graeme and Kenny had. He was wonderful. He praised me almost every time I did something well – even for things that, previously, he and I would have taken for granted. I was so worried about my future that in one pre-season training match I even treated Joe to the rare sight of me making a full-blooded tackle (albeit on one of the young players). Joe looked blankly at me, and said, 'That's different.'

From the start of the season, I clicked back into top gear again. However, the memory of my loss of form bothered me for the rest of my time at Anfield. Probably the only time I had ever felt as insecure was in my first season at the club, when I was given a first-team place earlier than I had anticipated, then dropped and wanted to go back to Scotland. I ended up playing in Liverpool's 1–0 win over Bruges in the European Cup final at Wembley.

# 7 As Green as Grass

Ray Clemence, Liverpool's goalkeeper when I made my opening first-team appearances at the start of the 1977/78 season, said that when he operated behind me on my First Division début (against Derby on 24 September), he thought, This lad is so good, he could add six years on to my career here.

Shortly afterwards, when I screwed up in my First Division match against Manchester United, he changed his mind. He told me, 'I thought that, far from putting six years on to my career, playing with you would take six years off it!'

In many ways I was as green as grass. That first season was the one in which I probably learned most about what is required of a top-class professional footballer, and it was one in which my Liverpool career could easily have been brought to an end.

It was a difficult season for everybody, given the changes in the team following the club's Championship and European Cup success the previous season. The most

111

notable of these were Kevin Keegan's transfer to Hamburg in June 1977, and the signings of Kenny Dalglish from Celtic in July – as Keegan's successor – and Graeme Souness from Middlesbrough in January 1978. Keegan was always going to be difficult to replace. All the players he left behind at Anfield spoke highly of him, and on the couple of occasions that I played against him later in my career – when he had returned to England to play for Southampton – I could appreciate why. His movement was exceptional and I was also impressed by his physical strength.

He was a different sort of player from Kenny: he did not have as much natural ability but other aspects of his game more than made up for that. It would have been difficult to separate them when they were at their peak, and all I can say is that it's a pity Liverpool did not have both. What a tasty combination that would have been! As it turned out, Kenny and Graeme settled in straight away, and as the record books show, their presence made Liverpool stronger than ever. But the club could not fully capitalize on their presence immediately as we were not settled in defence, especially at its heart.

Over my 18 First Division matches, I had three different partners: the redoubtable Tommy Smith, who had intended to retire after the 1977 European Cup final against Borussia Moenchengladbach but decided to carry on for another season, Emlyn Hughes and Phil Thompson. Of these three, Emlyn made 39 league appearances – but not all as a central defender – while Tommy and Phil were in and out of the side.

That was the season in which Nottingham Forest

emerged as our biggest threat and, indeed, overtook us in domestic competitions by winning the Championship – by seven points – and beating us in the League Cup final. I think it was mainly down to their having a more settled defence, in their case a rock-solid back division built around the brilliance of goalkeeper Peter Shilton, and two central defenders – Larry Lloyd and Kenny Burns – who took no prisoners and worked together superbly.

Forest, who went on to win the European Cup in 1979 and 1980, of course, were a bogey team to us for four or five years. While they had a number of good players, their biggest strengths were that those players worked exceptionally hard and played to a system that suited them. Forest were a counter-attacking team, who liked to get almost everyone behind the ball when the opposition were in possession and tended to defend deeper than a lot of other sides.

They also epitomized the importance of attempting to defend from the front. All their outfield players did their fair share of defensive work, and particularly the strikers. In most of our matches against Forest, we were streets ahead of them in terms of possession, but still rarely beat them.

Forest tended to operate with only one man up front against us and whoever was in that role – Peter Withe, Tony Woodcock or Gary Birtles – ran himself into the ground in trying to stop us building moves constructively from the back. Birtles was a particular pain in the backside to us. I can remember matches in which Phil Thompson and I would be knocking the ball back and forth to each other, with Birtles, who had no real chance of winning it, still chasing every pass. Phil and I never ceased to be amazed by his energy and commitment. When the ball had been directed somewhere else, I would turn to Phil and say, 'Where did they get this guy from?'

This commitment has been a feature of all the most successful teams in England, and it was certainly a feature of Liverpool in all the time I played for the club. As I have said, I had as much to learn from it as anyone, especially in that first season. It was unusual for Liverpool to put someone like me in their first team without first subjecting him to a lengthy apprenticeship in the reserves, and I'm still not sure whether this was a good or bad thing for me.

Liverpool didn't pay a fortune for me, by their standards, and in pre-season training they had been taken aback by my fitness and my skill on the ball in the training five-a-side matches. Those matches, though, are different from full-sided competitive games. They are used mainly to sharpen your control and passing in tight areas; the amount of tackling in them is virtually zero. Being judged on my performance in those games did me no favours because they showed off what I was best at and camouflaged my faults. It would have saved me a lot of heartache if those weaknesses – my lack of defensive discipline and the flaws in my tackling and heading – had been clearer.

In the circumstances, I owed a great deal to Ray Clemence, a great communicator who would virtually talk me through games. He was a lot different from his successor Bruce Grobbelaar. Bruce rarely said anything during a match, even if you were going for a ball which he intended taking, he would just come for it and clatter you out of the way. However, his lack of communication skills was no handicap to me because when he took over from Ray I did not need so much guidance.

Ray was brilliant at it, repeatedly shouting instructions about my positioning. But even he could not talk me successfully through every game. Take my first-team début, in the Liverpool winger Ian Callaghan's testimonial match against a North West Select XI before the start of the season. I did not play well – I had made the mistake of training on the afternoon of the game, so in the game itself I was knackered. So much so that the opposing striker, Duncan McKenzie, beat me no less than three times by flicking the ball over my head. I did not look much better in my first three reserve matches, in which Liverpool conceded a total of eight goals.

Some time later, Joe Fagan related a conversation between himself and Roy Evans, then Liverpool's reserve-team coach, about my performances. Apparently Joe asked Roy where I was positioned when the goals were scored, and Roy replied, 'To be fair, now you come to mention it, he was nowhere near the ball for any of them!' That, of course, should have caused the pair to become wary about me, but they continued to be seduced by my form in the five-a-sides.

In view of this, my First Division début against Derby went surprisingly well, especially when I had only just been told I would be playing. Following our morning training session, Bob Paisley pulled me aside and asked, 'Are you ready for a game?' I mumbled something which, roughly translated, meant yes. For the next three days, I was such a bag of nerves that I ended up feeling resentful towards Bob for not having waited until Friday night or Saturday morning to break the news.

In those days, the Liverpool squad would spend the Friday night at a hotel even when they were playing at home, and during the short coach journey to Anfield the following day no-one had to be an expert in human behaviour to see that I was struggling mentally. I remember that as the vehicle approached the stadium Ray Clemence, who was sitting opposite me, put his hand on my shoulder and said, 'You'll be fine – no problem.' Nevertheless, I spent most of the time in the dressing room going back and forth to the toilet. By two fifty, I was in such a panic that my only thought was, I can't play!

As always happened with me, I was OK when I got on to the field and the match started. On that occasion my confidence soared when I had my first touch of the ball after nine minutes and made a good pass. Liverpool went on to win 1–0 through a goal by Terry McDermott, thus stretching our unbeaten start to the season to seven matches.

But my euphoria evaporated in the next two games, when my flaws rose to the surface and hit me – *and* the Liverpool management – firmly on the chin. The other person who suffered was Tommy Smith, who then had the dubious distinction of being my central-defensive partner. For any young player, having Smith alongside you was a massive bonus, not least because of his reputation as one of the most intimidating 'hard men' in British football. He made opponents think twice about taking any physical liberties with him or the players around him.

I only saw this side of him once – in a five-a-side training match in which he created space to receive a short pass from Terry McDermott only for Terry to try a more difficult ball down the line. Tommy's rebuke was quite mild for him. 'Terry Mac, what's wrong with you?' he asked. 'That was the wrong pass.'

Terry got lippy with him. 'Tommy, you're dreaming,' he replied.

At that, Tommy's face looked like thunder, and it could easily have been Clint Eastwood talking when he growled, 'You watch what you say to me. If you're not careful, you'll be the one who's dreaming.' I don't think I need to add that Terry did not pursue the matter!

However, the side of Tommy Smith that made the biggest impression on me was his football. He was a much more skilful player than his macho image had led me to believe, and the other characteristic that struck a chord with me was his spirit. While I was the type of player who wanted to run off the pitch when things were not going well, Tommy would try even harder. When Liverpool were a goal or two down, he seemed to take it almost as a personal insult.

His character was badly needed when he was playing alongside me in the matches that followed my début against Derby. Central defenders should work off each other, but in the next game, a midweek friendly match against Gothenburg in Sweden, we were like strangers in the first half. When he was moving forward I was going backwards, and vice versa. It was my fault because, as the junior partner, I should have been following his lead. As it was, I thought I could play just like I had at Partick,

117

where the system of play in defence was not as regimented as it was at Liverpool and I could afford to be more individualistic. We were so far apart that almost every Gothenburg attack through the middle looked as if it could bring them a goal. Liverpool were 2–0 down at half-time, but it could easily have been 10–0.

In the second half I managed to keep more in contact with Tommy and Liverpool went on to win 3–2. But it can take time to develop a good central-defensive partnership, especially when one of the players is as wet behind the ears as I was.

The point was illustrated again the following Saturday in our clash with Manchester United. If anything, I was even more nervous for that match than I had been for the Derby game, and this time it showed on the field as well as off it. I had a shocker. I must have looked as if I was in a daze because most of the play seemed to pass me by and I felt little more than an observer. The worst moment came when I lost possession to Jimmy Greenhoff, while attempting to beat him with a drag-back in our penalty area, and Steve Coppell put the ball in the net from his pass. Fortunately for me it was disallowed for offside; but my good fortune did not extend any further than that. The scoreline at the end was 2–0 to United, and I knew that my inexperience had made me a liability.

I have never forgotten Bob Paisley's reaction to the error. He did not say anything to me about it immediately after the game, but the following Wednesday, when we were about to board a train to London for a match against Arsenal at Highbury, he pulled me to one side, put an arm on my shoulder and said, 'Look, lad, I know I'm getting on a bit, but I'm still too young to have a heart attack. Just watch it, will you?'

The likelihood that players will blow hot and cold at the start of their careers is always something that managers must consider when deciding whether to persevere with them as first-team players. Bob Paisley used to say, 'You need plenty of experience to win trophies.' When he left me out of the side in my first season, he explained, 'Experience is everything.' Indeed, it was with this in mind that I trotted out that statement on television: 'You cannot win anything with kids.' I was referring to Manchester United's chances of winning the Championship when they flooded their team with youngsters like Phil and Gary Neville, Paul Scholes, Nicky Butt and David Beckham, and no-one has allowed me to forget how wrong I was. Still, I would argue that United's case was the exception rather than the rule. Youngsters experience fresh problems at each match, and it is unreasonable to expect them to achieve the consistency of more experienced professionals. It is not unusual for a young player to start off like a house on fire, be swept along on the excitement of first-team football, only to lose impetus and 'die' as if he has hit a brick wall.

Generally, the stronger the team, the more a manager can afford to carry a lad. But it is not good for a young player to be kept in a side when he is not playing well, for the simple reason that when he has to drop out, the memory of the bad spell may be a considerable psychological barrier for him when he finds himself back in the team. It is for this reason that a lot of managers give a lad a rest when he's playing well rather than the reverse. It might be irritating for the fans, but I'm all in favour of it.

In my own case, the Manchester United match was followed by a run of games in which I did well. In addition to playing in Liverpool's next seven First Division games, I scored on my European Cup début in the 5–1 first-round defeat of Dynamo Dresden at Anfield (thanks to John Toshack's flick-on from a Jimmy Case corner). Things could hardly have been going better for me, but it wasn't long before I was brought down to earth again.

In the First Division, my first-team run had come to an end with an injury in the 2–0 defeat at QPR on 12 November. I was brought back for the return game against QPR five matches later on 17 December – a 1–0 win – but was injured again and missed five of the next 10 matches, including the four Christmas and New Year fixtures.

Off the field, it was the worst Christmas of my life. The opening match of the programme, against Forest on Boxing Day, was away and involved the first-team squad training on Christmas morning, then travelling to Nottingham for an overnight stay. After the Forest match, we were due to stay in Stoke that evening and travel back to Liverpool the next day for the home match against Wolves. But I did not make the trip as I had hurt an ankle and was told to stay at home. On top of this, my landlady and her other lodger were spending Christmas with their respective families in Wales and Ireland, so I was alone. As I had been expected to be away, there was no food or drink in the house. I had a memorable Christmas night dinner – fish and chips from the local carry-out.

When I look back, I can see that one of the biggest turning points for me at Liverpool was that, at the start of my second season there, I bought a small flat in Southport. It signalled my intention to establish roots in the area, and I stopped going home to Scotland every weekend. Until then, however, I felt very unsettled – to the extent that just before my first Christmas at Anfield I asked Bob Paisley if I could spend it back in Sauchie. He was not impressed. He said, 'Son, we have a long Christmas break at this club. It's in the summer!'

If this was not enough to make me feel sorry for myself, what happened when I started playing again for the first team on 14 January ensured that I did. In the five matches in which I played between then and 8 March, it was obvious to everybody – including myself – that I was struggling. Liverpool's results in those five games – one win and four defeats – said it all.

Ironically, it was against Derby County – the opponents at my encouraging league début for Liverpool – on 8 March that the need for me to wear L-plates became particularly noticeable. Derby beat us 4–2 – no other team put that number of goals past us that season – and I had a terrible afternoon against their former Arsenal striker Charlie George. Derby played a lot of passes through or over our defence for George to chase and, although I was able to match him for pace, it was amazing how many times he brushed me aside physically. It was an invaluable experience – and showed me yet again that I needed to get a grip on myself. I had to learn that lesson in the reserves and, initially, I struggled at that level too. Indeed, such was my misery both on and off the field that I became a small boy again. I wanted to go home.

Liverpool's solution? They left me to sort out my problems on my own. When it came to learning to play the Liverpool way, it really was 'sink or swim' for me. Nobody at the club told me what I had to do to fit into their defensive system – when the flat-back four had to hold their line and when they had to drop back – and as Liverpool players were encouraged to think for themselves I did not feel comfortable about asking for help. I think they viewed the situation as a test of my character and football intelligence, and reasoned that if I was going to progress I would do so more effectively through my own efforts than from any counselling or coaching they could give me.

I spent most of the next two months in the reserves, and during that period Liverpool played 10 First Division matches, two League Cup final games against Forest and the two European Cup semi-final ties against Borussia Moenchengladbach. Towards the end, I re-emerged on the first-team scene – on the substitutes' bench – but I was not brought on. Of those 14 matches, only two were lost (the League Cup final replay and the first match against Borussia) so the prospect of my being able to force myself back into the starting line-up for the European Cup final seemed an impossible dream.

Among the other players on the fringe were the more experienced Ian Callaghan, who had played in the previous year's European Cup final, and Joey Jones, who had the advantage of being a natural left-sided player and had proved himself at Liverpool as both a central defender and a full-back.

However, with three First Division matches left, the door swung open for me when Tommy Smith, Phil Thompson's central-defensive partner in a back line that included Phil Neal and Emlyn Hughes in the full-back positions, had to pull out after dropping an axe on his foot while doing some building work at home. I only found out about it when I came in for training on the eve of the match at West Ham on 29 April, and heard Ian Callaghan ask Bob Paisley which of us was going to be the substitute for the game. 'Tommy is injured,' Bob replied, 'so Al will be playing.'

This, of course, was disappointing for Joey Jones, who had hoped that he would be the one given an opportunity to stake a claim for a place in the side in such circumstances. Still, it was clear that Tommy had virtually ruled himself out of the final, so Bob promised Joey that if I played badly he would be the next in line to play.

But I did well. We won 2–0 at West Ham, beat Manchester City 4–0 at home, and maintained our run of clean sheets with a goalless draw at Nottingham Forest. So, having been miles away from a first-team place a couple of months earlier, and thinking of returning to Scottish football with my tail between my legs, I was playing in the European Cup final – at Wembley.

I think I was probably more shocked than elated. In previous years, my only experience of European Cup finals was watching them on television with my friends in Sauchie and a supply of six-packs. It was hard to grasp that I was now playing in one. Even after the game, when Liverpool's midfielder Terry McDermott and I were walking around the Wembley pitch with the winners' medals in our hands, I remarked, 'I still have the feeling that I'm going to wake up tomorrow morning and find that this was just a dream.'

It was so hard for me to get switched on to the leap I had made that in the dressing room beforehand I even took time to get nervous. I thought, I should be more nervous than this. Something's wrong! Then I remembered what I had been doing when Liverpool were in the final the previous year – watching it on television with my mates – and this was followed by images of the history of the European Cup, notably the achievements of the great Real Madrid teams. It was then that I needed to ask where the toilet was!

Everybody knows that playing at Wembley is special. The stadium itself, which is to be knocked down and rebuilt, could not be described as such. I have played in better-appointed arenas, but because of its history and tradition, you cannot help but feel excited at being there. The aspects of the stadium that got to me most on my first trip there as a player were those twin towers. I get a buzz out of them even now: whenever I go to Wembley on behalf of the BBC, they always cause a little chill to go down the back of my neck.

When people talk about the size of the Wembley pitch, they often mention its 'wide open spaces', as if it is twice the size of other pitches. In fact, it is only marginally bigger, but for some reason you always seem to have plenty of time on it. When you have the ball, there's rarely any reason to get flustered. The only explanation I can give for this is that the condition of the pitch – usually perfect – makes it easier for players to be spot on with their touch and passing. These are the key elements in deciding how much space a team can create for themselves. My own passing was perhaps the strongest part of my game and I felt that the Wembley pitch was made for me. I wish I could have played all my matches on it – although that's not to say that I never had an indifferent game at Wembley or never made mistakes there. I am still liable to break out in a cold sweat over the memory of the 1978 European Cup final against Bruges, which was settled in Liverpool's favour in the second half by a Kenny Dalglish goal from Graeme Souness's pass.

Some matches are so one-sided that it's virtually impossible to imagine anything going wrong. The game against Bruges was just such a match – the opposition were negative in the extreme, and I spent most of my time on the halfway line, with no Bruges player close to me, and had nothing to worry about except playing passes. It was one of the most boring games I have ever played in, although I cannot offer an excuse for my casual back-pass, which gave a Bruges player an outstanding equalizing chance six minutes from the end. As the ball was knocked over our defence, I read the situation and hit it back to Ray Clemence – but not strongly enough to prevent a Bruges player fastening on to it and getting in a shot. It looked a certain goal ... until Phil Thompson appeared, seemingly from nowhere, to scramble the ball off the line.

I suddenly became Phil's best friend for life. When the ball was heading towards the net, my whole life flashed before my eyes. Had the ball gone in, and Liverpool lost, the stigma would have remained with me for ever. No matter how much else I achieved in the game, I would never have been able to live that error down. 'I did that for you,' Phil joked afterwards, 'but you wouldn't have done it for me.'

The old Alan Hansen might not, but the Alan Hansen in a red Liverpool shirt had begun to change. The more I played for Liverpool, the more I realized that football is a team game in every sense of the word and that I needed to integrate myself into that way of thinking to make the most of my career. As individualistic as I was, I was forced to accept that Liverpool's team spirit was the factor most responsible for putting them head and shoulders above the rest.

# 8 Money Money Money

During my Liverpool career, you could only earn a fortune by winning major trophies. In my first season at Anfield, when my salary was £7,500 a year, the bonus each player was paid for reaching the European Cup final against Bruges was just £250. But as a member of the team that beat the Belgians I was paid a bonus of £6,000.

Over the years, my salary became an increasingly large part of my total Liverpool earnings. For example, in my second season – 1978/79 – it was increased to £15,000, more than double the £6,000 bonus I was handed for the winning of the Championship. For the top players of today, though, the salary–bonus differential has become wider than ever. The wages are so high that they can set themselves up financially for the rest of their lives without winning anything, or even performing particularly well. In the 1998/99 season, the lowest-paid first-team player in the Premiership was earning £200,000 a year. Is it any wonder that a lot of managers have detected a change for the worse in their players' attitudes?

Twenty years ago, there were many players who would give 100 per cent to their clubs irrespective of whether they were paid one pound or a million. I fear that this has been lost to English football and that the situation is going to get worse. This, indeed, is a totally different football world from the one I inhabited and I don't like it.

The extent to which players have gone into a totally different financial league was the subject of my 1999 BBC TV documentary, *The Football Millionaires*. The programme set out to show the change in earnings and lifestyle of players since I retired in 1991, and among those featured was Robbie Savage, the 24-year-old Leicester and Wales midfielder. He had started his career as a member of Manchester United's youth squad, with the likes of Paul Scholes and David Beckham, was given a free transfer to Crewe and hit the jackpot when he moved to Leicester in the 1997/98 season. At the time of our interview, he was about to sign a new contract with the club that would set him up financially for the rest of his life. No disrespect to him, but I couldn't help thinking of the outstanding players of my generation – including those at Liverpool – who were never in that position.

I was more than satisfied with what Liverpool paid me, and I was well rewarded for my loyalty to the club through what I received from my testimonial year in 1988. My benefit match in May that year – a Liverpool XI against an England XI – was particularly successful. Originally, I had wanted a match involving Rangers, a club with a massive fan base that extends far beyond their local Glasgow borders, which could be virtually guaranteed to attract a big crowd for any match against an

English team. In this instance, the added attraction in bringing them to Anfield was that my old Liverpool colleague, Graeme Souness, was their manager. However, while Graeme was keen, the Rangers chairman, David Holmes, vetoed it because of fears about crowd trouble.

Then, the publicity afforded to England's preparations for the European Championship finals in West Germany in June provoked the idea that Bobby Robson might provide a team for my game so that he could try different players and tactical possibilities. I phoned Bobby myself, and within 20 minutes he had rung back to say that he would do it. He was fantastic – his support was something that I will never forget. I would have had to fork out something like £10,000 in expenses to get Rangers to Anfield, but for the England team, I was charged only for the players' travel by coach – £300!

In a match that Liverpool won 3–2, the other big drawing card for the fans was the return of Ian Rush from Juventus to play for my side. The attendance was 33,000 and the receipts swelled my testimonial fund to more than £200,000. But not all testimonials have as big an impact as this. I was one of the lucky ones.

Nowadays, such financial good fortune is much more widespread. The millions that clubs are raking in from television and merchandising is one factor. Another is the Jean-Marc Bosman ruling, which has meant that players are now free agents and thus able to move to other clubs at the end of their contracts without a transfer fee being paid. It has caused them to become more self-centred than ever. Every time they change club, much of the money that would previously have gone to the one they left now ends up in their pockets, and is incorporated in their basic pay. It makes perfect financial sense for players to adopt the attitude of mercenaries and keep on the move. For a number of years at Anfield, and certainly when I was employed there, testimonial matches for Liverpool players were quite common. Significantly, since 1992, there haven't been any.

In the old days, when a player continued to be tied to a club – on the option clause – after his contract had expired, the set-up was bad for the player but good for the clubs. Following the Bosman ruling, it's the other way round. You cannot blame the players for capitalizing on the situation, especially as the formation of the Premiership, which has intensified the motivation of clubs to reach the top, has given them so much scope to do so. The Premiership might just as well be on a different planet compared with the Nationwide League, if only because of the difference in income between the two from television. The desperation of clubs to stay in that élite group, or get into it, has led them to stockpile the best players. The stakes are higher than ever before, and clubs have found it impossible to resist the temptation to take greater financial risks.

A report by John Ley in the *Daily Telegraph* in January 1999 said it all. Of transfer fees in 1998, he wrote,

Spending rose throughout English football by just 3 per cent but, importantly, Premiership spending in the year just past increased from £209 million to £245 million – an increase of 17 per cent, while combined spending of the Nationwide League was down by £35 million. The era of Bosman made the top players fantastically wealthy and prevented some transfer fees, but it has not prevented clubs spending lavishly in the pursuit of greatness.

In 1990 [the year before my retirement], English clubs spent £58 million; that figure has increased 450 per cent to £314 million.

Percentage-wise, players' wages have leaped accordingly!

During the 1998/99 season, Coventry's chairman, Bryan Richardson, stated that, on average, as much as 56 per cent of Premiership income goes on players' salaries. This was supported by a survey of six top clubs over their 1997/98 financial year, published in the *Observer* in January 1999.

At the top of this list were Liverpool, whose wage bill – £30.1 million – was 66.3 per cent of their income. It was slightly misleading, because their figures were given for a fifteen-month period, due to a change in their year end. However, many will have found their outlay disturbing. The same could be said for Chelsea (£22.5 million – 60.7 per cent), Tottenham (£17 million – 54.5 per cent), Leeds (£14.5 million – 51.2 per cent) and Newcastle (£22.3 million – 45.4 per cent). It seemed strange that Manchester United (£26.9 million – 30.6 per cent) were at the bottom of the list but, as the biggest English club to have become a public limited company, they are subjected to more rigorous financial control. An even greater anomaly, as far as I am concerned, is that, of the top six, Chelsea were the only club to win anything in 1998.

Too many clubs are chasing too few top-class foot-ballers, especially top-class British footballers, and no matter how poorly a player performs for one club, there is invariably no shortage of others prepared to offer him another platform.

The erosion of club commitment in England can also be attributed to the influx of so many foreign players. Undoubtedly they have raised the skill level of our game, but when you sign a player from abroad there is often a risk factor concerning his ability to adapt to our football culture. The temperament of many Continental players does not fit easily into the English concept of a team's strength being underpinned by the willingness to push themselves beyond the limit on behalf of those who pay their wages. That was one of the most important aspects of all the Liverpool teams I played for. It was not just the technical ability of those sides that enabled Liverpool to dominate the game over such a long period but their sense of unity.

If anything, Kenny Dalglish is probably even more obsessive about this than Bob Paisley and Joe Fagan were. In his post-match media interviews, it is significant that Kenny hardly ever talks about individuals, no matter how much he might be pressed to do so. I would be a million-aire by now if I had received a pound for every time he has talked publicly about his players 'working hard as a team'. It is what he believes in – and the fact that he keeps saying it shows that he realizes players read newspapers!

However, as I think Graeme Souness discovered during his troubled spell as Liverpool's manager from 1991 to 1994, a period in which the financial revolution in

England was mushrooming, the old Liverpool dressing-room culture became increasingly difficult to sustain. I had a great deal of sympathy for Graeme: he found it difficult to accept that not all Liverpool players shared his fierce will-to-win and pride in the club. For every player like him, he found twenty more who were quite happy to allow their generous salaries to keep them in a comfort zone.

He was the perfect choice to succeed Kenny Dalglish in the job – a better choice than I would have been. But the run of success Liverpool had experienced under his predecessors had to end at some time, and the same could be said about the luck they had with their signings. For many years, Liverpool made more successful signings than any other club – the number of players who were bought for relatively small fees and became great players is remarkable. There is a certain degree of luck in this as well as good judgement, and I believe that it was in the former department that Graeme came unstuck.

I also felt sorry for his successor, Roy Evans, over the headaches he was given by centre-forward Stan Collymore, who he bought from Nottingham Forest for a then British record transfer fee of £8 million in July 1995. It seemed a tremendous signing for Liverpool. Collymore has two great feet, he is good in the air and his pace and power are awesome. At a time when Liverpool were known to be interested in him, I watched him in a match against Manchester United, when he was up against Gary Pallister – in my view, the best central defender in the United Kingdom in the 1990s. But even Pallister couldn't cope with Collymore, who scored a superb goal by beating him for pace then hitting the ball past Peter Schmeichel from 20 yards.

I felt that Collymore and Robbie Fowler in partnership up front for Liverpool would represent a dream ticket and that he would lead them back to the Championship. True, Collymore was something of a rough diamond when he joined Liverpool: he was erratic when receiving the ball with his back to the opposing goal – he needed it in front of him – and there were question marks over his temperament. But if you can't improve at a club like Liverpool, you won't improve anywhere.

As it turned out, of course, signing Collymore was a disaster.

For most people, getting the chance to play for Liverpool is the ultimate dream. But I'm not sure that Collymore felt that way. I should be careful what I say on the question of his lazy appearance, bearing in mind how my running style created misconceptions of me during the early part of my career. It is a fact that when players with a languid or casual style are performing badly they give the impression – often wrongly – that they are not trying. However, when I watched Collymore in action, I did sometimes feel he could have given more. He made me look like Vinnie Jones!

There were problems with him behind the scenes too. He continued to live in the Midlands, which inevitably meant some difficulty in his getting to the ground on time for training, and when Liverpool instructed him to play for the reserves on one occasion – to improve his match fitness – he refused. Roy Evans was criticized left, right and centre for being too soft with Collymore. I think a lot of people wanted Roy to fine him, suspend him or leave him on the sidelines. But if he had done that, Collymore's saleable value to Liverpool would have dropped drastically. By keeping him in the first team – in the shop window – Liverpool got £7 million for him, a loss of 1.5 million on what they had paid for him but, nevertheless, it was a great deal for Liverpool in view of his lack of success there – and what happened subsequently with him at Villa.

It seemed the perfect move for him, but during the 1998/99 season, he voiced disapproval at being selected as a substitute. He came into conflict with the manager, John Gregory, and even more so when he dropped out of the squad on the grounds of stress.

The way in which players' attitudes have changed indicates that no club in the foreseeable future will be as consistent as Liverpool were. I suppose that if you had to put money on anyone doing it, it would be Manchester United, who have been as dominant in the 1990s as Liverpool were in the 1970s and 1980s. United, whose historic Championship, FA Cup and European Champions League treble brought their total of recent honours to 12 in 10 years – compared to Liverpool's haul of 24 in 20 – have reaped the benefit of having a number of talented young English players who have graduated together from the youth- and reserve-team ranks together, not to mention an outstanding manager in Alex Ferguson. However, I'll be surprised if anyone ends up with as many medals with one club as I did.

The importance of team spirit is a hobby-horse of mine. The commercial world has become increasingly switched on to this element in recent years, but it is probably in team sports like football that the advantages of the right group dynamics or chemistry may be seen most clearly. The Leeds United teams managed by Don Revie from the mid-1960s to the early 1970s were outstanding for that and it's worth bearing in mind that Revie – whose wife, Elsie, was Scottish – was a close friend of the Scottish managerial giants like Bill Shankly, Matt Busby and Jock Stein. In his three-part television documentary about Shankly, Busby and Stein, the respected football writer Hugh McIlvanney, drew attention to the remarkable sense of unity of their teams, and suggested that it stemmed from the trio having been brought up in mining communities and, indeed, having worked down the pits. The point, of course, is that mining is dangerous and miners work together to survive. Revie himself did not have that background, but, in view of his association with Shankly, Busby and Stein, it is significant that all the players in his Leeds teams would clearly have run through brick walls for each other. Revie took a lot of outside ridicule for subjecting his players to games of carpet bowls and bingo sessions on the eve of matches, and especially when he attempted to implement such 'bonding' ideas with his players when he was England manager. Yet at club level nobody could deny that his methods were effective. As his captain Billy Bremner once pointed out, 'We were so protective of each other that if any opposing player tried to intimidate one of our lads he would find all eleven of us wanting to pay him back.'

In a book about those Leeds teams, Paul Reaney, their England right-back, gives a good example of this protectiveness. In a match against Manchester United, when George Best, frustrated by his failure to get the better of him, took a swipe at him off the ball, he recalled, 'I wasn't really expecting it, and when it happened, Norman Hunter [Leeds's much-feared left-side central defender] immediately came over to me and told me to go into a different position. He said, "Paul, you just go over there for a minute," and he stood right in front of Best as if to say, "You've got me now." Frightening.'

Another team whose sense of unity stood out like a beacon were Arsenal, when they were managed by George Graham (another Scot). But, if we are judging teams solely on this aspect of their game, I honestly believe that the greatest success story in football over the last twenty-five years has been produced not by Leeds, Arsenal or even Liverpool, but by the 'Crazy Gang' at Wimbledon.

I'm not a fan of the pragmatic, highly physical football they play, nor of the way that some of their players conduct themselves. When we were lined up in the Wembley tunnel with Wimbledon before their shock 1–0 win over us in the 1988 FA Cup final, they made bizarre attempts to out-psych us through snarling and making threats about how they were going to knock us physically out of our stride. Intimidation is part of the game, I know, but their behaviour on this occasion should not have been allowed. However, part of me loves Wimbledon FC! When it comes to the art of bonding players into an effective unit, this is the club for which I have the greatest admiration.

Their rise from the Southern League to the top strata –

in just a few years – was remarkable in itself. That they have maintained their status there, with no ground of their own, meagre attendances and players generally less technically polished than those at most other Premiership clubs, has been a tremendous achievement. Even more astounding is that since Wimbledon reached the top division in 1986 only three teams – Manchester United, Liverpool and Arsenal – have had a better average record than them. Wimbledon are proof that money and outstanding technical ability are not essential for football success.

The all-for-one one-for-all mindset that has been their trademark is not acquired by accident. It is mainly down to good management – to the people at the helm recognizing the importance of the characters of the players they sign; of making sure that they treat their players as equals, no matter the differences between them in ability; and that when their players are on club duty, they are kept together off the field almost as tightly as they are on it.

It is asking the impossible for all the players to like each other. More important is that they have enough professional respect for each other to be able to combine effectively as a unit.

Bob Paisley never tired of stressing: 'You cannot play as individuals, you have to work as a team.'

The principle was not always as evident in the Liverpool team as Paisley and other Liverpool managers might have wished. Players cannot be selfless all the time, as was shown by my link with Liverpool's brilliant left-side forward John Barnes in the 1987/88 Championship-winning team.

John was a key figure in that side because he could take on three or four defenders or, at least, hold the ball long enough to disrupt the opposition's attacking momentum and rhythm. The last Liverpool player who could beat defenders as easily as Barnes had been Steve Heighway, the club's winger in the 1970s, who is now the club's youth director. But John was possibly even better. His strength meant that even if he was dispossessed, or did not have full control of the ball, he could be relied upon to win a throw-in or corner. He was great for me. Earlier in my Liverpool career, the first thing I thought of doing when I had the ball at the back was to play it to the feet of Kenny Dalglish. When I played with John, he was the one who became my favourite passing target. If anything, I gave him too much of the ball – it was an easy option for me. It got to the stage where John became tired of it, and deliberately took up positions in which he knew I couldn't reach him. Instead of 'showing' for the ball to be played to his feet, he would occasionally turn and start running away from me. He might have moved only five or six yards, but that was enough to make it difficult – if not impossible – for me to bring him into the play. I said to him, 'You've worked out how not to get the ball from me, haven't you?'

He smiled. 'Too right I have,' he replied.

I couldn't blame him, not least because I was quite happy to give him the ball in situations where it was inevitable that defenders would clatter him. There was the odd occasion that I made myself unavailable to receive the ball as well. I did it to Steve Nicol when Liverpool drew 1–1 on a mud-heap of a pitch at Derby in March 1988 to establish a club record of 29 successive matches without defeat. I paid for it, too, because Steve gave me the ball anyway, and as I tried to boot it clear, it hit my shin and flew over the goal-line for a Derby corner. The wry grin on Steve's face said it all.

However, while moments like these might suggest otherwise, the bond between the players at Liverpool when it came to helping each other was more powerful than that of most other teams. Before I joined Liverpool, it was well known among Anfield insiders that Tommy Smith and Emlyn Hughes (Tommy's successor as Liverpool's team captain) did not get on well. Tommy, who felt that Emlyn was self-centred, has said that the friction between the two dated back to when they first started playing together in 1967. It rose to the surface again in the early 1980s, when Tommy publicly revealed his dislike of Emlyn in his autobiography; and again in 1997, when Emlyn was initially the only member of Liverpool's 1977 European Cup-winning team not to receive an invitation to attend a gala charity dinner to celebrate the twentieth anniversary of the triumph. Tommy, who had scored the goal that brought Liverpool that win, apparently told the organizers that he would not support the event if Emlyn was going to be there, although he maintains that the remark was taken more seriously than it had been intended.

However, Bill Shankly made the most telling remark about the Smith–Hughes feud when he was the players' team manager. Tommy recalls that when he complained to Shankly about Emlyn, Shankly told him, 'Tommy, son, you don't have to live with him. All you have to do is play football with him.'

All clubs, of course, experience the occasional training-match clash between players. Perhaps the most disturbing example was the one involving John Hartson and Eyal Berkovic at West Ham, when Hartson aimed a kick at the Israeli midfielder's head. At Liverpool, the only training-match flare-ups I can recall were one between Graeme Souness and Alan Kennedy, and another between Phil Neal and David Fairclough. Yet in each case it lasted no more than a few seconds, and was then forgotten. As we were encouraged to be honest with each other, there were times during or after matches when someone would go overboard in his criticism of a colleague. But, here again, the team spirit was so strong that nobody bore any grudges.

Liverpool's management put a great deal of thought into it and it was tremendously important to my personal success at the club. I think I would have been more comfortable – and maybe more successful – at international level had that spirit been in evidence with the Scotland team. It is much more difficult to establish it in a national squad because of the limited time the players spend together, and because club cultures and methods are different. But, as the Irish Republic showed under the management of Jack Charlton, it is not impossible to imbue a national team with a club spirit.

Ironically, Scotland, too, have achieved it under the management first of Andy Roxburgh and now Craig Brown. However, when I was playing for my country, there were a number of little cliques in the camp – an obvious danger when you have players from so many different clubs – and the major ones involved the home-based players and the Anglos. Scottish players with English clubs were perceived to have hit the jackpot and become alienated from their roots, so there was bound to be an underlying feeling of resentment towards them. It is a pity that the problem wasn't properly addressed.

I remember that before international matches at Hampden Park the squad would stay on the coast, at Troon or Turnberry, and occasionally go for walks on the beach. The home-based players and the Anglos would split into groups, which could be as much as half a mile apart, and you could be sure that the two factions would be gossiping about each other.

This situation was never allowed to arise at Anfield, and the advantage this gave us was such that whenever I walked out of the dressing-room tunnel before a match, I never felt we could be beaten. No matter who we were playing, I was always confident that the team spirit alone would carry us through. I never had that feeling when I was playing for Scotland.

A number of simple factors helped Liverpool develop this feeling of togetherness. One of the most effective was that all the players had tea, biscuits and a social chat before their training sessions on Friday mornings. It was difficult to motivate yourself for the Friday session after a midweek match, because we were so conscious of the need to sharpen ourselves up for the Saturday game without taking too much out of ourselves. The players did not enjoy the training games on Fridays and the games reflected this. Kenny Dalglish felt that, before training, the players might benefit from a half-hour get-together where they could forget about football and just enjoy each other's company.

Our unity was also helped by the fact that Liverpool did not employ a 'kit man' to look after the players' strip on match days; the job was carried out by whichever first-team squad members were not in the side. The job, which included picking up all the players' dirty shirts, shorts and socks from the dressing-room floor, packing them in hampers and carrying them to the team bus, was not very pleasant, but there was no way that anyone could consider such tasks to be beneath his dignity when they saw players as accomplished as Graeme Souness, Kenny Dalglish and Ian Rush willingly doing them.

Such players were superstars, but their input into the team was as great as everyone else's, if not greater. This is one of the reasons why, of today's high-profile players, I admire Alan Shearer. Quite apart from his ability as a goal-scorer, the Newcastle and England captain is also a great dressing-room mixer. As Ray Harford, his former Blackburn manager, once said, 'He's a superstar without a superstar's ego.' Fabrizio Ravanelli was also a superstar when he signed for Middlesbrough, after playing a big part in Juventus's European Cup success in 1996. However, my main image of him in English football is of a centre-forward who, given a difficult ball to chase five minutes from the end with his team a goal down, was liable to shrug his shoulders and wave his arms in disgust at the quality of the pass. How many times have you seen Alan Shearer doing that? Or Kenny Dalglish, Graeme Souness or Ian Rush?

It was difficult for any player at Anfield to stand apart from the rest. When the Liverpool squad were on away trips, they all had to eat together at a big round table. The management did not take kindly to anyone who turned up late: 'If we cannot rely on you here, then we cannot rely on you when you are on the pitch,' an offender would be told.

Even when the players were having a drink at the bar it was never in twos and threes – if there were, say, sixteen players in the first-team squad, Liverpool wanted them all involved. The net for this fraternity did not contain only the players: it held the training staff and even the coach driver. Old habits die hard. For Scotland matches, the Liverpool players in the squad – Kenny Dalglish, Graeme Souness, Steve Nicol and myself – would all travel north together on a Sunday and, once we reached the hotel and put our bags in our rooms, we would immediately join forces again for a drink at the bar. We were often the only players there: all the others would be socializing in different groups in their rooms.

Liverpool were always looking for ways to maintain and strengthen this camaraderie. Even the board appreciated its importance. One of my responsibilities as Liverpool's captain under Kenny Dalglish was to negotiate with the chairman and secretary over the team bonuses for exhibition matches or competitions such as the British Championship game – involving the winners of the English and Scottish titles – in Dubai. I would always use the line: 'There is a great spirit in the camp and you don't want to undermine it by causing players to feel they have been short-changed financially.' While the chairman and secretary did not allow this to cloud their financial judgement, they were possibly more sympathetic to the argument than some of their counterparts at other clubs.

144

My addiction to golf clearly started much earlier than I think. Whoever put that club in my hands, during a holiday in Ayr when I was three, has a lot to answer for.

This picture was taken when I was given the medal for academic excellence at my primary school, aged eleven. It was quite a family hat-trick: the prize had previously been given to my brother, John (left), and sister, Maureen.

In signing for Partick Thistle, I gave up my dream of becoming a professional golfer. As indicated by this picture, taken at the start of my soccer career, the fantasy didn't totally die.

John and I when we were together at Partick Thistle, just before I made my first-team début for the club against Dundee in August 1973. He's the one with that dreadful moustache.

The fact that Bob Paisley was laughing when he signed me for Liverpool might have had something to do with the fact that the decision was taken on the recommendation of his scouting staff and that he personally had never seen me play!

My Liverpool league début against Derby in 1977. As heading the ball was hardly one of my strong points, this picture could be something of a collector's item.

The sight of Phil Thompson helping me out against Manchester United was more common! No disrespect to Tommy Smith and Mark Lawrenson, but Phil was my favourite central-defensive partner.

My first taste of European cup glory, in my first season as a Liverpool player.
Here I am with my fellow Scots, Graeme Souness (left) and Kenny Dalglish
(right), and the trophy, on the train journey back to Liverpool after our win over
Bruges in the 1978 final at Wembley.

The victory parade through the streets of Liverpool. At one stage I got off
the bus to use a pub toilet and, when I tried to get back on it, a policeman who
didn't recognize me barred my way. Fortunately, another policeman came to
my rescue and, with the bus some 400 yards up the road, took me back to it
on his motorbike.

As a defender who was comfortable on the ball, I loved nothing more than to be in possession and to display my creative ability. When I was running with the ball, I had a habit of doing so with my thumbs pointed outwards.

One of the goals I scored up to the mid-1980s, when the wear and tear on my knees forced me to stop trying to play like a forward. The volley brought Liverpool their late equalizer in the 2–2 draw against Manchester United in the 1979 FA Cup semi-final.

The faces of Kenny Dalglish and myself say it all. I was so elated that when I ran back I must have broken the world 50-metres record.

Eat your heart out Shearer! Another example of me as a scorer, this time in the 5–0 win over Coventry in 1984.

Here's me doing what most defenders are discouraged from doing – dribbling their way out of trouble. No wonder my Liverpool managers, Bob Paisley and Joe Fagan, had grey hairs!

We give our lungs an airing of a different kind as we celebrate winning the Milk Cup final replay against Everton at Maine Road in the 1983/84 season. It was the first leg of a remarkable treble – that season, we also won the Championship and European Cup.

Liverpool would not have been as successful as they were when I was there but for the scoring talents of Ian Rush. This Rush goal helped Liverpool win their penalty shoot-out against AS Roma in the 1984 European Cup final.

The climax to my first season as Liverpool captain: winning the FA Cup – at the expense of Everton in the final – to clinch the double.

Not for one moment am I suggesting there was never dissension in the ranks at Liverpool As with most clubs, and especially those with the biggest first-team squads, they found it difficult to make players accept not being in the team. No player is happy in this situation, no matter how many times you put your arm round him and tell him he is valued.

This, of course, is the tricky part of the rotation politics of Chelsea and Manchester United. It has proved a particular headache at Chelsea, where the rotation-selection policy implemented by Ruud Gullit and maintained by his successor, Gianluca Vialli, has meant the team being changed from match to match with most people in the dark about what the Chelsea management consider their first-choice line-up. This was not so at Liverpool, although the disappointment of players at being on the periphery of the first-team action was no easier to conceal than it has been for those at Stamford Bridge.

Liverpool's selection policy was the opposite of Chelsea's. Liverpool decided who their best 11 players were and, no matter how well someone had played when one of the 11 had been out of the team, he quickly found himself back on the outside looking in when the guy he had replaced was fit again – or judged to be fit again. As I have said, as someone who was regarded as one of the first choices, I was often selected for the team when I was not fully fit. Of course, it was a great compliment to me and boosted my confidence. However, as my inclusion in the side meant the exclusion of somebody else, it could get embarrassing. In 1982, I was brought back into the team after injury, even though Liverpool had experienced an inspired run of nine wins and a draw from 10 matches in my absence. On the day of the tenth match, at Manchester United, I had suffered a gash in my leg in an accident at home. The injury, caused by broken glass and needing six stitches, could hardly be construed as a blow for the team because they held United to a 1–1 draw, a good result by any standards. As Phil Thompson and Mark Lawrenson had played well together at the heart of the defence, there seemed no point in rushing me back into action. Liverpool, though, had other ideas.

I did not train on the Thursday morning, the day after the United match, but on the Friday, Liverpool's assistant manager, Joe Fagan, asked, 'Do you want to play tomorrow at Manchester City?'

I said, 'I'm not sure if I can run properly yet.'

'But do you *want* to play?' Joe persisted.

The fact that I nodded was all the justification that he and Bob Paisley needed to get me back into the team. I was selected to play alongside Phil Thompson and Mark Lawrenson was switched to midfield, at the expense of Terry McDermott. Needless to say, Terry was spitting blood. There were a number of incidents like that at Liverpool, and I think it says much for the excellent relationship between the players that it had no effect whatsoever on the way in which they dovetailed together. Paul Walsh, the clever little striker who played for Liverpool from 1984 to 1988, was also spitting blood after Kenny Dalglish omitted him for a match against Oxford. Kenny named the team just over an hour before the kick-off, and as he was giving some instructions to the players, Walsh could be seen muttering under his breath. Kenny ignored it for a while, but then he turned to Walsh and said, 'Have you got anything to say?'

Walsh, taken aback at having been put on the spot, blurted out, 'You can **** off.'

At that point, we expected an explosion. But Kenny handled it brilliantly. 'There's only one person who's going to do that here, Paul,' he replied calmly, and with that, he just carried on with his pre-match briefing as if nothing had happened.

Three or four players at Liverpool were known as the 'Pop-up Toasters', a reference to the frequency during matches with which their numbers would be dug out of the bag and held up to signal that Liverpool wanted to take them off. The first to get the nickname was Terry McDermott and the second was Craig Johnston.

Though Terry played for England, and some of the goals he scored were as good as you're ever going to get, I felt he was underrated. In fairness, he probably didn't have as much heart as other Liverpool midfielders, such as Graeme Souness and Jimmy Case – which caused us to view each other as kindred spirits. We spent a lot of time in each other's company off the field and would joke, 'The others have the heart, but we have the talent so we don't need it.'

Terry could usually find a release for disappointment or anger through his sense of humour. One day, a damaged thumb prompted Bob Paisley to substitute him, then leave him out of the side for the next match. Terry fumed, and what made it harder for him to accept was that he was one of the most prolific midfield goal-scorers in the country, and at the time Liverpool were struggling in the scoring department. He thought that one of the strikers should have been left out, not him. But he made a joke of it. He came into the dressing room, with his newspaper open at the crossword. 'Oh, this is interesting, boys,' he said. '"Liverpool striker, four letters."' Then he added, 'I've got it. None.'

But substitution or non-selection were no laughing matter to Craig Johnston. Born in South Africa and raised in Australia, he spent seven years at Liverpool in the 1980s and played a big part in their success. Bought from Middlesbrough in April 1981, by Bob Paisley, he operated on the right side of midfield and was super-fit and enthusiastic. But he was very individualistic – a sort of maverick, I would say – and although he was popular in the dressing room, he could be exasperating to play with. He was a little erratic when it came to reading the game, and he could be very erratic indeed with his crossing. Liverpool worked a lot on this aspect of his game in training, getting him to practise crosses to a specific area or player, instead of just hitting the ball into the middle and hoping. But he just couldn't do it. He would chip the ball when he should have driven it, and drive it when he should have chipped. Some players are like that – they find it difficult to look up when they get into a crossing position, and when they do they tend to select the wrong option.

He struck me as a complex person – the extreme version of myself, in that although he oozed confidence outwardly I had a feeling he was insecure inside. This, indeed, was illustrated when Joe Fagan became manager, and bought John Wark, another midfielder, from Ipswich in March 1984. Wark, though similar to Craig in physical power and the amount of ground he covered, played in the centre of midfield. As a box-to-box runner, he scored more goals than Craig, yet Craig, through his work in the wide areas, also did a valuable job in stretching defences. So it was not so much Liverpool thinking that John was a better player than Craig, merely that he was a different type of player who could provide another attacking option.

Craig, however, did not see it that way. Wark quickly established a place in Liverpool's starting line-up at his expense, and eventually, in the 1984/85 season, when Wark was the top Liverpool scorer, Craig exploded. The flashpoint was Liverpool's first home match, against West Ham, when Wark scored twice in a 3–0 Liverpool win. In the dressing room afterwards Craig told Joe Fagan, 'Well, you've got your wish. You want me out of here, and you signed Wark to get me out.'

Joe, rarely one to raise his voice, or get into a slanging match with anyone, calmly told Craig he was wrong. 'Lad, settle down,' he added. 'Just go away and think about it.'

The following season Craig became a regular member of the side, when Kenny Dalglish was manager and Liverpool achieved the Championship–FA Cup double. But, as if to underline his maverick side, he sensationally announced his decision to retire from the game in the week of the 1988 FA Cup final against Wimbledon.

He explained that he wanted to return to Australia to look after his sister, who had been involved in a serious accident, and to pursue other interests such as photography. Those who knew him argued that the decision also stemmed from the theatrical element in his temperament and personality, and his need to signal his independence.

It was a bold decision by any standards, and one that a person as conservative as me wouldn't have dreamed of taking.

It was beyond my comprehension that anyone would want to give up a football career with Liverpool. But, then, I was being paid the money I wanted, and outside my first season at the club, I was never dropped from the side. Above all, I had so much help from those around me. As a player with the responsibility of setting Liverpool's attack in motion from the back, the only thing I could have done with was a player up front who was good in the air and could therefore have given people like me at the back another passing option.

I am not talking about a John Fashanu; I mean someone like Andy Gray or Graeme Sharp – each of whom was a highly intelligent centre-forward who could involve himself effectively in any build-up play on the ground – or, indeed, John Toshack, the giant Welshman who formed an outstanding Liverpool striking partnership with Kevin Keegan but who left the club in my first season there.

The only subsequent centre-forwards who could provide this element were David Johnson and John Aldridge, who were good in the air but not exceptional. Having a big centre-forward, who can give a team the scope to take an aerial route to goal, has its drawbacks, as has been seen with Duncan Ferguson when he was at Everton. As

Ferguson is the best centre-forward in Britain in the air, there was a tendency for Everton to rely too much on this side of his game.

Liverpool's passing, the characteristic for which we were best noted, was another yardstick by which our team spirit could be assessed. Every player concentrated on giving the sort of passes that a team-mate wanted to receive, rather than the ones he wanted to play; and every player repeatedly made good runs off the ball to give the man in possession plenty of options. The playing philosophy of Liverpool FC was encapsulated in just three words: 'Pass and move.' Liverpool occasionally had a training-match rule that a player had to move two yards forwards, backwards or to either side immediately he passed the ball; if he didn't, his team would be penalized and the ball given to the other team. This helps to explain why Liverpool players were rarely seen running with the ball, trying to beat two or three players in a mazy dribble. Of course, we had players who could do it and, indeed, if anybody had the freedom to take chances in possession it was me. But the movement of the team, the willingness of the players to simplify the game for each other, meant that there were few times when it was necessary for them to dwell on the ball.

One of the advantages of stringing a lot of passes together as we did – apart from the obvious one that the opposition cannot score if they do not have the ball – was summed up once by Alex Ferguson when he talked about the hypnotic effect it can have on the other side. He pointed out, 'The ball is like a magnet to them. No matter how disciplined they might be, there is bound to be a time when a player will lose his patience, dive in for the ball and leave his team vulnerable.' But stringing a lot of passes together can also have a hypnotic effect on the team making the passes, and cause them to be viewed as robots.

I remember this criticism being made of me personally, by the Liverpool management, when we were beaten 4–3 by Crystal Palace in the FA Cup semi-final in 1990, after being a goal ahead at half-time, then 3–2 in front with about ten minutes to go. In the first half, when we pulverized Palace and could easily have been five up, I lost count of the number of times that I played our left-back David Burrows into good crossing positions. At half-time, David made a joke of it. 'Can't you play the ball somewhere else?' he asked me. 'I'm knackered.'

I said, 'Well, stop making the runs and I'll stop giving you the ball.' However, although my link with David had not amounted to much as far as Liverpool scoring went, I saw no reason to try something else in the second half. I did exactly the same then as I had in the first. I just thought, Well, the law of averages means that it's bound to pay off eventually.

The following day, as I was discussing the match with Ronnie Moran, then Kenny Dalglish's number two, he said, 'Did you not think about switching the ball to the other side?' He reminded me that the Liverpool player wide on the right, Ray Houghton, had had John Salako marking him, and that Salako, a natural attacking left-winger or left-side midfielder, was not the most efficient defensive player in the world. All of which shows that, whatever style of play a team favours, it is easy to become stereotypical.

The fans love to see players doing something unorthodox or spectacular on the ball, and I have to say that, as a football spectator, I do too. Ironically, the 'flair teams' I have criticized on television in the past for their lack of discipline – Tottenham, Chelsea, Newcastle and West Ham – are among the first teams I would want to see to be entertained. But, as a player who wanted to achieve major club honours, I would not have fancied playing for them.

I have had a number of conversations about this with my former BBC colleague Des Lynam, who is forever eulogizing the players who seem able to make the ball do everything but sing and dance. I take a more pragmatic view. One quality that the truly great players have had in common (and I am talking of stars of the calibre of Pele, Johann Cruyff, Michel Platini, Diego Maradona and George Best) is that their breathtaking technical ability was allied to considerable mental and physical strength: on days when things were not going well for them on the ball, they could still be relied on to do a good job in other ways for their team.

That is not to say that teams cannot afford to have a 'luxury' player, which was how some people viewed Platini, the inspiration behind France's World Cup and European Championship successes in the mid-1980s. At that time, I was amazed to hear one or two players describe him as 'lazy'. He wasn't lazy at all: it was just that he had been given a free role and, with plenty of team-mates who could do his running off the ball for him, he was encouraged to concentrate on exploiting his skills. However, this principle is riskier in English football, where there are so many competitive matches and so few easy ones.

One of my Liverpool colleagues who epitomized the best elements of English football was right-back Steve Nicol, who was with the club from 1981 to 1994. When I was switched from the left side to the right of the Liverpool back four towards the end of my career, when my knee problems had taken their toll on my running, it made me feel I could light a cigar and read a newspaper to have Steve on the outside. His fitness was astonishing. Dieticians would be horrified at the amount he ate. He could eat for Britain. He and I and our families once went on a Norwegian cruise together and he probably consumed more than the rest of us put together. It was not unusual for him to go through six or eight packets of crisps in one go. But he never carried any excess weight, hardly missed a tackle and gave the impression of being able to bomb up and down that right touchline for ever. Suffice it to say that after our first match together on the right, I thought, Where have you been all my life?

# 9 The Tartan Connection

The first thing that needs to be said about Kenny Dalglish and Graeme Souness is that they are my only former colleagues at Liverpool who are probably more dogmatic than I am. In football arguments neither would back down even when it was clear to everyone else within earshot which one was fighting a losing battle. As far as Kenny and Graeme are concerned, they have never lost an argument in their lives – and I'm not far behind them.

Kenny and I are close friends, but you'd never think so if you were sitting in on one of our football discussions. They reach absurd levels at times. If I make a comment on TV with which Kenny doesn't agree (not unusual), he's never averse to telling me. One such instance arose from my analysis of a Liverpool–Derby match in 1997 when I criticized Derby's central defender Jacob Laursen for giving Liverpool's striker Michael Owen too much space as the teenager fastened on to a ball played towards the touchline. Owen had drifted off Laursen, into a deeper position, and the Derby player, instead of staying tight with Owen, allowed him to turn and run at him with the ball.

If the ball had been played quickly to Owen's feet, and Laursen had not been able to get there, then fine – stand off him. But nobody will ever convince me that allowing Owen to run at you in one of the least congested areas of the field is not asking for trouble. As it happened, Owen's control let him down and Laursen won the ball, which prompted Kenny to point out that my criticism of the defender was irrelevant. But my attitude was that, nine times out of ten, Laursen would have been punished for giving his opponent so much space.

Our argument took up virtually the whole of the two-and-a-half-hour lunch I had with Kenny and his son Paul the following day. But for the intervention of Paul, who told us we were driving him crazy, we would have been going at it hammer and tongs for the rest of the afternoon. Needless to say, neither of us was prepared to back down.

Not long afterwards, I covered a Derby–Leeds United match in which Leeds scored as a result of Derby's Christian Dailly making exactly the same mistake as Laursen against Jimmy Floyd Hasselbaink. Leeds had been 3–0 down and that goal gave them a 4–3 victory. My first reaction was to telephone Kenny to point this out to him but I managed to stop myself – I didn't have time for another verbal set-to!

I have been involved in many such battles with Kenny and Graeme over the years. But of all the people I have mixed with in professional football, these are the players I feel the most protective towards. I will not hear a bad word said about either of them because if any players at

Liverpool can take most of the credit for helping me become as successful as I was, it's them.

Kenny, Graeme and I were bound to be drawn closely together at Anfield because from 1977, when I signed for the club, and 1981, when Liverpool bought Steve Nicol from Ayr United, we were the only Scots there. Newspapers often wanted to take photographs of us together – and I was nearly always in the middle of the group. I'm not sure if the other two were aware of this but I quickly realized that if I was at the side the papers could cut me out.

We were very much together when it came to national pride. We gleefully took advantage of any evidence we could lay our hands on to prove Scotland's greatness to our English colleagues. When one newspaper compiled a list of their 10 greatest men of all time in the United Kingdom, and included three Scots but no Englishmen, Graeme bought 20 copies and adorned the dressing room with them. In terms of getting one over on our brothers from the other side of the border, I reckon that was our finest moment. I feel a close affinity with Graeme and Kenny perhaps because, having worked with them, I have had an insight into the sides of them that the public do not see.

Graeme, who played with me at Liverpool for six years, from January 1978 to June 1984, was nicknamed 'Champagne Charlie' because of his glamorous lifestyle and sophisticated designer clothes. He had tremendous pride and self-confidence, and I think that many people who did not know him pigeon-holed him as arrogant. I remember someone once observing, 'If Graeme Souness were a chocolate bar, he'd eat himself!' When I first started mixing with him in the Scotland squad I just thought he was flash.

It is easy to make a snap judgement on people when you only see them for a few days every three or four months. Quite often, you're wrong, as I found with Graeme when I was with him at Liverpool. In the Liverpool dressing room he was just an ordinary guy who wanted to play to the best of his ability and do well. He is down-to-earth and takes a genuine interest in other people. If you introduced him to a friend and Graeme saw him again six months later, he would remember who the person was and go over and talk to him. Unlike a number of players who achieve fame and fortune, he never lost sight of his roots.

It has been the same with Kenny. When he was manager of Liverpool, and the team did not play well, he was as disappointed for the fans as he was for the club. He felt an immense sense of responsibility towards them. 'Think of the punters who have paid good money to watch you play,' he would say.

Some feel that one of the differences between Graeme and Kenny as players was that Graeme's view of the game was narrower; that he found it more difficult to accept that not everyone could have the same ability and style of play as himself. He was one of the few midfielders who are superb on the ball and also aggressive and combative in their general play. Indeed, he relished a physical battle, the macho, gladiatorial side of the game. To me, Terry Yorath, the former Leeds and Wales midfielder, provided a perfect insight into his nature. Having committed a bad foul on

Graeme, about five minutes later Yorath himself was flattened by a tackle from behind. As he was lying on the ground in a daze, he asked the trainer who had done it. He heard a booming Scottish voice proclaim, 'It was me – Graeme.' As I have said, this side of football was foreign to me.

It was perhaps typical of Graeme that, during one of my bad patches – times when he was among those who gave me the most encouragement and support – he also tried to convince me of the advantages of playing his way. 'You have to assert yourself and when you cannot do it by playing football, you have to do it in other ways,' he told me. 'Technically I'm not as good as you are, but I'll get in there and sort a few people out and that is what you have to learn to do.'

I took on board the advice to be stronger mentally. Needless to say, I ignored the rest! It wasn't in me to be like him. While this did not undermine our relationship in any way, I think it's fair to say that Graeme took longer to accept me for what I was than Kenny did. Apart from being more aggressive and confrontational than I am, Graeme was also more aggressive and confrontational than Kenny. This, indeed, came through when Graeme succeeded Kenny as Liverpool's manager. It is no secret that one of the men with whom he came into conflict at Anfield was Phil Thompson, who had been Graeme's predecessor as Liverpool captain. I don't know the reasons for the fall-out between them, which led to Phil being sacked from his job on the Anfield coaching staff, but I suspect that Phil, now back at Liverpool as first-team coach under the management of Gerard Houllier, still feels some pain over it.

My own relationship with Graeme was more harmonious, although I know what he can be like when he's angry with you. Managers do not take kindly to anyone pointing out publicly what is wrong with their teams, especially when they are not getting good results. I naïvely overlooked this when the BBC were covering a Liverpool Uefa Cup tie and volunteered to go into the Anfield coaches' room – the famous 'Boot Room' – to ask Graeme what his team would be. I had made a criticism about Liverpool's defensive set-up a week or two previously, and as soon as Graeme clapped eyes on me, he started having a go. He was virtually snarling as he said, 'Yeah, it's a hard job this – especially when people like you are telling me where I'm going wrong.'

The only other person in the room was Tom Saunders, Liverpool's youth development officer, and I tried to make a joke of it with him. 'Would you say that my visit to this room was a big mistake, Tom?' I asked.

He gave a wry smile. 'Think so,' he replied.

Graeme saw the funny side. He glared at me, shook his head, then handed me a sheet of paper. 'Before you go, here's the team,' he said. I met him again a couple of days later and this time he was all smiles. We were bosom pals again.

Of the two, Kenny is the one I have been particularly close to, of course. Our Liverpool careers ran almost in tandem: Kenny joined the club within months of my arrival in 1977 and left in the same week in 1991. When I joined Liverpool, I couldn't drive, and as Kenny and I both lived in Southport, he gave me a lift to and from training each morning. After a while, he invited me to have dinner with him and his family every Friday night. We have remained friends to this day (and he has the honour of being my golf partner). Our friendship had to be fine-tuned when Kenny became Liverpool's player-manager in May 1985, on the eve of the club's ill-fated European Cup final against Juventus, and appointed me his team captain. But, despite the pitfalls of his being both my boss and close friend, I think the balance we struck was excellent. At any club, there is a them-and-us divide between the playing and management staff, but even though Kenny and I were so close, the players looked upon me as one of 'us'. They trusted me. Had they not, and had they been afraid to talk about Kenny in front of me, my job would have been impossible.

Kenny's decision to make me captain must have seemed perverse. As I have said, I did not see myself as the type to motivate players when the team had their backs to the wall – I needed them to lift me. Even in the dressing room before a game it was a chore to find something to say that would provide a bridge between Kenny's team talk and our departure on to the field.

During a trip to Southampton, I thought I had been given the perfect script when I heard someone talk about the length of the journey and point out that it would be even harder for us to bear if we were beaten. Just before we took the field at the Dell, I shouted, 'Don't come off this pitch disappointed because, I'll tell you what, it's a long way back to Liverpool.'

We lost 4–1.

At times like these Kenny had no compunction about giving me as much stick as he gave anybody else. He went off his head with me when we drew 0–0 at Norwich towards the end of our 1987/88 Championship-winning season. About 10 minutes from the end, I intercepted a Norwich pass and played the ball back to goalkeeper Bruce Grobbelaar from forty yards. It was a negative move, but I felt it was a better option than trying to probe for a chance for us to score. Kenny disagreed.

Immediately we got back into the dressing room, Kenny, red-faced and almost frothing at the mouth, asked me, 'That ball near the end, what the hell were you doing? You took the easy option.'

We had an argument, and neither of us was prepared to back down. But Kenny then switched to something else and the whole episode was forgotten. He has never been one to bear a grudge.

Kenny never asked for my opinion, but I never felt I couldn't give it. I was very open with him, not just in my own relationship with him but about his dealings with other players. If Kenny upset a player, and I thought he was in the wrong, I would tell him so.

Today, my only criticism of Kenny is that he does himself no favours with his dismissive attitude to the media. Football has become a media-driven sport, and there is a greater onus than ever before for managers and players to be 'media friendly'. But Kenny is suspicious of newspaper, TV and radio people. I think he feels – with some justification – that they are trying to coax him into making undiplomatic comments about his team and the opposition. Whenever he is interviewed, he is very much on his guard.

I can relate to this because, as a player, I was not comfortable with the media either. I felt there was enough pressure on me on the field without my being in the spot-light off it. After training and matches, I just wanted to get away from the ground. I looked upon football as my job, not my hobby, and when I was at home with my family, I switched off and led a 'normal' life. I like to think I was always pleasant to the media, but if I could find a diplo-matic way to get out of being interviewed, I would. My present colleagues at the BBC remember discussions about players they could ask for their views on the games covered on *Match of the Day*. Apparently Des Lynam used to say, 'Well, you'll never get Alan Hansen, will you?'

Managers have no escape from this spotlight. Under the Premiership rules those at the top end of the scale have to make themselves available for post-match interviews and, indeed, the increase in media interest has meant many have had to devote what they would consider an unreasonable amount of their time to it. Not long ago I was interested to read Brian Little's comments about the change in his professional life when he parted company with Aston Villa and stepped into the Nationwide League with Stoke City. A step down? Maybe, but to Little it was also a step up because of the difference between Villa and Stoke in the media attention they attract. He found that being less in demand for interviews enabled him to spend more time with the players on the training ground, the part of the job that managers enjoy most, and have the occasional day off to recharge his batteries.

The press do not take kindly to managers they perceive as hostile or uncooperative. Thus, while I admire Kenny's determination to be true to himself, his media attitude is at odds with what is now required in our hyped-up modern football world, in which the so-called 'brand image' of the leading clubs is as important as their results. At a time when he was attracting particularly negative publicity, I telephoned him and joked, 'You need a personal image consultant. I'll do the job for you.' Shortly afterwards he laughed at my expense when one of the tabloids criticized my BBC performances at the 1998 World Cup finals, on the grounds that I was too outspoken, and he said, 'I should be acting as your image consultant.' However, it's a pity that Kenny comes across publicly as dour and uncommunicative. It explains largely why his managerial record – not so much with Liverpool, but certainly with Blackburn – has not had the acclaim it merits.

His achievement in steering Blackburn from the old Second Division to the Premiership title in three years was astonishing. People go on about how fortunate he was to be given £30 million to spend in the transfer market by Blackburn's benefactor, Jack Walker, and while I do not dispute that this helped him, nobody is going to tell me that any half-decent manager could have done what Kenny did at Ewood Park.

When Kenny became manager there, he inherited a long record of failure: in the light of their revival, it is easy to forget that Blackburn's title win under him was their first for eighty-one years. What's more, he broke the barrier with a team that was more functional than brilliant. As for money, a number of managers in the past had had plenty of dosh to buy players and had blown it; but the bonus for Blackburn under Kenny was that the big-name players who have subsequently been sold – like

Alan Shearer, Graeme Le Saux, Henning Berg and David Batty – have fetched more money than was paid for them.

Kenny's negative media attitude has rebounded on him in other ways. Some pundits, eager to undermine him, have used his self-imposed departures from Liverpool and Blackburn to question his staying power. That is a ludicrous suggestion. When Kenny left Liverpool he needed a break from football, and to recuperate from the strain of the Hillsborough disaster. He had been at the forefront of Liverpool's attempts to support the families of the spectators who lost their lives. As for Blackburn, the change of role that saw him hand the team manager's baton to Ray Harford and become director of football seemed a good idea at the time. In those days, though, the terms of reference of the post were not as clearly defined as they are now. I sense that the wide-ranging nature of the job, and the small detail involved, frustrated rather than stimulated him. On top of all this, there was reportedly a change of attitude by Jack Walker. It has been claimed that he began to adopt more of a hands-on approach in areas in which Kenny had expected to be the dominant force, particularly with regards to decisions on players that Kenny wanted to sign. So, despite the grandiose title of his new post, I think Kenny probably believed he was less in control of his own destiny than ever.

Another reason why some pundits think that Kenny's effectiveness as a manager is a myth is because he does not organize training sessions; he prefers to delegate that to his coach. But Bob Paisley did that, too. Managing and coaching are two different jobs, and nobody is going to tell me that Kenny is not a great manager.

Nobody is going to tell me either that he is not capable of being successful in his new job at Celtic – ironically as director of football – or that he isn't a fun person. He, his wife Marina and their four children all have a good sense of humour. Janet and I, with our two children, have often gone on holiday with them and laughed until we've dropped. Kenny can be dogmatic and awkward – he'll argue that black is white and white is black. He loves a strong debate. But those close to him know how to handle this and, in fact, you could say that his stubbornness is almost ironic and is partly what makes him so likeable.

No matter how much a manager is admired and respected by his players, he will always attract a degree of resentment from those he has left out of the team. It happens at every club and it was no different at Liverpool when Kenny was manager there. Yet, outside those circumstances, I have never heard any player with whom he has worked slagging him off. You could argue that when we were at Liverpool, players wouldn't have done it in front of me because they knew I was a mate of his, but, knowing the Liverpool players as I did, that just wasn't the case.

As with Graeme Souness, Kenny Dalglish the player was appreciated by me no less than Kenny Dalglish the person. He was noted as a moaner, especially over refereeing decisions. In training matches, he was also noted for not doing the straightforward things. You knew that if you were just three yards away from him and it was easy for him to give you the ball, you wouldn't get it: the best time to expect a pass from him was when you were twenty yards away and he had to thread the ball through 10 players!

He got worse as he got older: the older he gets, the more his love of playing football – and exhibiting the full range of his talents – has come to the fore. Players in the clubs he manages are liable to view him as the last person they would want in their side in practice games. I discussed this with Alan Shearer, before he and Kenny parted company after Kenny's sacking as Newcastle manager. I was with Alan in a golf tournament, and when I asked how Kenny was playing in the Newcastle five-a-sides, he said, 'Oh, just as bad as ever – in fact, worse!'

But in the Liverpool team, to have someone like Kenny Dalglish up front, to hold your passes to him and turn them into golden scoring opportunities, was manna from heaven. 'Look forward, look early,' he would tell me, meaning 'Look to play the ball to me.' When possible, we would give each other a little hand signal: mine let him know I wanted to pass to him and his told me which side he wanted to receive the ball. During the early part of his Liverpool career, he could always be relied on to turn a bad ball into a good one. It didn't really matter to him if it was hit five yards either side of him, or the pass was not properly weighted. This did wonders for my confidence. Whenever I hit the ball to Kenny, I was totally relaxed. Obviously, when Kenny was in his thirties, and past his peak, he became more choosy – as I like to remind him, you had to put the ball virtually on to his right or left toenail to make him happy! Also he wanted the ball to come smoothly to him on the ground, and you could expect a good grumble if this didn't happen – even if you had been trying to 'hit' him from 20 or 30 yards, and opposing players were in a position to intercept the pass. In that situation, I would chip the ball to him, and occasionally it would bounce around his neck. But, no matter how well I had done to get the ball to him, Kenny would just look plaintively at me and say, 'Don't bounce them in.'

It is often said that the key areas in any team are the positions down the middle – the spine – and I cannot think of anyone I would rather have had in the central positions in midfield and attack than Graeme and Kenny. Graeme, with his great first touch and intelligent distribution, was the Liverpool play-maker, who probably did most to link the play between defence and attack and to dictate the pace and pattern of a game.

There were players with more spectacular passing ability than Graeme – notably Glenn Hoddle, whose passing range and technical variation with either foot made him unique among the stars of my generation. In one of our matches against Tottenham, at White Hart Lane, Hoddle produced one of the most exhilarating midfield shows I have ever seen in the first half to steer Spurs to a 2–0 half-time lead. The accuracy of his passes – over 20 to 60 yards – was remarkable. For the second half, though, Graeme, who had been out because of injury, was brought on as substitute. From then, Hoddle hardly got a kick of the ball. I think it would have been asking a lot of any player to maintain the form he had shown in the opening 45 minutes, yet it is difficult to see how he could have gone to the other extreme. He was anonymous.

He never really stood out in matches at Anfield either, so while he was more gifted than Graeme, there is no doubt that Graeme had the edge in all the other ingredients necessary to be a top-class player. If I had a straight choice between the two for my team, I would take Graeme every time.

For a defender, having players in forward positions who were as comfortable on the ball as Graeme and Kenny was a bonus in itself. On top of this they were wonderful players for Liverpool – and me – in the defensive sense. Graeme operated from the 'hole' position, the space between the central defenders and the midfield, and was very much a back-line shield for us. In recent years, more and more teams have had a striker dropping into deep positions, thus giving the opposition the dilemma of whether a central defender or a midfielder should move forward to mark him. Either way, unless a team is exceptionally well organized, their basic 'shape' can easily be destroyed. When I was Liverpool captain, and Ronnie Whelan was operating at the centre of midfield, I would push him into the Souness job myself. Before a match, and especially a match away from home where we knew that at the start the other team would throw everything at us, I would tell him, 'For the first twenty minutes, I want you immediately in front of me. Don't move!'

Eric Cantona was arguably the best of the 'roving' strikers in England when he was with Manchester United. One of the most effective men to fill the space he tried to exploit was David Batty, the Newcastle and England midfielder. But Graeme was the *de luxe* version! As a defender Kenny was also in a class of his own – he was as good a tackler as any striker you'll ever see.

The way Liverpool tried to make it difficult for opposing teams – by compressing the play in the other half of the field and denying the opposition time and space to settle on the ball there – involved all the players. The strikers were as important as anyone in this: indeed, in situations where Liverpool lost the ball inside the opposing penalty area, our front players, by being closest to the ball, were the starting point for this 'pressing' game. The pressure they exerted on opposing defenders inevitably affected the quality of the passes the defenders were able to play.

I have never seen another team 'defend from the front' in this way more effectively than Liverpool when they had Ian Rush and Kenny operating together. Opposing back-four players always had difficulty in settling on the ball when Ian and Kenny were around, because of the speed with which Ian closed people down and Kenny's ability to step in and win the ball.

Lots of strikers will put themselves about off the ball, but tackling is an art which, inevitably, is foreign to them. Hence the number of times you see strikers conceding daft free kicks and penalties. As it happens, I think many defenders would have been proud to be able to tackle like Kenny – not least yours truly. Apart from his physical strength, he was an intelligent footballer who had an innate appreciation of what players in different positions would be thinking and where they would be at their most vulnerable in certain situations. To anyone who follows *Match of the Day*, I hardly need add that the art of defending is a pet subject with me. I don't necessarily know more about it than anyone else, but I do start with an advantage after my experiences in my second season with Liverpool, as a member of the team which established a defensive record that I cannot ever see being broken.

# 10 The Dream Team

At the reunions of the Liverpool teams I played for, one of the favourite questions in our after-dinner quiz is: 'Who were the players who scored against us in our 1978/79 Championship-winning season?'

Apart from Phil Thompson and Graeme Souness, who scored own goals, the easiest name to remember is Andy King (Everton). He was the only player to score against us twice. The others on the scoresheet were Paul McGee, Keith Eastoe (both QPR), Brian Kidd (Manchester City), Laurie Cunningham, Alistair Brown (both West Brom), John Ryan (Norwich), John Hawley (Leeds), David Price (Arsenal), Joe Royle (Bristol City), Allan Evans, John Deehan (both Aston Villa) and Nick Holmes (Southampton).

No, I haven't left anyone out – the list really is as short as that. Even today I still get a tremendous buzz from the memory of how Liverpool frustrated opposing forwards then. Just 16 goals conceded in 42 matches, an all-time Championship record, and no more than four let in at home: how's that for being sound in defence?

This was not the only mind-boggling aspect of Liverpool's eleventh Championship triumph. We also gathered a record number of points – 68 – and we scored a total of 85 goals. We finished eight points clear of second-placed Nottingham Forest, with a record of 30 wins, eight draws and only four defeats, all of which were away from home against Everton (1–0), Arsenal (1–0), Bristol City (1–0) and Aston Villa (3–1). Villa were the only team to score more than one goal against us in one match.

Not surprisingly, I rate the winning of that Championship as the best of all my achievements with Liverpool, and that team as the best I ever played in. Indeed, it still amazes me that the 1978/79 Liverpool side, who also won the title the following season, did not get more honours.

Despite turning the 1978–79 Championship into virtually a one-horse race, we were beaten by Sheffield United in the second round of the League Cup, by Manchester United in the semi-final of the FA Cup and Nottingham Forest in the first round of the European Cup. It was a similar story the following season when we lost to Nottingham Forest and Arsenal in the League and FA Cup semi-finals, and Dynamo Tbilisi in the first round of the European Cup. Other Liverpool teams won considerably more, but I feel that in individual ability and the team blend and balance, the 1979 model reigned supreme. The team was: Ray Clemence in goal; Phil Neal, Phil Thompson, myself and Alan Kennedy or Emlyn Hughes in defence; Jimmy Case, Graeme Souness, Terry McDermott and Ray Kennedy in midfield; and Kenny

Dalglish up front, with either Steve Heighway or David Johnson. For me, the only Liverpool line-up on a similar level was the one in the late 1980s when we had Bruce Grobbelaar in goal; Steve Nicol, myself, Gary Gillespie and Gary Ablett or Barry Venison in defence; Ray Houghton, Steve McMahon, Ronnie Whelan, Jan Molby, John Barnes and Craig Johnston competing for the midfield places; and John Aldridge and Peter Beardsley up front. Similarly, while they won the 1988 Championship by nine points, that side did not take as many trophies as might have been expected. For all their brilliant performances in the league that season, they are best remembered by the public for being turned over by Wimbledon in the FA Cup final.

In addition to John Barnes, Liverpool's other source of dazzling individual flair then was Peter Beardsley. The only criticism I could make of him was that if he was struggling to get into a game he would move too deep into areas in which his ability to create and take scoring chances was wasted. I suspect this explains why he was left out of the Liverpool team on a number of occasions when Kenny Dalglish was manager (even during a period when Peter was the league's leading scorer) and why, equally controversially, he was sold to Everton by Kenny's successor, Graeme Souness.

However, Peter, who had been bought by Liverpool from Newcastle in the summer of 1987 for a then British record transfer fee of £1.8 million, had as good a début season for Liverpool as any player I have seen. His most spectacular show came in the 5–0 win over Nottingham Forest, one of our closest Championship rivals, in April when he deceived the Forest defence with an array of feints and dummies that probably sent most of the crowd the wrong way, too. Such individualism was less evident in the 1978/79 Liverpool team, but I still feel that the latter had the edge in all-round ability.

When a team is not conceding many goals, the first player you tend to look at is the goalkeeper. But Ray Clemence had so little to do in a number of our matches that, if the weather was cold, he was liable to come off the field at the end shivering. Fortunately for Liverpool, it suited his temperament to be in this situation; had it been his successor Bruce Grobbelaar, the more assertive and excitable of the two, I should imagine that he would have come off with a nosebleed. The fact is that, because of the standard of the players in front of Ray that season, I could have stuck my mother in goal and we would probably still have won the Championship.

In my time with the club, Liverpool were never looked upon as an easy team to score against, but the 1978/79 side has been very much the benchmark for my analysis of the defensive strengths and weaknesses of the teams I study in my role as a BBC TV football pundit. They set the standards by which I now judge others.

I suspect that many viewers believe I place too much emphasis on this side of the game – there is hardly a goal I don't think could have been avoided. But while I accept that teams who play in an open style are good for the game from an entertainment viewpoint, the fact is that all the major honours have gone to the teams who have made tightness at the back their first priority. Even Manchester United can be put into that category. Their style of play has not been anywhere near as open as many seem to think. They have been very much a counter-attacking team. When the opposition have been in possession United have consistently had more players behind the ball than possibly any other team.

This is the essence of good defensive play, as was illustrated by Liverpool's 1978/79 side. My experiences in that eleven made me appreciate more fully than ever how much back-four players rely on their midfielders and strikers. It was in midfield that Liverpool stood out the most. The only midfield four from another club to compare with ours was that of Leeds United, with Peter Lorimer, Billy Bremner, John Giles and Eddie Gray.

Jimmy Case, Graeme Souness, Terry McDermott and Ray Kennedy were all good on the ball, and Ray was exceptional in the air, too. The attacking link-up between Graeme and Terry was brilliant: while Graeme would play the passes, Terry was the one who would make the intelligent forward runs to get on the end of them and finish. Terry and Graeme, who left Liverpool in 1983 and 1984 respectively, were an impossible act to follow.

Perhaps the most important characteristic of the 1978/79 Liverpool midfield unit, especially for the defenders, was that three of the four were exceptionally strong mentally and took no prisoners when it came to winning the ball. I am sure that my old pal Terry McDermott won't mind me saying that he was the odd player out in this respect: if the chance to win the ball was there, Jimmy, Graeme and Ray, all physically powerful, had no hesitation about putting the foot in. Terry was less enamoured of this side of the game.

Come to think of it, he was also like Phil Thompson. Phil was not the best tackler in the world either, and the other thing he and I had in common was that we could be shoved around. What a pair of central defenders we made. This is the one area of a team in which you expect players to be strong but, compared to some of the colleagues in front of us, Phil and I were as weak as water. The others used to joke about it: 'We must be the only team in the world with a pair of centre-halves who can't tackle.'

For some time it was thought that the best way for opposition teams to expose this was to put Phil and me under greater physical pressure by knocking the ball up to front players as quickly as possible, rather than trying to match Liverpool at their close-passing game. Neither Phil nor I was dominant in the air – although he was clearly better in that area than me – and therefore other teams were particularly confident about scoring against us from free kicks and corners.

All this would appear to be endorsed by some of our defeats against 'direct play' teams in big matches – notably against Wimbledon in the 1988 FA Cup final and Crystal Palace in the 1990 FA Cup semi-final. I say 'appear to be' because I think the argument has been exaggerated – it was hardly borne out by Liverpool's overall record against the likes of Wimbledon and Palace. Not only this, even in those specific games you could argue that we just happened to play appallingly badly against Wimbledon, and that we created enough chances against Palace to have slaughtered them.

Still, I accept that high balls pumped into the heart of

our defence, with a big centre-forward challenging flat out for them, was a type of play we did not handle as well as others. There was a period when Wimbledon, and their centre-forward John Fashanu, caused us so many headaches at free kicks that we tried to devise a system in which we could all move forward a split second before the kick was taken to catch Fashanu offside. As we are not used to doing this, someone suggested that when it was right for us to put this ploy into operation one of us should shout a codeword. It was a disaster. As the person elected to give the signal, I knew it would come to grief: for a start, nobody could quite make up their minds what I should shout (we eventually settled on 'Ready!') and I wasn't at all certain that I'd remember it.

I was talking to the former Leeds captain Billy Bremner about this, and he came up with the bizarre idea that we should have given the responsibility to the striker who wasn't involved in the defensive work in these situations. Billy's reasoning was sound enough: the Liverpool player loitering on or around the halfway line to provide a target for our defensive clearances could study the whole picture with a clearer head.

'But how is he going to communicate with us?' I asked.

'Easy,' Billy said. 'He doesn't have to say anything. If he stands in the centre circle, you know you have to run out. If he stands at the side, you know you have to stay put.' I can't be sure that this wasn't a wind-up, but the one thing I'm certain of is that the idea was too complicated for us.

In my experience, Liverpool was never the most intensely coached of teams, and when I was there, they rarely worked on any set-piece strategies, either for or against. They got by because of the quality of the players, not just in their technical attributes but in their intelligence as footballers and ability to use their common sense. Defensively, the other advantage for us, of course, was that Liverpool had so much possession of the ball, and were able to keep it in areas of the field where nobody in our side suffered a heart attack if it was lost.

While I have no illusions about the weaknesses of people like myself, I think Liverpool were also helped by their back four. I was helped by Phil Thompson, the only member of the quartet who had been with the club since leaving school and who, like me, spent 14 years as an Anfield player. Of my three main central-defensive partners throughout my career at Liverpool – the others were Mark Lawrenson and Gary Gillespie – Phil was the one with whom I had the best understanding. A number of people believe that Mark and I were the most effective duo for Liverpool, but that may be because the partnership was more recent than the one I had with Phil, and is fresher in the memory.

Mark, now my BBC *Match of the Day* colleague, was an exceptional defender by any standards. He was quicker than Phil and Gary and the strongest tackler. For his part, Gary was the best by a mile in the air, and had the slight edge on the ball. Where Phil came out on top was that he was the outstanding reader of the game. He could anticipate situations and took up excellent 'starting-point' positions in relation to his defensive colleagues. This was the area in which Mark was possibly at his weakest. No disrespect to him, but it seemed to me that this came through when he was Newcastle's defensive coach. While he improved their defensive play, their back men were still not particularly consistent in their positioning.

I think Phil and I had the biggest advantage over Mark here. In addition to our common flaws – in tackling and dealing with balls in the air when under a forceful challenge – Phil carried the burden of not being a good runner. He was the slowest of the central defenders I have mentioned. His knees were probably in even worse shape than mine. I used to say to him, 'My missus can run quicker than you.' When you added up what we had going for us as individuals, it didn't amount to much. Yet in my view our partnership was phenomenal. Our rapport, stemming from our ability to read the game, seemed almost telepathic. If the ball was played over my head, I knew he would be there covering me and vice versa. In my first season with Liverpool I had only played with him a few times, so you would have thought that we would need maybe the whole of the second season to gel properly. But we hit it off immediately, as if we had been together for many years.

While Phil and I were similar in a lot of ways, the full-backs, Phil Neal and Alan Kennedy, were poles apart. Phil, Bob Paisley's first signing for the club, from Northampton in 1974, was Mr Dependable, a player with a wonderful positional sense who went about his job in the steadiest, most disciplined way. Alan, signed from Newcastle in 1975, was less predictable.

Alan, or 'Barney', as he was called, because of his re-semblance to the *Flintstones* character, was the back-four colleague I knew best. In addition to operating on the left side of the defence, alongside me, he was my Liverpool room-mate for seven years. I benefited from that arrangement more than he did. During those seven years, I cannot recall ever having to get out of bed to answer the door or make our morning tea or coffee. Janet had a go at me when I told her about it. 'It's disgraceful that he should have to do everything for you,' she said. All I could say in mitigation was, 'Well, Alan enjoys doing it.'

The one thing he did *not* enjoy was me stealing his duvet while he was asleep one freezing night before a match against Sheffield Wednesday at Hillsborough. When he woke up the next morning, you could hear his teeth chattering.

As a player, Alan, one of England's best attacking left-backs, was the only member of our back four who could be described as a loose cannon. It was typical of him that he should score the goal – with a shot any striker would have been proud of – which brought us our 1–0 win over Real Madrid in the 1981 European Cup final. He also scored the penalty shoot-out goal that gave us victory in the 1984 European Cup final against Roma in Rome – after looking hopeless at spot-kicks when practising them a few days before the game. Perhaps the best example of that loose-cannon side to him came in a European Cup tie against CSK Sofia at Anfield, when the Bulgarians made a dangerous break down our left side with Alan nowhere to be seen. As the player cut inside with the ball, I nicked it off him, played a one-two with Graeme Souness, then found myself going down the inside-right channel with it. Suddenly, as I was beginning to struggle to keep the run going, who should I spot on the outside of me but Alan. I had no idea why he was on that side of the field (he probably didn't know either) but I was very glad to see him there. This sort of uninhibited play summed up Alan to a T, although it should be added that when it came to defending, to holding a certain position when the opposition had the ball, Alan was no less disciplined than the rest of us.

If you are looking for a solid back four, that word 'position' is the key one, as far as I am concerned. As long as the back players are in the right positions, it is amazing how difficult it can be for the opposition to create clear-cut scoring chances. In a flat-back four – where the four defenders are in line with each other and operate as far up the field as they can to compress the play – the basic requirements are that the two central defenders work off each other, and provide the positional lead for the full-backs to follow. If the two central defenders are in the right places, you're laughing.

While Liverpool were the masters of the flat-back four system in England in the 1970s and 1980s, the best exponents of it over the last ten years or so have been Arsenal, with their renowned quartet of Lee Dixon, Tony Adams, Steve Bould or Martin Keown and Nigel Winterburn. They are different types of players from the ones we had and therefore they have deployed the system differently. While I had greater 'recovery' pace than the Arsenal central defenders, neither I nor Phil Thompson was as powerful as them in the air or such strong tacklers, so it has suited Arsenal to defend deeper than we did. Liverpool would defend from anywhere between the 18-yard line and the halfway line, but when things were going well for us, we were closer to the latter. In the

1978/79 season, I reckon that our back four took up more advanced positions than any team in the history of British football.

The only time Liverpool defended from the 18-yard line was when we were playing on Luton's artificial-grass pitch, a surface on which the bounce of the ball made it tantamount to soccer suicide for a back four to be too far forward. I found it a doddle to be so close to our goal, because of the limited amount of chasing back you had to do from that position. But Liverpool could not afford to play like that all the time, especially if we were up against a team with a striker who was good in the air.

The other difference between Arsenal and ourselves is that they have deliberately played for offside decisions whereas we did not. We pushed up with the intention of making it difficult for opponents to give their strikers the service they wanted to give them, and to keep the ball a safe distance from our goal. True, a lot of opposing teams kept hearing the referee's whistle for offside, but we took the view that this was hardly our fault. If anybody wanted to run behind our back men into an offside position, that was up to them.

Any system requires work to perfect it but, compared to Arsenal, the time Liverpool's players devoted to our defensive formula was minimal. I have read several times about the intensive formal coaching to which the Arsenal back four were subjected each day when George Graham was the Gunners' manager. But the Liverpool back four were never schooled in that way, either individually or collectively. The only defensive work we were given in training was that we would occasionally put on a function where the goalkeeper and the back four would 'play' against eight other players – who were the only players allowed to attack.

It was exceptionally tiring for the defenders – you could only do it for about 10 minutes – because every time we won the ball, or it went wide of the goal, we had to give it straight back to the attackers. I'm not sure how many other teams do this, but it was certainly advantageous to us. It was a tremendous way of teaching us how to work effectively as a unit.

I could talk for hours on the finer points of defensive play which the public inevitably does not see. For example, one area rarely brought into the public domain concerns the side of the defence on which central defenders prefer to be positioned. I preferred operating on the left, partly because I'm a naturally right-footed player, which meant that my angle of vision, in terms of all the passing options available to me, was much wider. Also, I was quicker turning to my left than my right, and there-fore more confident about getting to balls played down that touchline or the inside-forward channel. If a team was attacking us down the flank, Liverpool preferred the defenders closest to the ball to try to push them inside, into a more crowded area. But because of the pace of Alan Kennedy and myself I did the opposite. I was so confident about my sharpness in turning to the left that even when the people on the Liverpool bench shouted, 'Bring them inside,' I tended to ignore them. At the risk of upsetting Kenny Dalglish, I even ignored him. When he asked me after the game, 'Did you not hear me?' I would say, 'No!'

The point about central defenders operating on their

favourite sides was uppermost in my mind last season when I saw the way Chelsea used their French World Cup central defenders, Frank Leboeuf and Marcel Desailly, in the pair's Premiership début at Coventry. In the World Cup final, Leboeuf and Desailly had played on the right and left respectively, but against Coventry their positions were reversed. I did not think it suited Desailly, an impression borne out by Coventry's first goal. In attempting to stop the scorer, Darren Huckerby, he turned to his favoured left side when it would have been quicker for him to go right.

Leaving aside the numerous adjustments that need to be made according to the play, the basic principles of the flat-back four system are quite simple, and I am surprised that so many teams get it wrong. I see so many Premiership matches in which teams don't have to do anything special to score. When I see videos of the games featured on *Match of the Day* each Saturday night, my most common thought about the standard of defending is 'Dear me, how bad was that?'

Nowadays there are mitigating circumstances for defenders, such as the extra dimension given to attacking play in the Premiership through the introduction of so many foreign strikers and the football rule changes that have been introduced by Fifa, the game's world governing body, in an attempt to produce more goals. As a defender, I think that whoever came up with those changes – relating to back passes to the goalkeeper, the offside rule and the tackle from behind – deserves to spend a year in a straitjacket. However, it would be wrong to use them as excuses for bad defending – for back-four men taking up poor positions.

It does not matter what system a team plays at the back: all the players have to work together. The very nature of their jobs means that being able to work as a unit is more important for defenders than it is for midfield players and strikers. But few teams get it right in that department. The most common mistake is the positioning of full-backs when an opposing attack is developing on the other side of the field. If people see scoring chances being created by moves down, say, the right, they immediately assume that the defending team have a weakness there. Quite often, the weakness is on the other flank.

In a flat-back four, the defending full-back on the opposite side of the field to the ball should be in line with the other defenders so that, even if the ball is played across, the opposition are kept too far out to have much chance of scoring. But I have lost count of the number of times I have seen players in that position fall into the trap of following an opponent behind the line. The only time this makes sense is if the full-back is in a position to influence the play – that is, if the central defenders are in trouble and he is able to move far enough in-field to cover them. More often than not, though, he would need to be jet-propelled to get there and he's caught in no man's land.

It should be so easy for a full-back to look along the line, to where the central defenders are, and adjust his position accordingly. Even if the central defenders are in bad positions, the full-backs must play off them, not vice versa. However, in the heat of the moment, the instinct to mark someone is clearly difficult for a lot of them to resist. For me, this is the major defensive curse of the modern game.

One point about defensive systems that cannot be stressed enough is that the further up the field you stand – the more space you leave between the back men and the goalkeeper – the more the positioning of the defenders needs to be spot on. You can get away with bad positioning in or around the penalty area, particularly with a dominating goalkeeper, but if you get it wrong on the halfway line, you're stuffed.

Equally important, if we're talking about the pressing game, is that the midfielders and strikers must be as switched on to it as the defenders. As we were fond of saying at Liverpool, 'You attack from the back and defend from the front.'

I have found that teams newly promoted to the Premiership – teams used to getting away with their defensive mistakes in the Nationwide League – have tended to look the most vulnerable. The classic case were Barnsley in the 1997/98 season. They are a lovely club and they gave me a lot of pleasure in their first season in the Premiership – they played a lot of good football. But I only needed to watch them for five minutes when the opposition were in possession to appreciate why they conceded the highest number of goals in the Premiership – 82 in 38 matches – and finished second from the bottom. It is impossible to play the way Barnsley did and not lose goals.

I remember their 2–0 home defeat by Arsenal, caused partly by their midfielders and strikers giving the Gunners too much scope to settle on the ball in their build-up play. No less of a problem was the Barnsley back division's attempts to push up and hold the line. After about half an hour, as Arsenal broke quickly into the

Barnsley half, Barnsley's central defender, Adrian Moses, could be seen with his hand up near the halfway line, appealing for offside, with their other central defender, Arjan de Zeeuw, more than 15 yards behind him. Suddenly Arsenal found themselves in a three-against-one situation and, fortunately for Barnsley on that occasion, the player with the responsibility for applying the finishing touch – Marc Overmars – somehow missed the chance. However, Barnsley's lack of defensive organization was noticeable to me every time I watched them.

Yet they are hardly alone in this, which begs the question, why?

Some believe that the change in the rule concerning the pass-back to the goalkeeper has been the biggest problem: they argue that it has caused play to swing more quickly from one end of the field to the other, thus making it more difficult for teams to get themselves properly set up defensively. Mistakes are inevitable under this sort of pressure – it's a bit like driving a car when you're stressed – and the intense television spotlight means that mistakes are harder than ever before to cover up.

Sometimes, though, as with television probes into refereeing decisions, the camera can come to your rescue. In a 1–1 draw against Ipswich in 1981, Liverpool conceded a goal stemming from a bad square pass to me by Phil Thompson, which was cut out by Alan Brazil. As I was chasing Brazil, he leaned into me, fell over and got a penalty. In the dressing room afterwards, Bob Paisley blamed me for the goal, arguing that I had not taken up a position to receive the ball from Phil. 'You were a disgrace,' he told me. 'When Phil was ready to give you the ball, you turned away from him and started walking up the pitch.'

I knew I hadn't done that, and that the only thing Bob could possibly have hauled me over the coals for was that maybe my concentration wasn't what it should have been. But he continued to insist that he was right, as did Joe Fagan. However, when the highlights of the match were shown on TV the following day, it was proved that they'd got it wrong.

The most glaring error by a defender is to score an own goal, although when I was at Liverpool there were times when we felt we could get away even with that. One of our tongue-in-cheek golden rules was that if anyone put the ball into his own net, in a situation where the picture was confused by the involvement of other players, he should just walk straight up the field pretending that he had not been the one to make the *faux pas*. It worked, as I found when I scored my only own goal as a Liverpool player through deflecting a John Fashanu shot past Bruce Grobbelaar in a 2–1 win at Wimbledon in 1990. Unlike our centre-back Alex Watson, who was positioned just two yards behind me, I showed no emotion – almost everybody thought that the OG was down to Alex.

But there was no hiding-place for me when the match highlights were shown, just as there is no hiding-place for the defenders who come under the scrutiny of television people like Andy Gray and me. It seems unfair that it has become so close and critical – you could say that all the so-called great defenders of the past can count themselves lucky that they were not subjected to it, and that their counterparts today are much better than they might appear.

I often discuss this with Kenny Dalglish, who is adamant that fewer players think as deeply about the game as they did during his and my playing careers. 'The difference between then and now is that they sometimes cannot think for themselves,' he says. 'As a manager or coach, you have to hold their hand.' The other way of looking at it, of course, is that some managers and coaches do not give the players the freedom to think for themselves.

It takes time for any player to adjust to a different way of playing or the different styles of play of those around him. In the 1998/99 season, the Dutch World Cup player Jaap Stam became the world's most expensive defender when Manchester United bought him from PSV Eindhoven for £10.75 million. I was impressed by his individual ability, his strength, quickness and power in the air. However, while he was adjusting to English football, he caused United a number of headaches. In Holland, Stam had operated as a man-marker, and therefore when the United defence pushed forward, he remained with his opponent behind the line. This happened a few times in United's two matches against Chelsea. On one occasion, when Stam's positioning had the effect of playing Gianfranco Zola onside, and almost led to a Chelsea goal, you could see United's left-back Dennis Irwin signalling agitatedly to Stam that in these situations he needed to move forward with the rest of the defence.

But like all exceptional players, Stam was a quick

learner. He went on to become the best central defender in the Premiership in my view.

Two Liverpool central defenders with the same problem as Stam have been Glenn Hysen, the Swedish international who played with me in my last season with the club, and Mark Wright, who was signed by Graeme Souness before the start of the following season. Glenn, previously with Fiorentina in Italy, was used to playing in a sweeper system, as the spare man responsible for patrolling the space behind the defenders with specific marking jobs. It was hardly surprising at Liverpool that, when I was holding my position, he would take three or four steps backwards. During the early part of Mark Wright's Anfield career, he was inclined to do the same. He was superb in a five-man defence, as one of the three centre-backs, but in a flat-back four, he created problems.

As I've already said, I, too, found it difficult to change my usual habits when I joined Liverpool and this was also the case when I was in the Scotland team. Although they, too, played with a flat-back four, their personnel meant that the interpretation of it was different. This was bound to create problems for me and it did. I had played such a high number of matches for Liverpool that their approach to the game came to me instinctively.

When I look back on our defensive ability at Anfield, it's difficult to avoid sounding boastful. Phil Thompson, Mark Lawrenson, Gary Gillespie and I were able to get the flat-back four system down to a fine art. At the time, I think I was inclined to take this expertise for granted. It is only since I started watching other teams that I have become truly proud of it.

I am also proud of how I learned to make my attributes – and especially my ability to read a game – work for me as an individual.

# **11** Tricks of the Trade

Nothing highlights the lack of football intelligence in a defender more than situations in which he has to deal with something by himself, outside the protection of other players or the system. In that department, the game is hardly overflowing with Bobby Moores.

If I had to pick the finest piece of individual defending I have ever seen, it would be Moore's challenge on the brilliant Brazilian winger Jairzinho during England's match against the South Americans in the 1970 World Cup quarter-final in Mexico. When Jairzinho received the ball outside the England penalty area, Moore allowed him to run 25 or 30 yards with it into the box instead of trying to force him away from the goal. Then, with virtually no margin for error, in terms of not bringing Jairzinho down and conceding a penalty kick, Moore made the cleanest of tackles and strode off with the ball in the cool, imperious manner that was his trademark.

Moore could afford to handle Jairzinho in that way because he was in a class above other defenders in his reading of the game and his timing; if an average defender had been in that situation, he would have been crazy to let Jairzinho get into the box. But the times I see defenders take that sort of gamble in English club matches! I always say on television that when a goal is scored as a result of someone bursting forward with the ball the defending team should look at the number of challenges he had to overcome between gaining possession and releasing the ball. On what I have seen, the answer is none. Arsenal's Marc Overmars benefits from this strange feature of the modern English game as much as anyone. I have seen a number of Overmars goals, where he has run maybe 40 or 50 yards with the ball, with the other team backing off him until he has arrived in a shooting position – by which time it has been too late. If there is only one defender between the striker and the goal, then backing off him is excusable, especially if the striker has as much pace as Overmars. But if there are two, then one man must attack the ball to try to force the attacker to make a mistake, if not actually to win it. Another Premiership forward who has benefited from defenders not putting enough thought into their play is Alan Shearer, especially where he is receiving the ball with his back to the opposing goal. He is superb at getting his body between the ball and the defender marking him, and when that happens, the first priority for any defender surely must be just to keep close enough to him to deny him the scope to turn with the ball and run at his team.

Shearer, the most complete centre-forward in Britain, is always liable to knock the ball to one side, and spin and shoot in the same movement. But you can usually tell if he is going to do that by his body position as the ball is played up to him. So why is it that so many defenders try to tackle him from behind instead of taking up a position where he has to play the ball the way he is facing?

In the old days, it did not matter if a central defender clattered into the opposing centre-forward, especially if he did it in the first five or 10 minutes and it was his first foul. Referees rarely took action that early. In fact, both central defenders would be moved to chance their arm in that way. These days, with referees instructed to show them the red card for such challenges, it has become much riskier. But still defenders persist in doing it, often when there is no need. Some defenders have claimed that Shearer makes such challenges seem worse than they are. But even if it were true – which I do not think it is – the argument surely misses the point. A foul is a foul.

This is a subject on which I have tended to invite quite a lot of criticism in recent years. Take the question of fouls by defenders inside the box. If a defender goes for the ball, misses by a mile and catches his opponent, then the opponent is entitled to go down as far as I am concerned. For me, the issue of whether he could have stayed on his feet does not really come into it. Many might look upon it as 'cheating' but I prefer to describe it as the opponent being 'clever'.

For example, I have seen a number of situations in which a forward with only the goalkeeper to beat has virtually invited the keeper to knock him off balance.

Obviously, there is a dividing line; I agree that it can be taken to the extreme. The real play-actors are the men who, despite hardly being touched – or not being touched at all – will fall over and roll around on the ground as if they have been hit by a bullet. Generally, though, the way I look at it is that if a forward is able to seek an advantage through being on the receiving end of an inadequate challenge, it is basically the defender's fault for giving him the opportunity to do so.

The clamp-down on the tackle from behind has led to a raw deal for defenders, inasmuch as referees have struggled to differentiate between the good and the bad. Whenever it was necessary for me to tackle from behind, I would do so by getting my foot around the opposing player, so that my contact with him was usually minimal. However, now even that method is seen as a sending-off offence by some referees. The most bizarre example of this in the 1998/99 season was when Everton's Alex Cleland was sent off against Aston Villa for a challenge from behind on Dion Dublin which I felt was perfectly legitimate.

But I repeat – I have no sympathy with defenders who are shown the red card for going through opponents.

At Liverpool, Craig Johnston seemed to think it was a slight against his manhood to let himself be knocked over, no matter how bad the challenge on him. But he did not get any plaudits for this from the rest of us because it irritated us: his apparent bravery and honesty often caused us to lose a chance of giving the opposition problems through a free kick.

Shearer, a centre-forward who takes more stick than most, is no different from any other central striker when it comes to looking for ways to protect himself and gain the maximum advantage for his team. While criticism of his so-called 'gamesmanship' was particularly rife, I had to laugh over newspaper articles that compared his approach to the sportsmanship of Gary Lineker when Gary was a top striker. Does anyone really believe that, had Gary been playing today and someone caught him on the back of the legs while he was trying to shield the ball, he would not have jumped out of the way or gone down as readily as Shearer has?

Central defenders, like players in all the other positions, have to learn from their mistakes. If you do, it is probably the easiest of the outfield roles in the physical sense. At Liverpool we referred to it as the 'armchair' position – and had Phil Thompson and myself been strong in the air, it would also have been the 'light a cigar' position! However, for a number of central defenders, who do not learn from their mistakes, the role remains hard work.

I greatly admire Arsenal's Tony Adams and Middlesbrough's Gary Pallister: they both had glaring basic faults when they first started playing at the top level, but have improved beyond recognition. Adams became less headstrong, learned to read the game and stay on his feet more, while Pallister improved his positional sense. I would say that Pallister, who like Adams is tremendous in the air but is quicker and more skilful than the Gunners' captain, has been the best all-round centre-half in Britain over the last 10 years. But I could not have anticipated the stature he has achieved when I saw him start playing for Manchester United, alongside Steve Bruce, in 1989.

As I stressed earlier, it is important for two central defenders not to become isolated from each other. One has to be in the middle at all times, with the other working off him. But in his first season at Manchester United, it struck me that Pallister was not working off anybody. Though his general play was impressive – as you would expect of someone with his talent – I could not believe how bad his positional sense was. To his credit, however, he learned quickly. I see the same development pattern in Tottenham's Sol Campbell, perhaps the most exciting member of the next generation of English central defenders. In his early days with Tottenham, when he operated at the heart of their defence with Colin Calderwood, the pair were so split down the middle that you wondered whether they'd had a row and weren't speaking to each other. Campbell's positioning off Tony Adams in the England team left much to be desired, too. But the more I see him, the more he appears to be mastering this aspect of the game.

For any central defender, it is the one-against-one situation, the personal battle of wits with the striker you are marking, that provides the most intriguing part of the learning process. The basic aim is to force the striker to do something special to get past you. The strikers who present the most difficult technical challenge are the few who can go past a defender equally easily on either side. If a striker is running at a defender with the ball, the defender's first aim is to force him to use his 'weaker' foot, but if the striker is good with both feet, it inevitably becomes more complicated.

Central defenders also hate facing a striker with a lot of pace, even if they are quick themselves. A lot of them give themselves the extra insurance of standing two or three yards off the striker, but as explained earlier on the subject of defenders backing off Marc Overmars, it can be suicidal to give such players the scope to run at you. The closer I could get to such a striker, the more comfortable I felt.

Generally I didn't mind playing against what you would call the 'class' strikers – it was the highly physical types like Billy Whitehurst who tended to worry me most. If I was up against any striker who had pace, and was also strong and aggressive, I would get twitchy.

I would get even twitchier if the centre-forward had as much football intelligence as Everton's Graeme Sharp, the British striker for whom I had probably the greatest respect. In my view, it is a terrible indictment of the game that Graeme has not landed a top job as a specialist centre-forward coach, because if anybody had a perfect grasp of all the aspects of number-nine play, all the tricks of the trade, it was him.

Graeme was not the type who could dribble past three or four defenders, yet in all the less noticeable facets of a centre-forward's job, he had as much right to call himself an artist as anyone. One feature of his game was that when the ball was in the air the position he took up made it virtually impossible for the defender marking him to get the ball without fouling him. He was a physical player who developed into a good technical player because of his intelligence. The other thing that made him special was that he was an unselfish player – possibly the most unselfish centre-forward I ever played against. Some centre-forwards will think only of trying to score themselves when the ball is heading towards them at the back post. They play the percentage game: they work on the premise that for every 10 scoring attempts, at least one will go in. Graeme wasn't like that. If a player was better placed than himself, he would give the ball to him.

I had to be on my toes all the time when Graeme was around, especially when we operated in the same area and were in direct opposition. When I played on the left for Liverpool, he played on Everton's right – the ideal position for him because of his potential threat as a target for the long, sweeping diagonal passes from Everton's left-side midfielder, Kevin Sheedy. I was on the right when Liverpool beat Everton 3–2 in the 1989 FA Cup final, so the player in closer contact with Graeme was my central-defensive partner Gary Ablett. Yet while I had anticipated that this would be like a day off for me, the reality was that Graeme created problems for both of us. The one thing you could be sure about in any match against Graeme Sharp was that the experience would drain you mentally.

I learned a lot from him, as I did from Kenny Dalglish. Of all the strikers I played with or against, Kenny, on top of all his attacking ability, was probably the best ball-winner. He recognized that the last thing players in this position wanted was for the defenders marking them to trigger indecision. Phil Thompson, who would occasionally take small, subtle steps sideways and backwards before he committed himself, was superb at this. We referred to those challenges by him as 'spider' tackles.

I attempted to develop this in my own game. The first time I remember using it was when I played for Scotland against Argentina at Hampden in June 1979 – Diego Maradona's first game in Britain. It wasn't a great success.

As Maradona ran towards me with the ball, I took one small step one way, another step the other way – and by the time I was ready to make the next move, he was 20 yards past me! Maradona, I should add, scored one of Argentina's goals that day and ran rings around us to inspire a 3–1 Argentina win.

Still, my attempts to gain a psychological edge over strikers paid off for me many more times than they failed me. The outstanding examples concern my battles with Mark Hughes and Karl-Heinz Rummenigge when they were with Manchester United and Bayern Munich respectively. Hughes, like Kenny Dalglish, has been a master at receiving the ball with his back to the opposing goal and bringing other players into the attacking picture. He is immensely strong and has a good first touch so once he is in possession there is little his marker can do about it. Other defenders would just stay goal-side of him, but I would occasionally burst in front of him as the ball was played to his feet. That meant that the next time he was about to take possession his attention would be focused on where I was as much as on the ball.

I played against Rummenigge – the Teutonic equivalent of Alan Shearer – in the 1981 European Cup semi-final, when Liverpool drew 1–1 with Bayern and went through to the final against Real Madrid on the away-goal rule. With his physical power and pace, Rummenigge – who won the European Footballer of the Year award for the second time that year, gained 95 international caps and also had a successful career in Italy with Inter Milan – was probably the European attacking player who presented the biggest challenge to me. I cannot say that I passed it with flying colours because he scored the Bayern goal in the last minute of the second leg of that semi-final against Liverpool in Germany. But it could have been a lot worse. The aspect of his play that caused me most trouble was his movement, especially his diagonal runs. When Bayern played the ball forward, Rummenigge was brilliant at making runs for it across my body. I had never experienced this before and only my speed enabled me to stop him getting away from me and creating a shooting chance. As it was, I was living on borrowed time. I knew that if I did not find an answer to those runs of his then I was bound to pay the price eventually.

It wasn't until about 20 minutes into the second leg that I was able to come up with a plan to stop him. It was very simple: as the ball was about to be played through for him, I took a step or two towards the space into which he wanted to move. In other words, I moved before he did, which put him off.

By and large, the Rummenigge types – indeed, any Continental strikers – were the players I most relished facing. First, their main strengths – pace, movement, anticipation – were also my main strengths. Also, once I gained possession, Continental strikers would anticipate what I would do with the ball as opposed to attempting to win it off me. For example, if the ball was approaching me, they would get behind me in the hope that I would miss it or try to play it back to the goalkeeper. Instead of concerning myself about a striker barging into me, I could relax and concentrate fully on expressing my creative ability. Some British strikers also enabled me to do that, particularly those who were out-and-out goal-scorers and only really interested in getting into positions where they could put the ball in the net. One in that category at Liverpool was John Aldridge: if I did not waltz past him with the ball at least half a dozen times in training matches, I would consider myself to be having a bad day. Ian Rush kept me guessing: sometimes he would try to win the ball from me and sometimes he would drop off.

The most 'Continental' of all the strikers I played against was probably Gary Lineker, when he was at Everton and Tottenham – which is why, given a choice between playing against a Gary Lineker or a Graeme Sharp, I would choose the former every time. Indeed, when pondering the number of Gary Linekers in other European countries, and how much I enjoyed Liverpool's European Cup campaigns, I have never been able to switch off the idea that maybe I did not get the most out of myself in the technical sense in England.

I still fantasize over the thought of operating not in Liverpool's flat-back four but in the defence of a top team in Italy's Serie A – as a sweeper.

# 12 If Only I Could Have Been a Sweeper

A lot of men dream about being in the shoes of someone like Richard Gere or Mick Jagger. Trust me to be different. If there was anybody I would have wanted to swap places with it was Franco Baresi. While I was at Liverpool, Baresi, the AC Milan and Italy player, was regarded as the world's outstanding sweeper. Whenever I watched him, I always felt that I was born to fill his role and play in Italian football, too.

In the last 20 years, only two British central defenders have realized the dream of playing for clubs in Italy: Paul Elliott and Des Walker. Elliott, who joined Pisa from Aston Villa in July 1987, was judged to have done quite well there, but his career in Italy lasted only two years.

For Walker, it appeared to be a disaster. He was at the height of his career when he moved from Nottingham Forest to Sampdoria in July 1993, but he lasted little more than a year, during which time he ended up at left-back. Sampdoria had visualized him as their Baresi but his struggle to adjust to Italian football prompted such a drop in confidence that shortly after his return to the UK – with Sheffield Wednesday – he was bombed out of the England squad. Indeed, Walker has never regained the status that he achieved before he went to Italy, although on the most recent occasions I have seen him playing for Wednesday he has been excellent.

It was Walker's pace that initially caught Sampdoria's eye. I think they overlooked that he was not a particularly good positional player. When I watched him playing for Nottingham Forest, and even for England, there were times when he had to use his pace to get himself out of trouble because he had not taken up a good position in the first place. If a defender is not a good reader of the game, then the higher the standard of football in which he plays, the less his pace can compensate for it. In a sweeper system, Walker would be ideal as a marker, but I would always have reservations about him as the spare man because he is not skilful enough on the ball.

So, as I considered that my ball skills and my positioning were among my strong points, I see no reason to allow Walker's experience in Italy to influence my thoughts on what I might have been able to achieve there. As a defender who put the emphasis on playing football, I cannot help thinking that being a sweeper in Italy would have suited me better than operating in a flat-back four in England. I would not have achieved as many honours – the great Baresi himself does not have the collection of winners' medals that I have accumulated – but I feel sure that I would have been a better player.

English football is probably the most competitive in the

world, but I doubt that it is the most skilful. Though my career coincided with English teams, and notably Liverpool, dominating the European Cup, I think that even then it was recognized that the majority of the most technically accomplished players in Europe and the most sophisticated styles of play could be found in Italy's Serie A. Despite the hype surrounding the Premiership, and the high number of foreign players who are earning their livings there, I would suggest that this is still so. I think Watford's chairman, Sir Elton John, was spot on when he said recently, 'Only three or four English teams would survive in Italy.'

Technically, most of the foreign players who have come to England are superior to their English, Scottish, Welsh and Irish counterparts and they have improved the skill level in our game. The downside is that, apart from their problems in integrating into the dressing-room culture, few have been able to adjust to playing in a higher number of competitive matches and the more cut-and-thrust, pacier game here. Generally, I think it's fair to say that British players have been more consistent and that the failure rate of foreigners has exceeded their success.

Among the most notable exceptions was Eric Cantona at Manchester United. Moreover, it would be wrong to ignore the impact in recent seasons of men such as France's World Cup-winning stars at Chelsea (Marcel Desailly and Frank Leboeuf) and Arsenal (Emmanuel Petit and Patrick Vieira). The Arsenal Foreign Legion not only lifted the Gunners to the Championship–FA Cup double in 1998 but made them arguably the best team to watch in the country. The following season, this mantle was assumed by the overseas players at Chelsea: no team could match their movement and passing skills.

However, there is little doubt that many have been attracted to England by the money rather than the football; and how many of the big names who have moved to Premiership teams have done so when their careers were at their peak in their previous environments? Especially when their home is the Italian league.

One foreign player who has made a big impression on me has been Paolo Di Canio at West Ham. Described by the Hammers' manager, Harry Redknapp, as the most gifted player he has ever worked with, the Italian forward has had a lot of adverse publicity in England – notably over that infamous shove on referee Paul Alcock when he was playing for Sheffield Wednesday against Arsenal. However, while his temperament might not make him the easiest of players to handle, it says much about his place in the pecking order of top-level strikers in Italy that he was allowed to leave that country.

No less surprising is the fact that West Ham were able to get a player of his technical quality for just £1.4 million. What a bargain.

Dennis Bergkamp is another foreign star who has stood out in England. He is a phenomenal player but, here again, it is questionable whether one could describe him as such by the standards of Italian football. Would he have joined Arsenal had he been more successful at his previous club, Inter Milan?

The question, of course, is no less hypothetical than the one about my own inclination to play in Italy. At least Bergkamp accepted the challenge whereas I didn't. I didn't even consider it – a thought which is particularly difficult to push aside when I think of Baresi. One of the main reasons I envied him – and most of the central defenders in Continental teams – was that he had more space to settle on the ball than I did.

Not long ago, Coventry's manager, Gordon Strachan, in an article in the *Observer* on the change in the pass-back rule, expounded the view that it had highlighted the lack of skill among British defenders, especially in European competitions.

Before the change, the pass back to the goalkeeper was an ideal outlet for English defenders when they pushed up to the halfway line to compress the play. If they were in difficulties or wanted to waste some playing time, they could always pass to the keeper. Now, with the keepers not allowed to handle, their defenders need to be closer to them. Instead of playing in half of the pitch, they have been forced to use three-quarters of it.

There is more space for players to exploit their skill – or, to put it another way, more space for those who lack skill to have this shown up! This has not been a problem for Continental sides because they have always played with more depth than the British and, by and large, they have always had defenders who can 'play'.

Gordon, a member of the Leeds team when they won the Championship in 1992, added, 'It was significant that the following season, when the new pass-back rule was put into operation, Leeds finished sixth from bottom and were knocked out of the European Cup by Rangers in the second round.'

Of the English teams who did well in Europe in the 1970s and 1980s, Nottingham Forest, with two central defenders who weren't good runners – Larry Lloyd and Kenny Burns – defended as deep as any of the Continental sides they played against. Liverpool, outstanding at adapting to different conditions and styles of play, approached many of our European ties in the same manner. Most of the teams we met were excellent at drawing the opposition towards them and hitting them on the break, so in a lot of our European ties, and especially those away from home, we didn't leave anywhere near as much space behind our defence as we did in our domestic matches.

Unlike the teams Gordon Strachan was referring to, Liverpool, with all their players being comfortable on the ball, benefited considerably from giving ourselves extra room in which to play. In any event, we didn't need to hit many balls back to the goalkeeper because all our defenders could retain possession just as well by knocking the ball around among ourselves.

I loved this side of the game and always considered it to be one of my greatest strengths. Because of their emphasis on technical ability, the European Cup ties were, indeed, the matches I generally enjoyed most. I played in more than 50 ties and there were only a handful of occasions on which I felt I did not play well. That was another reason why I kept visualizing myself in the boots of my AC Milan and Italy hero.

As the spare man in his defences, Baresi, with his

Gary Lineker made me look a mug when he gave Everton the lead in that final. It was one of my worst Wembley moments.

The silver lining – Ian Rush beats Everton defender Kevin Ratcliffe and goalkeeper, Bobby Mimms, to score his second goal and give us a 3–1 victory.

A tussle with Everton's Graeme Sharp, one of the players I least enjoyed facing, as we beat our Merseyside neighbours again in the 1989 FA Cup final.

Goodbye, Wembley, and thanks for the memories. My last match at the stadium as captain of the Liverpool team who beat Arsenal in the 1989 Charity Shield.

My eighth experience of being in a championship-winning team; what a way to mark my last season as an active Liverpool player. The others hogging the trophy in the dressing room are John Barnes (right), Ian Rush and Ronnie Whelan. Me guarding it again, (below) this time with all the players who made the success possible.

Graeme Souness does my job in the Scotland–Brazil World Cup match in 1982.

My Scotland appearance against Argentina, then the world champions, in 1979.
One of the rare occasions when I could do more than just defend.

The tributes laid at Anfield in memory of
those who died at Hillsborough on 15 April
1989 – the blackest day of the club's history.

John Barnes and I at a Hillsborough
memorial service.

Arsenal's Tony Adams, the general of the only club defence that has seriously challenged the record of the 1978/79 Liverpool rearguard in conceding only sixteen league goals.

Another Arsenal favourite of mine, Emmanuel Petit. Of today's players, he is the one I would most like to have had in my Liverpool teams.

The dreaded Billy Whitehurst – my least favourite opponent – in action for Sheffield United against Leeds in 1990. All I can say is that you should spare a thought for the Leeds man marking him.

Germany's Karl-Heinz Rummenigge, one of the strikers who played a major part in my education as a central defender.

The Manchester United players I most admire. David Beckham (above) did not deserve the stick he took after the 1998 World Cup finals. Roy Keane (right), the driving force behind United's treble. Jaap Stam (below), worth every penny of the massive fee United paid for him.

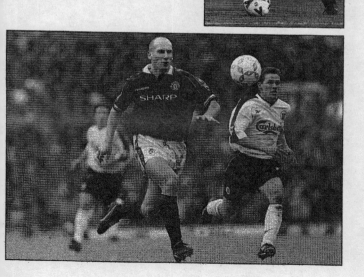

The best of all my team-mates: Janet, Adam and Lucy.

ability to organize his colleagues at the back and also to orchestrate many of his team's attacking moves, cut a majestic figure. The team-mates immediately in front of him might have had to get their hands dirty by involving themselves occasionally in the physical side of the game – the unarmed-combat side – but Baresi could concentrate on using his head.

Oh, how I would have loved that!

Now 39, he is five years younger than me. He was among the world's greatest players for much of the 1980s and 1990s. He joined Milan in 1977, the same year that I went to Liverpool, and in his 18 years there, he played a major part in their European Cup triumphs in 1989, 1990 and 1994 and also helped them win the European Supercup and the World Club Cup. That burst of success had been sparked by the financial power of Silvio Berlusconi, the media magnate who became president of the club when they were on the brink of bankruptcy in the mid-1980s. Berlusconi's investment in Milan – initially some £20 million – led to the signing of the Dutch trio of Ruud Gullit, Frank Rijkaard and Marco van Basten.

The other intriguing aspect of that Milan team was that, under the coaching regime of Arrigo Sacchi, they switched to a British-type pressing game, based on a flat-back four defensive system. Apparently, Sacchi became a devotee of this style of play through having once attended a lecture on it by Scotland's coach Andy Roxburgh, and he managed to develop what I would call a flat-back four/sweeper system rolled into one.

Previously, Italian teams defended very deep, with two or three back players in marking roles and a player operating behind to cover them – the 'true' sweeper system. The change of style at Milan meant that their spare man, Baresi, while continuing to fulfil the basic sweeper function did not do it in such an exaggerated fashion. He was more in line with his fellow defenders than previously, and he was the 'boss' when it came to deciding their positions as a unit. However, when Baresi pushed forward his defence, he would only hold the line for a few seconds. If the ball did not come through, he would drop back 10 or 15 yards behind everybody else to become a man apart again.

The one thing you could be sure about was that he had it easy compared to British central defenders like me. He did not do as much running as I did, and he did not have an opposing striker snapping at his heels whenever he was in possession of the ball. In that situation, he enjoyed the luxury of his immediate opponents backing off quickly and allowing him to do whatever he liked with the ball. The difference between us was driven home to me when I watched him playing for AC Milan against Genoa just before Liverpool faced Genoa in the Uefa Cup quarter-finals in March 1992. I had gone there with commentator Ray Stubbs to provide an assessment of Genoa for a BBC preview of the tie. About 10 minutes into the game, I turned to Ray and said, 'If I had played all my career in Italy, as Baresi has, I would have played until I was 45.'

In Italy, it struck me that the role Baresi filled was a central defender's dream. He was 33 then and, great reader of the game that he was, he hardly moved. Moreover, when he gained possession of the ball, he just made a square pass. If that had been a match in England, Baresi's approach would have caused the crowd to go berserk. In England, spectators hate it when they see back players knocking the ball around among themselves. They demand plenty of goalmouth action. But the crowd watching that match in Italy were quite happy because that was the football they had been brought up with – they knew no different.

The next best scenario for a player of my attributes – and, more specifically, my mentality – would have been the sweeper role in England. Unfortunately, this was never going to be more than a pipe-dream for me, if only because so few players in England were accustomed then to the sweeper format. The most effective team patterns are the ones the players are comfortable with, and British players, almost all of whom have been brought up on 4–4–2 or 4–3–3, have never handled any new frameworks particularly well.

They are not alone in this. Wherever you go in the world you will find that all players are creatures of habit who like their jobs to be made as simple as possible for them. When a manager or a coach attempts to introduce something different from the norm into their game, and a player does not understand his instructions, the player is unlikely to stand up and say so: no player likes to admit to any lack of football knowledge. Even at Liverpool, where the words 'keep it simple' would have made an appropriate club motto to go beneath the Liver Bird emblem on our jerseys, there were occasions when players were given instructions they did not truly grasp. The manager or coach would end his team talk by asking, 'Do you understand what we're trying to do? Do you have any problems with it?' The players would say, 'No problems.'

Immediately the manager or coach walked out of the door, they would be shaking their heads and asking, 'What was all that about?'

Any British player who wants to be a sweeper – or wants to learn to be one – should go to a country like Italy or Germany, where teams have been using the structure for many years and the game is less frenetic than it is in England. The obvious flaw with the system is its rigidity, the fact that the defenders in man-to-man marking roles can get ridiculously narrow-minded about their jobs. In my experience, the most glaring example came in the Liverpool–Borussia Moenchengladbach European Cup final in 1977, when the former Germany defender Bertie Vogts was assigned to shadow Kevin Keegan. For Liverpool's first goal, by Terry McDermott from a Steve Heighway pass, Vogts took up the most bizarre position I have ever seen from a player of his stature, alongside Keegan, when he could easily have left Kevin and moved across to deal with the threat posed by Steve and Terry. In trying to do his job, he did not leave enough room for common sense.

Vogts must shudder when he looks back on that match. He was run ragged by Kevin and it was his foul on Kevin near the end that led to Phil Neal making it 3–1 from a penalty. However, the Germans are usually superb with this system, as the national team showed when they won the 1996 European Championship. With Mathias Sammer as the spare man at the back and their midfield anchor man, Dieter Eilst, filling in for him whenever he supported the attack, they played the sweeper game to perfection.

They were able to reach that level because, through being accustomed to the style of play with their club teams, every member of the German squad was switched on to it. In any formation all 11 players have a part to play. It is impossible to overstate the importance of this. Hence my misgivings about the trend of teams in England to use three central defenders, each covering a specific zone or area, and two wing-backs. I do not think any team has looked entirely happy playing that way. Aston Villa are the best of the bunch, but while Villa have been impressive defensively, they have lacked someone at the back to involve himself in the attacking play.

The wing-backs have a big responsibility in the attacking sense, but few teams have consistently mastered the problem of covering the space behind them. The other headache is that, with five men available at the back, teams are liable to become too negative. Instead of playing a flat-back four, it is almost a flat-back five.

This was how Liverpool missed an excellent chance to beat Manchester United at Old Trafford in the 1998/99 FA Cup fourth round. For obvious reasons, I would love to have seen Liverpool win that game – it is impossible for me to be a totally neutral pundit where my old club are concerned – and they were given the perfect start with a Michael Owen goal after three minutes. So why did United win 2–1? My old colleague John Barnes, commenting on the match in the *Daily Telegraph*, pointed out that Liverpool's wing-backs, Stig Bjornebye and Vegard Heggem, were often in a straight line with the three central defenders and that Liverpool were outnumbered in midfield as a consequence. Perhaps the most important factor in any defensive set-up is that you should always have one extra man. If the opposition have, say, one man up front, he should have two defenders to beat. But I have seen matches in which teams have had all three central defenders back even when there has been nobody to mark.

Liverpool experienced headaches like these even during my period with the club. In addition to playing occasionally with three central defenders against teams such as Wimbledon to give ourselves extra protection against their high-ball bombardment, we adopted the sweeper format for a run of games during the early part of the 1982/83 season, under the management of Bob Paisley. The only difference between our interpretation of the system and that of the Italians and Germans was that the two men who worked with the sweeper did not have man-for-man marking jobs: they covered specific zones. But I had reservations about the change from the start. Operating with a flat-back four had stood us in good stead in the past and as we were still better than most teams at the back, my attitude was, 'If it ain't broke, don't fix it.' However, you had to give Bob Paisley credit for being prepared to try something new – and for admitting he was wrong.

I struggled to come to terms with the system as much as anybody. In any defensive set-up, the spare man has to be able to move forward and play in midfield, which I considered my speciality. At my physical peak, I probably went forward more than any other central defender in Britain. In knowing when to go and when to stay put, the number of matches I had played in a 4–4–2 system meant that I never really had to think about it when I was in a flat-back four. But, as one of three central defenders, it was a different matter.

This is where I have mixed feelings about the possibility that West Ham's young central defender, Rio Ferdinand, will emerge as the Baresi or Sammer of the England team. Ferdinand is probably the only English-born central defender who has the ability for the job. But if he does not play as a sweeper for West Ham for a reasonable amount of time he's going to have problems. Sooner or later, he is going to cost England a goal through going forward at the wrong time.

While I and the other Liverpool players would have adjusted to the sweeper system eventually, the expectations of our fans meant that arguably we were the team who could least afford to persevere with it. After so many years of Liverpool being among the strongest contenders for the major trophies, how could Bob Paisley tell our supporters, 'Sorry, we won't win anything this season because we are trying to get used to this sweeper system'? The only other time that I might have filled the sweeper role was when Scotland faced Belgium in a European Championship qualifying tie in Brussels in December 1982. It was rare for Scotland to play this way, and on that occasion the manager, Jock Stein, handed the job to Celtic's Roy Aitken and used Dundee United's David Narey and myself as the markers. A number of people found it a curious decision, as I did.

It is possible that Stein was influenced by both David and me having a lot of pace, which tends to be more of an advantage in a man-for-man marking job than it does in the spare-man position. Nonetheless, I felt that our abilities and styles of play screamed out for either of us to be in Roy's position I am not saying that Stein's decision caused Scotland's 3–2 defeat, but I would not have thought that our cause was helped by it.

Some players in England have the ball-skill to operate as the spare man at the back but not the defensive ability, while with others it is the reverse. In the first instance, despite what I have said about the importance of sweepers involving themselves in the creative play, their first priority must be defence. They have to be able to think like defenders. This is particularly so in the Premiership or Nationwide League, where the ball gets played into the box more quickly than it does in other countries and defenders are under greater physical pressure, especially in the air. For this reason I become quite irritated when I hear that attacking midfield players are being touted for the sweeper role. For me, it underlines how good defensive play can be taken for granted.

Several people insisted that Bryan Robson, the former Manchester United and England captain, would make an ideal spare man at the back at international level. He had the tackling ability to be a defender, but I doubt that he would have had the necessary positional discipline. More recently, Liverpool's England midfielder, Jamie Redknapp, has also been envisaged as a sweeper and, in fact, has been tried in the position by England's B team. It did not go well for him, from all accounts, which was only to be expected because, as a defender, Redknapp has less going for him than Robson did. He is not as good a tackler as Robson was, nor as strong as Robson in the air.

As these were areas in which I was found wanting, too, it could be argued that I would have been in the same boat as Redknapp. However, my reading of the play offset these weaknesses in defensive situations. Inevitably, for someone who had played at the back for so long, I instinctively thought like a defender.

However, although I like to think that I showed a midfield player's creative skills, I needed to be in defence to exploit my ability. I apply the same argument to Redknapp, and all the other top-class attacking midfielders who have clearly been at their best in positions from which they are able to create the highest number of scoring chances.

Glenn Hoddle seems a strong believer in the sweeper concept. He attempted to fill the role when he was a player-manager for Swindon and Chelsea. I was never impressed with him in the position. For a natural creative midfield player such as himself, Hoddle's defensive positioning and ball-winning ability were impressive. For a defender, though, they were indifferent. When Hoddle signed Ruud Gullit in the summer of 1995, he initially gave Gullit the job of replacing him in the role. I saw his Premiership début against Everton, and on *Match of the Day* that night I said I did not think Gullit could play as a sweeper and that his creative ability was wasted in the position. His greatest quality was that he could play the 'killer' pass and there was no way he could open up a team as well from the back as he could from midfield.

Later, Gary Lineker told me he thought I was talking rubbish, but I had predicted that, before long, Gullit would find himself back in his more familiar midfield position. I was right.

All managers have their own ideas on how they want their teams to perform, but some cling to them too closely.

They aren't practical. I cannot stress enough that managers have to tailor their systems and styles of play to the ability of their players. The 'right' way to play the game is the way that brings the best results. When Hoddle's Chelsea team was struggling in the 1993/94 season, I said on television that the worst thing any side can do is try to play intricate football if they haven't the players to do it, and especially if they are in danger of relegation. In an interview on *Match of the Day*, Hoddle had insisted that he would never abandon his 'principles and philosophies', but my reaction was, 'Nice words, but I'll give you a better one. Survival. To get better results, Chelsea will have to battle harder and stop stringing so many passes together. They have got to get the ball through to the front more quickly.' I was reminded of that comment when watching Chelsea beat Luton 2–0 in that season's FA Cup semi-final at Wembley with the sort of route-one approach that must have made even Wimbledon green with envy. Both Chelsea's goals, scored by Gavin Peacock, came from long punts from deep within their own half.

I often think of Hoddle's 'principles and philosophies' when I hear people like him talk about the need for English teams to play with a sweeper. It's a great notion, but whether it's realistic is a different matter.

All managers make mistakes, and in Hoddle's case the other mitigating factor is that his teams have generally been very entertaining.

I had a lot of admiration for Kevin Keegan when he was manager of Newcastle. I stated on *Match of the Day* that Newcastle could never hope to win the Championship with their cavalier attacking football. I found it strange that Kevin was happy for his team to take so many attacking risks away from home because the great Liverpool sides he played for were much more disciplined.

At the same time, while I would not have liked Newcastle to play as they did if I had been their manager, I had to concede that their approach had been successful in lifting them into the top flight – remember they were in danger of relegation to the old Third Division when Kevin was appointed in February 1992 – and they were the team I most enjoyed watching. So much so that when Kevin was criticized in the 1995/96 season over Newcastle losing a 12-point Championship lead and eventually finishing fourth, I found myself playing devil's advocate when I pointed out, 'But for their open style of play, they might not have got to the top of the table in the first place.'

On the principle of a team's system or style depending on the players available to them, Liverpool were more fortunate than most in having teams who could perform effectively in a number of different ways. Because we favoured a passing game, and did not take as many attacking risks as other sides, we were categorized as a negative side. I remember that when the three points for a win system was introduced in 1981, it was widely felt that it would prove the end of us as a major Championship force. Indeed, in March that season, we were in the bottom half of the table. But we won our last 11 matches to pip Ipswich for the title by four points.

But I didn't gloat when people got it wrong about Liverpool: there were two occasions when I was proved wrong about the team myself.

# **13** How Liverpool Conquered Europe

There are plenty of options for me when I'm asked to single out the Liverpool achievements that gave me the most satisfaction, but outside Liverpool's European Cup success in 1978 and their record-breaking Championship triumph the following year, two other high spots will always stand out in my memory: the winning of the European Cup, for the third time, against Roma in the Olympic Stadium in Rome in 1984 (when Liverpool also took the Championship and the League Cup) and the Championship–FA Cup double in 1986, when I was captain of the side. These achievements meant more to me than most of the others, because they were the least expected.

Such was my conservative nature that, when assessing Liverpool's chances of winning a trophy, I would tend to lean towards the negative rather than positive. I often expected the worst – even with a unique goal-scorer by the name of Ian Rush in our line-up. I feel a little awkward about discussing Rush's value to Liverpool in those seasons because he was something else I was proved wrong about.

I am being kind to myself when I say that in emerging as the most prolific goal-scorer in Liverpool's history, with more than 330 goals in 600 first-team games, Rush blossomed in a way I found impossible to envisage when he was bought from Chester for £300,000 in May 1980. He did not score in any of his first seven First Division matches the following season, and having watched him in training over this period, I honestly felt he had nothing to offer us.

About six months after his arrival, when I was trying to regain match fitness after an injury, I played with Rush in a reserve match at Preston where he was marked out of the game by my old friend from Scotland John Blackley. John, the former Hibernian and Scotland defender, had an easy match and later, when we were discussing Rush, I said, 'Liverpool don't usually make mistakes but I reckon they've made a big one with this signing. At the end of the season, I'm sure they'll get rid of him.'

'I agree,' John said. 'I can't believe Liverpool bought him for three hundred thousand pounds.'

Three or four years later, when John and I were playing golf together and I happened to mention Rush's extraordinary scoring feats, he burst out laughing. 'You and I are both good judges of players, aren't we?' he said.

The only explanation I can give for my misjudgement was that Rush was initially overawed by the size of the club and the big-name players there. As he was quite a shy, introspective person, it was bound to take him time to settle. The point at which I began to think differently

221

about him was when he was brought into the side for the League Cup final replay against West Ham in April 1981. He did not play a big part in Liverpool's 2–1 win, but I still remember being taken aback by his pace and sharpness in latching on to a Graeme Souness pass and firing in a shot that hit the bar.

As his self-confidence soared, he kept getting better and the partnership he established with Kenny Dalglish up front was just in a different class. Kenny never had a lot of pace, which is why he and Ian complemented each other so well. While Kenny could concentrate on having the ball played to his feet, Ian would be looking for the ball over the top or through the defence for him to chase. No defenders relish playing against strikers who attack the space behind them, especially a striker with Ian's lightning pace, and Ian terrorized them. The goals he scored were hardly likely to put them in a confident frame of mind either. In the 1983/84 treble season, he scored 32 goals in his 41 Championship matches, eight in the League Cup and four in the European Cup.

However, despite Rush's presence, and Liverpool's success on the home front, I still felt I had good reason to worry about the date with Roma. As if the venue for the match was not enough to make me neurotic about it, their players had reportedly landed a bonus of £12,000 for reaching the final and been promised £64,000 if they won. Our win bonus was £6,000.

For a while, I kept my misgivings under reasonable control. There was a two-week gap between Liverpool's last league match and the clash with Roma, and while Roma's players were locked away in some mountain training retreat, Joe Fagan took us for a short break to Israel and encouraged us to unwind. A couple of Italian journalists had been assigned to join us there to provide daily reports to their newspapers on our build-up to the game, and I don't think they could believe how laid-back we were.

But as the game drew closer, I became increasingly uptight. My sense of foreboding started to get the better of me three hours before the kick off, when I switched on the television in my room and tuned in to the Italian channel covering the match. I was amazed to see that the Olympic Stadium, with a capacity of almost 70,000, was already three-quarters full. Although 20,000 Liverpool fans had bought tickets for the match, you would have been hard pressed to spot any of them there.

We had another glimpse of this intimidating sight on the coach journey to the stadium, when we were able to see inside the ground as the vehicle went over a hill. Again, Liverpool supporters were conspicuous by their absence. The thought that the Liverpool followers were probably all in the boozers and that none would be posted missing by the time of the kick-off was of little consolation to me. I suffered from pre-match nerves at the best of times, but when I saw that Roma crowd, with their smoke bombs, flares, klaxons and flags, I have to admit that I was not far short of being petrified.

It was only when we were in the dressing room and I looked at the other Liverpool players that my anxiety started to evaporate. The more I studied them, and thought about their strengths, the more I realized that if my nerves got to me on the pitch, or I made a bad mistake,

I could rely on all 10 of those other Liverpool players to help me out.

When we were in the dressing-room tunnel, ready to take the field, the others were clearly as anxious as I was. Suddenly our substitutes, Mike Robinson and David Hodgson, started humming Chris Rea's 'I Don't Know What It Is But I Love It'. Within the next few seconds, the whole team had latched on to this as an outlet for their fears and were singing it.

Liverpool's teamwork and strength of character enabled us to hold Roma to a 1–1 draw at the end of 90 minutes, then through extra-time, and finally overcome them in a penalty shoot-out. It was the sort of success story that was very much a feature of our European Cup challenges. Nevertheless, it was when Liverpool were in Europe that I was always inclined to be at my most pessimistic. Indeed, even if we had been playing Roma in Rome again the following week, I would have been only marginally less worried about our chances than I had been the first time.

The vast majority of the teams we faced in the competition were technically better than we were. Their individual skill was often breathtaking, especially when they were on their own ground. Liverpool were streets ahead in other important aspects of the game, and once we put them under pressure they collapsed, but I never really got into the habit of putting all my faith in that scenario. Indeed, after the opening 10 or 15 minutes of a European tie, I would often be thinking, We cannot possibly beat this side.

Generally, I found Eastern European teams the most

difficult to handle. My first European Cup tie was against Dynamo Dresden in 1977, and I scored one of our goals in a 5–1 first-leg win at Anfield. Yet in the second leg in Germany, they could easily have wiped out that four-goal lead. I still cannot work out why they only beat us 2–1. In the first 45 minutes they were light years ahead of Liverpool in skill and pace, and Ray Clemence had to make half a dozen great saves to keep us in the game. Dresden made their breakthrough with two goals at the start of the second half, but then their performance suddenly fell apart.

It would be nice to think that Liverpool's tenacity had something to do with it but the nature of Dresden's collapse militated against such an explanation. Although he had no real evidence to support it, the collapse even prompted Bob Paisley to wonder whether their players had been taking stimulants. This would not have been the only time that speculation has arisen over whether a team has used drugs in a big match, and in the light of our match against Dynamo Dresden – and the amount of money at stake in professional football at the highest levels – I would not discount the possibility of some of the stories being true.

Call him paranoid if you like, but Bob Paisley was always on his guard against the possibility of the opposition trying to drug us. Before we played Widzew Lodz in the 1982/83 European Cup quarter-final first leg in Poland Bob was furious with me for taking a cup of tea from a pot that had been put in our dressing room by a Widzew club representative half an hour before the kick-off. I was one of four or five Liverpool players drinking it, but I was the first person Bob saw as he came through the door. His reaction was little short of hysterical. He swept the pot off the table, and shouted, 'What have I told you? Drugs! Don't drink anything they give you.' They beat us, 2–0, and went on to clinch a 4–3 aggregate victory. But, of course, these blemishes on Liverpool's European Cup record were rare.

Liverpool's achievements in the competition, and those of the other English teams in the 1970s and 1980s, look even more impressive nowadays when set against more recent performances. In the eight seasons before the ban on English clubs – imposed by Uefa in 1985 as a result of the shameful crowd trouble at that year's Liverpool–Juventus European Cup final at the Heysel Stadium in Brussels – teams from this country won the trophy no fewer than seven times. Liverpool were top of the list with four triumphs, followed by Nottingham Forest (two) and Aston Villa. But it has been a different story since the lifting of the ban in 1990, with England having had to wait nine years to celebrate another victory, courtesy of Manchester United.

Why? Some believe that it has become more difficult to win the competition than it was when Liverpool did it because of the change in its format – it is now a league rather than a cup competition – and the fact that there are more matches. Liverpool had only nine matches to get through, while Manchester United's route to glory encompassed 13.

However, without wishing to detract from United's success, I believe that the change in format has made it easier. It is often said that the best teams have more chance of coming out on top in the Championship than in a straight knock-out competition like the FA Cup or League Cup, where so much depends on the luck of the draw and who happens to get the right breaks on the day. To a degree, I think the same logic applies to the European Champions League.

I wish the Champions League had been in operation in the 1978/79 and 1979/80 seasons, when Liverpool, with a team I considered to be as good as any side in the world, didn't survive the European Cup first round. In the first instance, Nottingham Forest beat us 2–0 at home and held us to a goalless draw at Anfield, and in the second, Dynamo Tbilisi lost 2–1 at Anfield but beat us 3–0 in the return leg. In a Champions League we would still have been in the competition, with enough points in the bag to justify confidence in our chances of going all the way.

I think the main reason for England's lack of European success at club level is simply that teams in other countries have caught up with the English in terms of attributes like strength and determination, while the English have not made sufficiently big strides in improving their technical expertise. That five-year European exile led to English teams losing the European football habit: they couldn't adjust to the style of play necessary for European Cup success. Though the influx of foreign players in recent years has helped alleviate this problem, the number of foreigners good enough to form the nucleus of a European Cup-winning team has been limited.

Liverpool's success in Europe had its roots in our ability to keep the ball and play opponents at their own cat-and-mouse game. For all my faults, I don't think any central defender in Britain was better at holding the ball than I was. As I've said, this was one of the hallmarks of the Liverpool back four as a whole. Whenever I played the ball to another defender, I was never inhibited by the thought that it might give the opposition the chance to nick it and get a clear run at our goal.

One of the things I remember from our match against Roma was the huge amount of energy expended by their Brazilian forward, Cereza, in his attempts to dispossess our back players. I had played against Cereza when Scotland were thrashed 4–1 by Brazil in the 1982 World Cup finals in Spain. He was some player – he had to be to get into a team that included the likes of Socrates, Falcao and Zico and which, indeed, was the best side I ever faced. But playing for Roma was clearly not the same for him. As we knocked the ball around at the back, Cereza did so much chasing after it that he ended up with cramp and had to be substituted. However, I have to reiterate that there were few European ties in which the opposition did not make it difficult for us to get the ball in the first place. Roma apart, the other teams we faced in the European Cup during the 1983/84 season were Denmark's Odense BK, Athletic Bilbão, Benfica and Dinamo Bucharest. Any of the latter three could have easily knocked us out, especially as they had all done the most difficult part of the job by getting a good result in the first-leg ties at Anfield. In those matches, we were held to a goalless draw by Bilbão, and only managed 1–0 wins over Benfica and Dinamo Bucharest. Yet in the away ties, we beat Bilbão 1–0, Benfica 4–1 and Dinamo Bucharest 2–1.

The Benfica triumph, an outstanding example of a

team having players making runs through a defence from midfield or defensive positions, was one of the best in Liverpool's history. It was the first time that Liverpool operated with only one man up front, a revolutionary policy in those days. In this instance, the Lone Ranger role was filled by Ian Rush, who scored one of the goals and was supported well enough for Ronnie Whelan to get two and Craig Johnston the other. Rush, who had scored the only goal in Bilbāo, also helped himself to both our goals in Bucharest.

I just wonder what the results would have been if this unique Welshman had been playing for the other sides. For example, Dinamo Bucharest had the chances to score five against us. I also wonder what might have happened to Liverpool had Graeme Souness been playing for the opposition. If ever there was a game that showed how much Graeme meant to Liverpool, it was the second-leg semi-final in Bucharest. I would not have fancied being in his shoes. Following his clash with a Dinamo player in the first leg at Anfield, when his opponent was left nursing a fractured jaw, the hostility shown towards Graeme in Romania was something else. On our arrival, even the soldiers at the airport had no compunction about drawing his attention to it, with gestures that indicated Graeme could expect to leave the country on a stretcher.

During the pre-match warm-up, Graeme was booed by the 70,000 crowd every time he touched the ball, which prompted us to give him as much of it as possible. Suddenly, he did something that I think only he would have had the bottle to do: as the ball was played to him, and the crowd geared themselves up for another verbal blast, he played a joke on them by producing a great dummy and stepping over it. Even they had to laugh. Surprising as it might seem, despite my pre-match fears about Roma, I found the final itself – or, at least, the 120 minutes that preceded the agonizing ritual of the penalty shoot-out – almost a doddle compared to the tie against Dinamo. It must have been a terrible match to watch, as were our triumphant 1978 and 1981 European Cup finals against Bruges and Real Madrid. The obvious explanation is that the bigger the prize at stake, the more cautious teams become, and in the Liverpool–Roma match, the fact that Roma were playing at home put them under particular pressure to avoid mistakes.

Liverpool took advantage of the nervousness in Roma's play by going ahead after just 15 minutes through Phil Neal. It was a massive psychological blow to Roma, who felt that the goal should have been disallowed for what appeared to be a foul on their keeper by Craig Johnston. They did well to get back into the game, equalizing just before half-time, but then the fear of defeat took over and the game became a bore.

I doubt whether any team in England could have played the way Roma did in the second half and through 30 minutes of extra-time – the fans would not have stood for it. The goalkeepers hardly had a save to make. I think Roma were mainly to blame because the onus was on them to attack, not us. It takes two to tango, and as they were not interested in committing themselves in front of their home supporters – risking leaving gaps in their defence – there was little scope for us to do so. For both teams the match was a wonderful exhibition of the art of stringing a lot of passes together without going anywhere.

The penalty shoot-out was an exhibition of a different kind: how to reduce the players involved, and those watching them, to nervous wrecks.

Over the years, I have been involved in numerous debates about whether the penalty shoot-out – a tremendously exciting spectacle for the fans – is the right tie-breaker as far as the teams are concerned. One of the most popular alternative ideas I have heard is that of awarding victory to the team that has gained the most corners. Some people have even suggested a change in the rules of the 'golden goal' system, which provides for an additional period of extra-time in which the team that scores first wins the game (as Germany did in the 1996 European Championship final against the Czech Republic). As even this does not always obviate the need for a penalty shoot-out, it has been suggested to me that, to make scoring easier, each team should 'lose' a player for every five or 10 minutes that the scoreline remains blank.

In fact, there is no perfect answer, and I still feel that the penalty shoot-out is as good a system as any. Having said that, I should add that I was the last player who could be expected to relish taking part in one. As one would expect of someone with my aversion to pressure, I tried to steer clear of taking spot kicks at the best of times. I never took any for Liverpool in a competitive match, and when our five nominated penalty men were going through the ordeal in Rome, I remember being haunted by the thought that in the event of it ending 5–5, I might be forced to have a go in the 'sudden death' part of the competition.

Defenders who are the epitome of composure in their third of the field can be exactly the opposite when they get the ball close to the opposing goal. Perhaps the easiest scoring chance of my career came in a home match against Sheffield Wednesday, when I swung my left leg at the ball – in front of an open goal and the live TV cameras – and missed it. Had I been making a clearance near my own goal, I would probably have been inch-perfect. As for penalties, I knew that the secret was to make your mind up about how and where you were going to hit the ball, and not change it. But I also knew that as *I* approached the ball I would be thinking, No, don't hit it there, hit it somewhere else!

Imagine what I would have been like had I been in the shoes of Liverpool's spot-kick players – Steve Nicol, Phil Neal, Graeme Souness, Ian Rush and Alan Kennedy – in Rome. Phil Neal was supposed to take the first kick but Steve Nicol showed bravery beyond the call of duty, as far as I was concerned, by pushing himself into the job. It backfired horribly for him: he missed. However, Liverpool scored from each of their next three attempts (through Neal, Souness and Rush), and Roma missed two of their corresponding four kicks. So with Liverpool 3–2 ahead, it was down to Alan Kennedy to apply the *coup de grâce*. At this point, a number of the players were confused about the position. Their attention was so focused on each kick that they forgot the score, which I think is quite common in such situations. It was a bit like waking up after an operation – you know where you are, but you're in a haze. When Roma missed their fourth penalty, our players were asking each other, 'What now?' Then someone said, 'If Alan scores, we win.' It was appropriate that he should use the word 'if' because when Alan had been practising his penalties two days earlier at our Mellwood training ground, he had been hopeless. The same could be said about Steve Nicol, Phil Neal, Graeme Souness and Ian Rush. We had had a penalty-taking competition against five of the club's youth players and they beat us 5–0.

I immediately thought of that during the 1998 World Cup finals, when Glenn Hoddle was getting stick from the media because the players defeated in the penalty shoot-out against Argentina had not practised them in training earlier in the week. I particularly remembered Alan Kennedy's attempts against our youth-team keeper. He tried to direct every kick to the keeper's left and every kick was pushed wide of the post. Joe Fagan, who was watching him, shook his head incredulously. 'Alan, son,' he said, 'you're turning me into an old man. Haven't you ever thought of trying to put the ball to the other side?' Before Alan could answer him, Joe was walking away, still shaking his head.

I have never asked Joe what was going through his mind when Alan stepped up to take that kick in Rome but I think it was pretty obvious. So, too, was the reaction of all of us when Alan scored . . . with a shot to the keeper's right.

From that pinnacle, the only way for Liverpool was down. After a season like that, it was perhaps only to be expected that we would experience a sense of anticlimax and take time to get going again. Another problem was the loss of Graeme Souness to Sampdoria during the close season. Denmark's Jan Molby, the first player signed to help fill the gap, in November 1984 from Ajax, took time to settle in English football. Though he clearly had many of Graeme's technical qualities, it was difficult for him to exude the same air of authority. It was the same with Kevin MacDonald, signed from Leicester in December 1984, and Steve McMahon, who was Kenny Dalglish's first Liverpool signing, from Aston Villa, in September 1985. While they, too, were excellent players, I just felt that Graeme's leadership style was unique.

For all these reasons, in the 1984/85 season Liverpool failed to win a trophy for the first time in nine years. What made it worse was that Everton took over from us as the Champions, and also won the European Cup-winners Cup.

In terms of my own performances it was a good season for me – probably the best of my Anfield career. But this was inevitably overshadowed by our results. The season began on the low note of Everton beating us in the Charity Shield, and when they won 1–0 at Anfield in October – their first win at our place in 15 years – we were as low as eighteenth in the table. We eventually reached second place, but Everton finished no fewer than 13 points ahead of us. Our bid to keep the League Cup ended with a third-round defeat by Tottenham, and in the FA Cup we lost to Manchester United in a semi-final replay.

On top of all this, there was the horror of the European Cup final against Juventus at the Heysel Stadium, where rioting between Liverpool and Juventus fans before the kick-off led to 39 deaths and English football being vilified by the rest of the football world. Heysel cast a giant shadow over Liverpool – and English football – the following season, and I do not think anybody can have envied Kenny Dalglish his task of undoing some of the damage to the club's reputation through their performances on the field. Kenny had been confirmed as Joe Fagan's successor on the eve of the Liverpool–Juventus match, and as the player chosen by him as the new Liverpool captain, I would have been the last person to suggest, publicly, that he might struggle to succeed.

Although Liverpool had never had a player-manager before, I felt that if anyone could make a success of it, it was Kenny. The only other contender was Phil Neal, who was so upset about being passed over that he initially refused to comply with Kenny's request for the players to refer to him as 'boss'. I thought Phil had a lot to offer, but it seemed to me that he was more of a coach than a manager, and that Kenny would be more effective in getting the players to work together. That has always been one of his great strengths.

However, while I was confident that Kenny would get more out of the players than Phil could, if only because of his stature at the club, I also believed that he needed time to produce a trophy-winning team. The only player he had bought during the early part of the season was the tenacious Steve McMahon, so, as far as I was concerned, we would still be considered a workmanlike team rather than a skilful one.

This view was strengthened in February 1986, when Everton beat us 2–0 at Anfield to forge some six points ahead of us in the title race. While I was having dinner with Kenny that evening, I told him, 'Individually, this is the most limited Liverpool team I have played in.'

'You might be right,' Kenny acknowledged. 'But the team spirit is still excellent, and if we see a run of good results, and build up some momentum, I think we could still do something.'

I could tell that Kenny genuinely believed this. Yet I remained sceptical. Still do something? I thought. You must be joking.

What happened next was amazing. In the following game, Liverpool came from behind to beat Tottenham 2–1, thanks to a late Ian Rush goal when our defence was taking the mother of all batterings and we would have gladly settled for a draw. Liverpool went on to win 10 and draw one of our last 11 First Division matches, to pip Everton for the title by one point.

The worst Liverpool team I had played in also overcame Norwich, Chelsea, York, Watford and Southampton in the FA Cup . . . not to mention Everton in the final. Only two teams since the Second World War had achieved this double – Tottenham in 1961 and Arsenal in 1971 – and while I think that most people would have expected Liverpool to emulate them at some time in the 1980s, the possibility of our doing so in that 1985/86 season really was beyond my wildest dreams.

How could I have been so wrong?

The Liverpool team spirit and Ian Rush's scoring ability only partly answer the question. Kenny Dalglish had brought himself back into the team for the last seven matches, after appearing in only 14 of the other 35, and it was tempting for people to suggest that it was his presence that made all the difference. But Rush apart, the other player who deserved special praise, in my view, was Kevin MacDonald, who was brought into the starting line-up in December in place of the injured Steve McMahon. I would say that at the tail-end of that 1985/86 season, he was far and away our most influential player.

The amount of ground he covered in supporting team-mates in possession was remarkable. It irritated me that so many Liverpool fans and the media seemed to take him for granted. It was as if they were saying, 'Well, you can get anybody off the street to run up and down a football field.' What they overlooked was that Kevin could *play*. He probably got more touches of the ball than anyone else in the side and, while his passing was safe rather than spectacular, he hardly ever gave the ball away. During those crucial final hurdles of the season, he was the man who did most to knit the team together. He was in the starting line-up for our last five Championship matches, and I think it was significant that, although four of those games were away, we won them all.

I was delighted for Kevin that he kept his place in the side for the FA Cup final. You had to sympathize with the players who did not make it, among them Steve McMahon, who was named as a substitute. However, the journalists who suggested that Kevin was not a 'true' Liverpool player, and was lucky to get the nod over players like Steve, were not living in the real world, as far as I was concerned.

The most vital of those remaining league matches was the last one at Chelsea, which we had to win to be sure of taking the title. I cannot say I was optimistic about our chances because Chelsea, in sixth position, had drawn 1–1 at Anfield in November and badly wanted to end the season on a high note after taking just one point from their three previous games. They were a talented team, but liable to blow hot one moment, cold the next. You never knew quite what to expect from them. On top of all this, Liverpool did not have a good record against them.

Unfortunately for Chelsea, however, their controversial chairman Ken Bates took it upon himself to indulge in some public Chelsea drum-beating. 'Liverpool', he declared in his inimitable bulldog fashion, 'will win the Championship over my dead body.' I thought it was silly of him to get involved in the build-up to the match in this way, given Liverpool's habit of being motivated by indiscreet comments from the opposition. But we could understand where he was coming from. Liverpool's domination of the major honours had inevitably provoked a sense of resentment and envy towards us, especially in the south. It became an important source of motivation to us. Indeed, opposing teams had to be very careful what they said about us because if they uttered a word out of place someone in our dressing room was bound to get fired up about it. It was daft, I know, but in the build-up to a big game professional footballers are touchy people and the paranoia that encroaches on every dressing room at such times is infectious.

The scoreline at Chelsea was 1–0, and such was my elation at the end that I was virtually out of control. This was unusual for me: I was never one to show much emotion, and whenever Liverpool clinched a major honour, my reaction was usually one of relief more than anything. At Stamford Bridge, though, some of the other

Liverpool players said they had never seen me celebrate in such an uninhibited manner – they thought I'd gone berserk. Hours after the game, I was still shaking my fists and exclaiming, 'Yes – we've done it!' I could have done with retaining some of that adrenalin for the FA Cup final the following Saturday.

The Everton team we faced at Wembley was superior to the Goodison side beaten by Liverpool in the 1984 League Cup final, and also the one we overcame in the 1989 FA Cup final. Their 1984/85 team – with Neville Southall in goal, Gary Stevens, Derek Mountfield, Kevin Ratcliffe and Pat van den Hauwe at the back, Trevor Steven, Peter Reid, Paul Bracewell and Kevin Sheedy in midfield and Andy Gray and Graeme Sharp up front – was one of the best exponents of the 4–4–2 system that I have seen. But for any opposing defenders, Everton had become even more intimidating before the start of the 1985/86 season through the signing of Gary Lineker from Leicester. The transfer replaced Everton's bludgeon with a sword: Gray's power and aggression were replaced by Lineker's explosive pace and clinical finishing skills.

Liverpool did brilliantly to get the better of them at Wembley because for most of the match – and particularly the first half – my performance meant that we were as good as down to 10 men! It was my most indifferent appearance in a Wembley final and I was lucky that Everton did not capitalize on it more than they did. I still cringe when I see the photograph showing my desperate body language as Gary Lineker beat me to give Everton a half-time lead.

I had known something was badly wrong with me

during the pre-match warm-up. It was a blisteringly hot, sunny day and my legs felt so heavy that, whenever I ran, it was like treading water. I never felt as restricted during a match as I did in that game, not even when I was carrying an injury. I was in a daze.

The Lineker goal, from a simple ball over the top of our defence by Peter Reid, underlined it. In normal circumstances, it would have been the easiest thing in the world for me to read the pass. I knew it was coming, and even if Gary had been Carl Lewis, my anticipation would still have enabled me to get to the ball before him. But instead of starting to move into position, I just stood there watching the ball. That moment of hesitancy must have made Gary feel as if it was his birthday. By the time I started to make my move, Gary was away from me.

I did manage to catch up with him, but then made another mistake by just sticking my left leg in instead of making a sliding tackle to ensure a stronger contact. I stumbled over as Gary hit the shot, and Bruce Grobbelaar came to my rescue by saving it. But as I was scrambling to my feet, even Bruce had no chance of preventing Gary putting the rebound into the net. Gary still winds me up over it – and I never tire of reminding him that the exuberance with which he celebrated the goal was made to look somewhat hollow at 4.50 p.m. when I was preparing to walk up to the Royal Box to collect the trophy.

There had been little to suggest I would be in that position when Gary scored. But Everton began to wilt in the heat and Liverpool, thanks to the spirit of players like Kevin MacDonald and a double strike from Ian Rush, seized control in the second half. As for myself, it was a good thing I could brush aside my errors over the Lineker goal and hold myself together for the rest of the game. Had I been 21, not 31, I think I would have folded.

I also owed a great deal to the Liverpool management team. If you felt you were doing really well, they would bring you down a peg or two to keep you on your toes, but if things were going badly, they built you up. At half-time against Everton, while everybody knew I should have prevented Gary's goal, nobody said a word to me about it or about the way I was playing. Everything that was said was positive. We were getting thumped, but all I could hear were remarks like, 'Oh, it's not going too badly, we're only a goal down. The game's bound to open up – there's plenty of time for us to get back into it.'

## 14 The Scottish Bombshell

One of the lessons you have to learn as a professional footballer is never to take anything for granted. Whenever I
achieved a major honour, I was always worried about the
possibility of it being followed by a kick in the teeth. But
when I learned that Scotland had left me out of their
squad for the 1986 World Cup finals, in the week of the
FA Cup final against Everton, it still came as a massive
disappointment.

No-one can truly be looked upon as a world-class
player unless he has proved himself at World Cup level. I
do not think I looked out of my depth in the 1982 finals in
Spain, but the most abiding memory of my performances
in Scotland's three first-round group matches was the
collision between Aberdeen's Willie Miller and me in
the last game against Russia, which scuppered Scotland's
chances of getting the win we needed to reach the last
phase. Everybody knows that Scottish teams often shoot
themselves in the foot, but even by the standards of past
cock-ups, the mix-up involving Willie and myself was

something special. Seen by millions of television viewers, it enabled Russia to take a 2–1 lead, and their eventual 2–2 draw meant our being knocked out of the competition on goal difference.

The memory of that incident has remained so strong that a lot of people have overlooked the Scotland matches in which I did well. Fans still ask me, 'Why didn't you play well for Scotland?' The 1986 finals would have been a great chance for me to give them more positive memories of me as a Scotland player.

The first sign that the chance was going to be denied me came on the day after Liverpool's last First Division match at Chelsea on Saturday, 3 May, three days before the Scotland squad was due to be announced. Immediately after the Chelsea game, I had travelled to Glasgow with Steve Nicol and Kenny Dalglish for the testimonial match that had been granted to Kenny by the Scottish Football Association. I found it impossible to get to sleep that night at our hotel – mentally, I was still on the pitch at Stamford Bridge – so at 5 a.m., I got up and bought the Sunday newspapers. I should have stayed in bed, with the covers over my eyes and ears. I had two tabloids, the *Sunday Mail* and the *Sunday Post*. Both had published a list of the players they expected to be left out of the final World Cup squad. In both cases, my name was on it. I thought, You must be joking.

Then, when I arrived at Hampden Park for the match – between a side of home-based Scots and a team comprising Anglos like myself – I was given further cause to worry. The first person I saw when I went into the ground at midday was Alex Ferguson, who had taken charge of the Scotland team after Jock Stein's death the previous year, and was manager of the home-based side for Kenny's game. I knew that he had seen me – and I found it significant that he did not even acknowledge me. Most players will confirm that it is not unusual for a manager to blank them when they are preparing to give them bad news, although when I mentioned it to Kenny he said I was being oversensitive. According to him, there was no way that Alex could leave me out. But the following day, when I was back home, I received a telephone call from the *News of the World*. 'Do you want to say anything about being left out of Scotland's World Cup squad?' they asked.

'Wait a minute,' I replied. 'It's not being announced until Wednesday.'

'We can tell you you're not in it,' they said.

I just told them I didn't believe them, then immediately made contact with Kenny again to tell him what had happened. Kenny maintained that the papers had got it wrong.

On the Wednesday, though, the dreaded phone call came from Alex to confirm that they were right. He did his best to explain the decision to me: he felt he had to keep faith with the players – and especially the home-based ones – who had made more appearances in the qualifying ties than I had. I was not at my clear-minded best so I wasn't sure if he was referring to the players who had been seen most often in the team or in the squad, but either way I was confused by his logic.

I accepted that the central defenders in Alex's club team at Aberdeen, Alex McLeish and Willie Miller, were the first choices for the positions in the national team. They played together in all the Group 7 ties, while I had been involved in the action only once as a substitute. However, I felt that my claims to at least an understudy spot should have been considered on a broader base than the number of times Alex had seen my face around the place. As he was talking, I felt like reminding him that Jock Stein, while installing McLeish and Miller as his preferred partnership – on the not unreasonable basis of their excellent understanding at club level – had described me as the best central defender in Britain.

Then Alex found firmer ground: 'I can only pick twenty-two players, and I have to do what I think is right for the overall blend and balance of the squad,' he said.

I tried as best I could to hide my disappointment. I told him that I appreciated his predicament and even agreed to his request to go on the list of World Cup standby players. The situation could not have been easy for him. Indeed, Alex has since been quoted as saying that having to tell me that I was surplus to Scotland's World Cup requirements was one of the most dreaded moments of his career, and that the way I took it made him feel even worse. But I can assure him that he did not feel as bad as I did. After our conversation, I rang Kenny and tried to make a joke of it. 'You're some judge of football,' I said. 'I'm not in the squad – Alex has just phoned me.'

I was happy to leave it at that but, as my club manager and close personal friend, Kenny – who had a greater influence than most in the Scotland set-up – immediately took it upon himself to try to persuade Alex to change his mind. Within 10 minutes of me telling him about my conversation with Alex, he was back on the phone to me. 'I've told Alex he's making a big mistake,' he said. 'Don't say anything to anybody and I'll ring you back as soon as I can.'

To this day, I don't know what Kenny told Alex. However, when he telephoned an hour later, he had to admit defeat. According to Kenny, the decision could not be changed because all the letters to the players informing them of their selection for the squad had been posted. Kenny himself, then 35, was not included in the squad because after his demanding first season as Liverpool's player-manager he was unsure about his fitness. It has been suggested that his stance would have been different had Alex Ferguson showed the same faith in me that he did. But this is nonsense: there was no way that Kenny would have allowed my position to influence his thoughts about his own.

To Alex, I think my fitness had been no less of a worry to him than Kenny's. Halfway through the season I had sustained a tear in a muscle in the right knee, and was told by a specialist, 'It's not serious. You're going to have to get it stitched sooner or later, but it isn't going to get any worse and you can play with it as long as you want.' When I asked, 'What about the World Cup?' he said, 'I can't see any problem – you can have it stitched afterwards.' For obvious reasons, although the operation would have kept me out for two weeks at the most, Kenny did not want me to have it done until the end of the season. It was not as if the injury hampered my performance. All it meant was that I had to be careful about pushing myself too hard in training, but it was not necessary for me to train very hard anyway because we were playing two matches a week.

As the season reached its climax, I became increasingly conscious of the need to protect the knee, not just for Liverpool but for Scotland. When Kenny withdrew from the Scotland squad for the match against England at Wembley on 23 April, because of an injury he picked up in the match at West Bromwich Albion four days earlier, I suggested to Alex that, because of my own fitness, it might be best for me to leave, too. Had the match been a World Cup qualifier, I would have had no qualms about playing. However, despite the rivalry between Scotland and England, this match was only a 'friendly' and I felt that I'd be better off staying at home and resting the knee. Alex seemed unperturbed about this.

In hindsight, I can see how this incident might have played on his mind. For some time before the finals, Alex had stressed that he had to be 100 per cent sure of his players' fitness.

However, I played in all but one of Liverpool's 39 First Division matches up to the England game, and went on to take part in all their subsequent games. It could be that Alex was concerned not just about my fitness but my general attitude towards playing for Scotland. In an interview on his spell as Scotland manager, he claimed that, when he was assistant manager, Jock Stein told him he had always to be on his guard against me pulling out of the squad. To me, the suggestion that I made a habit of it – and the implication that I was not committed to playing for Scotland – was outrageous.

As time has gone by, though, I have become increasingly philosophical about Alex's decision. Although I still maintain I deserved to be there, I have no hard feelings towards him. With Scotland again failing to reach the second phase, after goalless draws against Denmark and Uruguay, and a 2–1 defeat by West Germany, it was tempting for the pundits to claim that Alex's decision had been a mistake. Scotland were certainly found wanting in the creative sense and I do think that the conditions in Mexico, where the altitude alone made it important for players to be good on the ball and thus able to conserve their energy, would have suited me.

But I also believe that Scotland were unlucky in having to face three teams of the calibre of Denmark, West Germany and Uruguay so early in the competition, and that my presence would not have made a great deal of difference – if any – to the outcome. Also, Alex Ferguson was not the only Scotland manager who did not use me as much as one might have expected. It seems anomalous that, although I was generally comfortable against the top players in club teams from other countries – as reflected by my Liverpool European Cup performances – I did not gain more than 26 Scotland caps. Alex McLeish and Willie Miller accumulated 77 and 65 respectively. As I was a central defender whose ability and style were considered more conducive to international football than theirs, some people reckon that I should have ended up with 100.

There are a number of reasons why I didn't. Generally, I would say that British players find it more difficult to shine in international football than those in other countries. Their biggest problems concern the higher number of competitive matches they have to play for their club teams, and the diversity of playing styles at that level.

The gruelling fixture schedule proved a handicap to Liverpool's international players during my time at the club, especially when they were representing their national teams at the end of the season.

I was interested to note that Manchester United played a total of 59 matches in their 1998/99 treble-winning season. In the 1983/84 season, when Liverpool won the Championship, European Cup and League Cup, our number of fixtures was 66. Moreover, in those days, the squad system at clubs – their scope to chop and change their first-team personnel to give key players a rest – was not as pronounced as it is now.

One Liverpool player who buckled under the strain was John Barnes in 1988. He played brilliantly during the season to be voted Footballer of the Year, but by the end of it – when Liverpool won the Championship and reached the FA Cup final – he was almost on his knees.

I have never accepted that John's disappointing performance in the final against Wimbledon was down to Wimbledon double-marking him: a lot of teams had done that in our earlier matches and he had still destroyed them. Wimbledon were just lucky to face him at Wembley when the physical and mental strain of playing for Liverpool had caught up with him.

England also suffered because of his 'burn-out' when John played for them in the European Championship finals in West Germany that summer. In addition to John, the team included Peter Beardsley, his Liverpool teammate, Tottenham's Chris Waddle and Gary Lineker, so England could hardly claim that they were lacking goalscoring flair. In normal circumstances, any defenders in the world would have been worried about facing a group of attacking players of this calibre. But, as Bobby Robson said, those four players – and especially Barnes and Beardsley – were 'gone'. Hence the fact that England scored only two goals in their three group matches against the Irish Republic, Holland and the USSR – courtesy of Bryan Robson and Tony Adams – and lost them all.

In most other countries the professional game is structured around the needs of the national team rather than the clubs, but in Britain it is the other way around. This also applies to the way that teams perform. In Germany, for example, the national team and the club teams use much the same system, so that when a player is brought into the international squad, there are few grey areas in terms of what is expected of him. This is not so much the case in Britain where the range of styles is wider: each manager or coach is concerned only with getting players to perform in a way that suits his particular team. To him, what the national team manager wants is immaterial.

Of course, there are a number of cases in which players have only themselves to blame for not making a bigger impact in their national teams. Take Glenn Hoddle. Although he gained 53 England caps – not bad going for any player – it is widely felt that he was often hampered by being in a different role from the one he filled at Tottenham. The latter were more prepared to build their team around him than England were. He was not the most defence-minded of players, so Spurs took a lot of defensive responsibility off his shoulders by using him in a free attacking role just behind the front men or in a midfield unit of five. England, though, took the view that this was a luxury they could not afford.

Ron Greenwood, one of Hoddle's England managers, has said, 'On the ball, Hoddle was prodigious, a delight. But he did not shape a game enough. It had to be shaped around him. He also tended to float into bad positions and it was difficult for team-mates to find him.' Harsh? Maybe, but Hoddle has to take some of the blame for not being sufficiently adaptable.

To a great extent, I blame myself for what happened to me in the Scotland set-up because I know that I did not adjust to their style of play quickly enough. Liverpool's defence pushed up more than any other back line in Britain and when I first got into the Scotland team, there were situations in which I would try to push up and hold the line only for other defenders to take a step or two backwards. It's difficult to change something that you do instinctively for your club team, but I should have made more of an effort to get on the other back players' wavelength, or at least discussed the problem with them more extensively.

It was particularly noticeable when I played with Willie Miller because Willie, never the quickest of covering central defenders but a great tackler in the penalty area, preferred to defend deep and be the last man. At Liverpool, I had become accustomed to holding my ground and, before the ball was played, allowing an opponent to run past me into an offside position. But it was difficult to do that with Willie because his instincts were to get 10 yards or so behind me. That was the way he played at Aberdeen, with Alex McLeish attacking the ball and Willie taking up a covering position. I had good Scotland matches in partnership with both players, but I preferred playing with Alex. If Willie was my partner I had to attack the ball, which just wasn't my game.

You could say that I had a stronger case to play in Willie's position in international football than he did because I was a better passer of the ball but, against that, the rapport between the Aberdeen pair – a vital ingredient for central defenders at any level – was first class. I, too, would probably have had them both in the national team had I been the manager. The other problem for me as an international player was that Scotland did not function effectively as a team, and therefore my sense of vulnerability – always prevalent even at Liverpool – was greater. As I have said, the spirit in the Scotland camp was nothing like it was at Liverpool so I always felt I had to look after my own corner more, as opposed to concentrating on the needs of the team. I think it was the same with a lot of players.

This is where I think Andy Roxburgh, who succeeded Alex Ferguson after the 1986 World Cup, was good for Scotland. In my experience, he was the Scotland manager who did most to instil the tremendous team spirit that is one of the team's hallmarks today. Roxburgh was forced to address this aspect more closely than others because his spell at the helm coincided with a decline in the number of great individual players available to the national team, and I thought he did it superbly.

I played only three matches under Roxburgh, Luxembourg in the 1986/87 season and the opening 1988 European Championship qualifying ties against the Irish

Republic (two), but I enjoyed working with him. It is said that players with my sort of record are sceptical of managers who have never been big names in the professional game themselves. Roxburgh, the Scottish Football Association's director of coaching when he took charge of the senior national team, had never been a top player; nor did he have any track record as a manager. In fact, when he was appointed to the post, the media reaction was, 'Andy who?'

I am not naïve enough to deny that it is an advantage for managers to have had an accomplished background in the game, especially at international level where they are dealing with the best players. In terms of credibility the stature of the men Roxburgh followed meant that he was a couple of goals down before he even started.

Jock Stein had charisma with a capital C. He was a big man, physically, and he had a big record of success. Quite apart from his European Cup triumph with Celtic in 1967, his CV also included a Scottish record of nine successive Championships. Knowledge is power, so if he told you something, you listened because there was no doubt he knew what he was talking about.

Paddy Crerand, the former Manchester United and England wing-half, has said that if Stein and his fellow managerial greats Bill Shankly and Sir Matt Busby had appeared together on the Old Trafford pitch to talk about football for an hour and a half, there would have been a capacity crowd to hear what they had to say. Of the three, Stein cut the most intimidating figure. He did not have to say much to players who had stepped out of line: just a look was enough to put them on the right track. The players respected him to the point where some were almost scared of him.

I remember a meeting between Stein and the players before the 1982 World Cup finals in Spain to discuss a squad sponsorship deal which had been put up to him and which he felt would be beneficial to us. Some players were not sure about him, and suggested that it might be best for the team to discuss it among themselves. 'Oh, you don't have to worry about talking about it in front of me,' Stein said. 'I'm not going to be offended or hold anything against any of you.'

At this point, striker Maurice Johnston, who had joined Celtic from Watford a few months earlier and was a relative newcomer to the squad, suggested, 'That's OK, boss, but I think we should have a secret ballot.'

Stein eyed him coldly, and muttered, 'What's it got to do with you? What do you know about World Cups?'

Suffice it to say that Stein got his way.

There can be no doubt that he was an ideal Scotland manager, even though the appointment came late in his career, when he was in his mid-fifties, and was not in the best of health.

While my experience of working with Alex Ferguson was more limited, he also stood out as a manager who could be relied on to command his players' respect. In the light of his success at Manchester United, it is easy to over-look Alex's impact as manager of Aberdeen, when he turned them into the major force in Scottish football, at the expense of Rangers and Celtic, and steered them to European glory through their Cup-winners Cup triumph in 1983.

Roxburgh had nothing like this to influence his own relationship with Scotland players. Also, as you would expect of someone responsible for the training of would-be coaches, his technical knowledge of the game was somewhat theoretical. However, he compensated for this with his organizational skills, his enthusiasm – he was the most enthusiastic manager I have ever worked with – and his willingness to listen to the views of his players. In the latter respect he wasn't obsessed with the playing guide-lines laid down in his coaching textbooks.

I have never attended an English or Scottish FA coach-ing course, but a number of those who put themselves through the English version when Charles Hughes was the director of coaching at Lancaster Gate have told me that they were disenchanted by it. Bill Shankly and Bob Paisley both started the course but left in the middle. They did not agree with a number of the teachings, and found that there was no scope to apply their own interpretation to them. The FA's attitude was, 'This is the way to play football, and if you want to gain our coaching badge, you have to do it our way.'

Andy Roxburgh, however, seemed more flexible. Indeed, instead of telling his players how they should play, he had no qualms about letting them decide. The European Championship qualifying match against the Irish Republic at Hampden in February 1987 was a good case in point, although cynics might well argue that the result – a 1–0 win for the Irish, who went on to qualify for the finals – suggests otherwise.

We were concerned about the number of tall players in the Irish squad and the threat that Jack Charlton's team were liable to pose at near-post corners, so Andy tried to come up with a counter-plan which I thought too stereo-typed and simplistic. For example, one of the basic arts of defending a short corner is to have a defender in front of the player at the near post and one behind. However, in this instance, a number of factors have to be taken into account. Some believe that the tallest of the two marking defenders should be behind the near-post opponent, but I would prefer him to be in front. And what happens if the opposition put two men on the near post, or put one of their smaller players there and use the bigger ones to attack other areas? Andy did not fully appreciate that no team can afford to be too specific in their tactical planning. It is folly to go on to the field with too many preconceived playing methods because there are so many things that the other team can do to negate them. To his credit, Andy gave his own thoughts as the starting-point for our dis-cussion before the Irish game but was happy to give us the freedom to do whatever we felt the situation demanded. He did not interpret it as a threat to his authority.

For all this, some players were not very receptive to him. Among those who found it difficult to accept a man with his background in the job was Richard Gough, the Rangers central defender who was my centre-back colleague in my matches under Andy. Richard felt that Andy's manner with the players was similar to that of a headmaster organizing his pupils. Richard was independent-minded, a loner, and unhappy about Andy's insistence on group activities to help bond the players together.

I welcomed Andy's approach: as you will have spotted,

the principle behind his methods was what I had been used to at Liverpool. I wish it had been more prominent in the national set-up earlier in my international career.

In those days, the rift between Scotland's Anglo and home-based players was accentuated by the fact that the latter group tended to be favoured by the Scottish media and the fans. We used to joke that if Scotland were beaten, all the Anglos in the team would be best advised not to read any of the next day's Scottish papers. From time to time, the media conducted a campaign for the Scotland team to be restricted to players with Scottish clubs, their argument being that these players derived more pride in representing their country than those living and working outside it. The view that players like myself had undergone a Scottish culture bypass operation was one that I deeply resented, and I was not alone in this.

I remember Billy Bremner's look of horror when the former Leeds and Scotland captain was asked once whether he ever wished he could have been a member of England's 1966 World Cup-winning team. 'You must be ******* joking,' he replied. 'Once a Scot, always a Scot.' Billy was more fortunate than me as a Scotland player because of his style of play: Scottish supporters always take to players who perform with passion and Billy, one of the most fiery characters in the game, fitted the bill perfectly. My style was much more understated.

I think the fans were inclined to look upon me – and indeed other Scotland players at Liverpool – in the same way that they looked upon Graeme Souness. Graeme's problems in being accepted by them were summed up in an article about him in the *Sunday Times*, after his resignation as Rangers manager in April 1991. As it pointed out:

> The Souness who had returned to Scotland [to join the Ibrox club in 1986] was a very different man [from the one who had left the country as a youngster to join Tottenham, and had then played for Middlesbrough, Liverpool and Sampdoria]. He had become wealthy and sophisticated. He had won three European Cup medals, he had married a divorced heiress, and fathered two sons who attend Millfield School. But there is also the question of belonging. Souness has never been comfortable in Scotland. Indeed, in his autobiography, he has a chapter titled: 'Sometimes I wish I was English'. He dislikes the weather in Scotland. He dislikes the mentality of the fans and he has never been accepted by them. By going south, he became labelled as an Anglo, which some see as little more than a traitor. Souness, who thought he had bettered himself, who used cologne and gold credit cards, was regarded as too dandy by half.

The prejudice against Anglos in general, and those at Liverpool in particular, was illustrated for me by the comments I heard from spectators when I watched Scotland matches from the Hampden Park stand. On one such occasion, I could not believe the abuse directed at Steve Nicol. Almost as soon as he stepped on to the pitch, the message to him from the crowd around me was, 'Get back to Liverpool, Nicol, you're a ******* dud.' Some dud: Steve was one of the most versatile players in Britain. I was sitting with another Liverpool player, John Wark, and once our initial incredulity had faded we started laughing our heads off. The reaction stemmed from relief more than anything. As John remarked, 'It could easily have been one of us!'

Although the Anglo and home-based Scots seemed to get on well enough on the surface, I was always conscious of an undertone of resentment. One incident that showed this was not a figment of my imagination was my conversation with Willie Miller before Scotland's 1–0 win over Sweden in a 1982 World Cup qualifying tie in Stockholm. It was my fifth Scotland match, and Jock Stein envisaged using Alex McLeish and Willie as his central defenders with me in the 'hole' immediately in front of them. I was not happy about it because I had never filled that role before, not even when I operated in midfield for Partick. The gamble of going into it at a stage in my Scotland career when I had yet to establish myself at international level, and was feeling quite vulnerable after poor performances in my opening matches, was not one I was prepared to take. This, after all, was my first World Cup game for Scotland.

Stein was great about it: he agreed to allow me to play in my usual position, and put Willie Miller in the midfield anchor role. Willie was less happy with the decision. I tried to make a joke of it when we discussed it before the kick-off, but there was no trace of even a smile when he retorted, 'I'm a home Scot. I've got to play where I'm asked.'

It was before that game that Jock Stein probably put his

finger on another reason why my Scotland career was so patchy when he told me, 'If you get into a difficult position, just kick it.' It was not so much that he disliked central defenders showing skill on the ball, more that at that stage in my career I was not disciplined enough.

When I first came into the Scotland team, my temperament and personality were mirrored by what I would describe as a 'looseness' in my play. International football is obviously a step up from club football and it took me time to appreciate that the way I played at Liverpool – in a team that was arguably stronger as a unit than the Scotland side and certainly more dominating – needed to be curtailed. Hence the fact that my first three Scotland games were a nightmare.

I made my début in the British International Championship match against Wales at Ninian Park, Cardiff, on Saturday, 19 May 1979, alongside my former Partick colleague Alan Rough, who was then at Hibernian, Paul Hegarty, the Dundee United defender who was my centre-back partner, Leeds United's Frank Gray, Ipswich's John Wark, Manchester City's Asa Hartford, Coventry's Ian Wallace and my Liverpool friends Graeme Souness and Kenny Dalglish. Things started badly for me, and got worse.

Early in the first half I was caught in possession by John Toshack, who put Wales ahead. To add insult to injury, the former Liverpool centre-forward who had left Anfield to become Swansea's player-manager the previous year, went on to score a hat-trick to give Wales a 3–0 win.

My preparations for the game had been far from ideal. Liverpool had played their last First Division match at

Leeds just two days earlier, on the Thursday night, and all the players from these clubs who were in the Scotland and Wales squads did not get to Cardiff until Friday morning. It had been a long, hard season, especially for the Liverpool players who had brought the club the Championship for the second successive year, and also helped steer them to the FA Cup semi-finals. The Leeds United match was one of three First Division fixtures for Liverpool in the space of 10 days, and when I had to make my first sprint at Ninian Park, I thought, Where are my legs? But I do not offer any of this as an excuse for my performance against the Welsh. Despite the tiredness, I should have done better.

I did not play in the 1–0 win over Northern Ireland on the Tuesday night, or in the 3–1 defeat by England the following Saturday and then, with Scotland scheduled to face Diego Maradona and his 1978 Argentina World Cup-winning team on 2 June, I rejoined my Liverpool colleagues for an exhibition match in Israel. I should have been feeling great by the time I arrived back in Glasgow two days before the Argentina game – but I had been on the beach for three days and spent the Wednesday in bed with sunstroke.

On buying an evening newspaper *en route* to the Scotland squad's headquarters, I started to feel dizzy again, this time over a report that Manchester United's Gordon McQueen, then our first-choice centre-half, was doubtful because of injury and that I was virtually certain to confront Maradona and company in his place. Even without Maradona, Argentina would have given us a lot of problems. With him, the difference between the two teams was frightening.

In view of the world-wide publicity he subsequently attracted as the best player on the planet, not to mention the most controversial, I would love to have been able to claim that I had hardly allowed him a kick, but I never got anywhere near him. In leading Argentina to their 3–1 win, he produced one of the greatest individual performances ever seen at Hampden.

My problems in proving myself continued in my third match, the European Championship qualifying tie against Belgium in Brussels, five months later. Partnered by Willie Miller for the first time, I was so concerned about my Scotland form by then that I kept diving in for the ball in situations where I would usually have used my head and tried to force my opponent to make the first move.

Scotland were beaten 2–0 and when I returned to Liverpool, Bob Paisley, who had watched the television highlights of the game, told me, 'You don't play for Liverpool the way you played for Scotland. I've never seen you make so many rash challenges.' He added, 'All players have matches like that at times. Just forget about it.' The Scottish media were less supportive: one newspaper said I would never be seen in a Scotland shirt again!

I felt they might be proved right when Jock Stein left me out of the squad for the return match against Belgium the following month. But for the next match, against Portugal at Hampden in March 1980, I was brought back in. The decision appeared to have been prompted mainly by Stein being present at Liverpool's match at Manchester United on Boxing Day, a game in which I scored the best goal of my career and produced a performance that he reportedly described as being 'as near perfect as you could get'. As a result of that performance, I was also brought back into the team, with Alex McLeish making his international début alongside me.

The Portugal game was my Scotland turning-point, thanks largely to a chat I had had with Stein the day before. I felt under enormous pressure from the media and the fans to produce better form for the national team, but Stein insisted, 'You're under no pressure whatsoever from me. Just relax and enjoy yourself.' I did. It was my best game for Scotland, we won 4–1 and I quickly became established in the side.

From October 1980, I played in all but four of the 19 Scotland matches leading to the World Cup finals in Spain, and generally I played well. Ridiculous as it might seem, my best game was the 3–0 defeat by Spain in Valencia in February 1982. Because of the space Spain allowed me when I was in possession, I was able repeatedly to involve myself in our attacking play – so much so that Ruud Krol, the famous Dutch sweeper then at Barcelona, paid me the compliment of describing me as Scotland's most important player. I also maintain that I played well in the 1982 World Cup finals.

There were a number of reasons why Scotland didn't get beyond the first phase, not least because three days after beating New Zealand 5–2 in the opening match, we had to confront the best team in the world – Brazil – in Seville.

The Brazil team who won the 1970 World Cup in Mexico have been rated the best national side of all time. However, the Brazilian eleven we played against in 1982 were not that far behind them in my view. They certainly lived up to the 1970 model in the openness of their play and their willingness to show off their creative talents. Therefore, far from being depressed by Scotland's 4–1 defeat – after David Narey had given us the lead – I felt privileged just to have been on the same pitch. It was without doubt one of the most memorable experiences of my career.

To me, the most extraordinary aspect of that Brazil team was that they played with virtually 10 men. I say that because they had a centre-forward, Serginho, who was the most uncharacteristic Brazilian footballer I have seen. He appeared quite clumsy; compared to all the others he looked hopeless. Yet Brazil were still able to string countless passes together and force us to do a lot of chasing after the ball in the searing heat. That night Seville was like an oven, and what Brazil did to us can be summed up by one word: 'torture'.

Brazil should have won that World Cup. They had greater attacking flair than Italy, who knocked them out of the competition by beating them 3–2 in the next group to decide the semi-finalists, and who went on to overcome West Germany in the final. However, there was bound to come a time when the lack of discipline in their play would rebound on them.

In addition to meeting Brazil so early on in the competition, the other handicap for Scotland concerned the Scottish Football Association's choice of a golf complex in Sotogrande as their World Cup base. The road to Malaga, where we had to play our matches against New Zealand and Russia, was atrocious, and the journey by coach – made on the afternoon of each match – took about an

264

hour and a half. I found those trips very uncomfortable and tedious; hardly the ideal way for players to prepare for an important game.

I also had misgivings about where the Scotland squad was staying. Because of the heat, we were discouraged from spending a lot of time outdoors – on the golf course and around the swimming pool – but unfortunately there were no indoor leisure facilities available. Outside training and playing, I spent virtually all my time during that World Cup eating and sleeping. Not that I'm offering this as an excuse for my experience in our last match against Russia.

Publicly, the subject of Russia's second goal 10 minutes from the end has always been a tricky one for me because I cannot accept responsibility for it. The consensus of opinion among Scottish pundits was that I was mainly to blame, but the more I have thought about what happened, the more I have struggled to pinpoint something to support their view.

The only area in which I concede I was culpable was that, when attempting to get my head to a flighted ball going towards the player I was marking on the left touchline – Ramaz Shengelia – I did not get a proper contact and misdirected it into the space behind me. However, I was able to turn quickly enough to stay in front of Shengelia in the chase for it and I felt I was in control of the situation. I saw Willie moving towards me, but all I needed him to do was take up a position to receive a pass from me. As he was approaching me, I was thinking, He's got to stop. But he kept coming until he was almost within touching distance of me. Then it really was nightmare time. We bumped into each other as he tried to boot the ball into the stand, the ball ran loose and Shengelia beat Alan Rough to put the Russians ahead.

What was particularly strange about Willie's action was that, with Scotland needing to beat Russia and time running out for us, it was important for us to keep the ball in play. I'm not trying to knock Willie, but I'm absolutely convinced that had our positions been reversed – had I been the sweeper – there is no way that we would have collided.

From then on, my Scotland career went downhill. I played 17 times for Scotland up to and including the 1982 World Cup finals, but only nine times after that. Four of those appearances came in the first post-World Cup games the following season against East Germany, Switzerland (two) and Bulgaria. East Germany was the only team we managed to beat, and of the other games the one I most wanted to forget was the European Championship qualifying tie against the Swiss at Hampden in March 1983.

I was not in the best of form for Liverpool at the time and the Hampden fans, still clearly experiencing a hangover from the World Cup disappointment, even laid into me as I was warming up with Steve Nicol before the game. I said to Steve, 'I would take it as a tremendous compliment if these were the away supporters. When it's your own supporters doing the booing, you know you're in really big trouble!'

It got worse for me, because about two minutes into the game there was a misunderstanding between myself and left-back Frank Gray, which led to the ball running between us and, luckily for us, going out of play. Switzerland established a 2–0 lead, but after I was substituted by Alex McLeish in the second half – because of a thigh strain, let alone the fact that my mind was all over the place – Scotland made it 2–2.

The match reports in the papers the following day suggested that I was the reason why Scotland had conceded those goals. Switzerland's second goal had come from a tremendous move that caught out the whole Scottish defence, but I was singled out for most of the blame. 'Hansen', one report stated, 'was just standing around watching.'

Thereafter, I had plenty of scope to do just that for the Scotland team because I was left out of the squad for the rest of that season and the whole of the 1983/84 campaign. I got back in after Liverpool's European Cup final win over Roma in the summer of 1984, but it was not until March 1985 that I returned to the team. The match was the Mexico World Cup qualifying tie against Wales at Hampden, and even then I was not in the starting line-up – I was brought on in place of Manchester United's left-back Arthur Albiston, when Ian Rush and Mark Hughes were causing numerous headaches for the Scotland defence. Not that my presence made any difference: a superb move between Rush and Hughes led to the latter scoring the goal that brought the Welsh the distinction of being the first team since 1965 to beat Scotland in a World Cup tie at Hampden.

My only other pre-Mexico appearance, and the only one when Alex Ferguson was manager, came as a substitute for Willie Miller in the 3–0 win over Romania at home in March 1986.

The sad irony about my situation was that in the 1984/85 and 1985/86 seasons, I was arguably in my best-ever form for Liverpool. However, though there was obviously an element of frustration in not getting more opportunities to exploit this in a Scotland jersey, it honestly did not affect me as much as some might imagine. When I started my career, I would have settled gladly for just one cap. And my Scotland disappointments were more than offset by my record with Liverpool.

I have always appreciated that there are many more important things in life than football. Though it could be argued that this was one of my faults, I would suggest that at times of adversity my less than intense attitude to the game proved one of my strengths. Certainly, being left out of a World Cup squad meant nothing compared to the horror that I and thousands of others experienced on an April afternoon in 1989 at Hillsborough.

# 15 Heysel and Hillsborough

In the opening few minutes of Liverpool's FA Cup semi-final against Nottingham Forest at Hillsborough on Saturday, 15 April 1989, I felt happier than I could have anticipated. Two months short of my thirty-fourth birthday, I had been out of Liverpool's first team for nine months – the result of a dislocated left knee sustained in a pre-season friendly against Athletico Madrid in Spain – and had only started playing again, for the reserves, four days before the semi-final. The Liverpool fans gave me a tremendous reception as I came on to the pitch, and I made a great start to the game. In those opening minutes, I hit three good passes – two long balls over the top of the Forest defence to Steve McMahon and the other to Peter Beardsley, who hit a shot against the Forest bar.

All my fears about my fitness evaporated. I felt as if I had never been away.

Then, suddenly, I started to fall into the blackest period of my life.

Seconds later Hillsborough became a death chamber as

95 of the Liverpool followers, who packed the central terracing behind the goal at the Leppings Lane end, were crushed to death in the worst crowd disaster in the history of English sport. One person spent some two years on a life-support machine before his death so the toll finally reached 96. The number of broken hearts was incalculable.

Ten years on, it bothers me sometimes that I tend to think only of the people who perished at Hillsborough when the subject is raised or when I see the memorial to them just outside the Anfield main gates. I have attended a number of services to mark the anniversaries of the disaster, and at the third, in 1992, Bruce Grobbelaar and I had the honour of reading the lessons, but Hillsborough has always been something I have tried to shut out of my mind: the more I dwell on it, the more I am forced to imagine how my life would have changed had the catastrophe claimed anyone close to me. That so many youngsters were among the victims was particularly heart-rending. People can find tremendous strength through adversity, but if either of my children had been lost at Hillsborough, I honestly cannot see how Janet and I could ever have recovered from it. Adam was only eight at the time, but had he been 15 or 16 and wanted to go to the match, I might well have made arrangements for someone to watch it with him from the terraces rather than the stand. I could imagine myself saying to him, 'You don't want to go into the seats, you'll get a better atmosphere on the terraces.' To think of him at the Leppings Lane end of the ground is just too painful.

It was certainly thus at the time of Hillsborough. The immediate aftermath, when Kenny Dalglish and the players attended the funerals and tried to show support for the grieving families took more out of me emotionally than any other experience I have gone through.

I thought I had already experienced a big enough tragedy for one lifetime with the events at the Heysel Stadium in Brussels four years earlier. To be involved in another, this time so close to home and involving people who were an integral part of my professional life, inevitably hit me even harder.

Whenever I think of Heysel, the first image that springs to mind is the expression on Joe Fagan's face as the terrifying scenes of crowd violence escalated to the point where the game that had been his whole life no longer meant anything. Following the announcement the day before that the European Cup final against Juventus would be his last as Liverpool manager, Joe deserved good memories of the occasion, no matter what the result. But, at the end, he looked a broken man.

Of all the men at Liverpool who went through the ordeal of Heysel, Joe, who was then in his mid-sixties and had decided to retire, was the one for whom I felt most sorry. In one way, though, he was lucky: at least he was not subjected to the nightmare of Hillsborough. It says much about the inner turmoil experienced by people at Liverpool FC that Kenny Dalglish, inevitably the focal point of Liverpool's attempts to bring some measure of comfort to the mourning families, brought his Liverpool career to an end two years later and took a complete break from the game.

It affected everybody.

It is incongruous to attempt to draw a parallel between

the two disasters, given that the cause of Heysel was hooliganism and that Liverpool supporters were the perpetrators. At Hillsborough, they were the innocent victims. However, if there was one common denominator, it concerned the inadequate crowd arrangements.

I would not dream of attempting to condone the conduct of the Liverpool fans whose war-like charge towards the Juventus followers' section resulted in many Italians being crushed under a crumbling wall. However, I would suggest that whoever was responsible for putting the two sets of supporters within such easy reach of each other, separated only by a flimsy wire fence, was failing in his duty.

Because of the poor security arrangements, and the dilapidated, outdated Heysel Stadium, Liverpool had been edgy about the match for some weeks. About 10 days earlier, I remember bumping into Jim Kennefick, who handled the club's travel, as he was leaving the ground following a meeting with the directors. 'They are paranoid upstairs about the Liverpool and Juventus supporters being together,' he told me. Even outside the stadium, the security system – or lack of it – was crazy.

During the 1998 World Cup finals in France, police ensured that no-one without a ticket could get within a mile of the stadiums on match days. There was no such security blanket in operation for the Liverpool–Juventus European Cup final. Indeed, from what I can make out, there was no security blanket at all. It did not matter if anyone turned up without a ticket; it seemed that everyone got in and could go to whatever part of the stadium he wished.

The first I knew of the tension building among the two sets of fans was about an hour and a half before the kick-off, when we – the Liverpool players – came out to look at the pitch. We could not get on to it because a boys' match was taking place, so we decided to stretch our legs with a walk around the running track, towards the section where most of the fans were situated. As we approached, the Juventus followers started throwing what I took to be bricks. I remarked to Alan Kennedy, 'This is unusual – you don't often find supporters taking bricks into a stadium.'

'They're not throwing bricks,' he replied. 'They're throwing the stadium at us.' We were indeed being pelted with bits of concrete from the crumbling terraces. It's hard to believe, isn't it? This was the showpiece match of the season in Europe, and it was being staged in a stadium that was not far short of a ruin.

When we were back in the dressing room, we were unaware for some time of the extent to which the trouble had escalated. We kept getting reports of what was going on, but none were official and they were contradictory. Inevitably, our first thoughts were for the safety of our friends and families. My own group at the match were Janet and her family, my father and uncle, all of whom seemed to me to be too far away from the madness to be swept up in it. We were getting so many conflicting reports that it was difficult for us to put the football in its proper context: it sounds terrible to say it, but my over-riding anxiety was that we had a European Cup final to play, and I had to get myself ready for it. I succeeded in getting myself so psyched up for the match that what was happening on the terraces was pushed into the background.

Eventually, a Uefa official came into the dressing room to ask our captain, Phil Neal, to go over to the Liverpool fans to try to calm them down. When Phil came back, he said, 'People have died out there.' But even at that point, neither he nor anyone else in our dressing room could say how bad the trouble had been. There was further confusion when the kick-off was delayed, amid deliberations about whether the match should be postponed or cancelled. Here again, the players were too isolated from the trouble to be able to take it in – so much so that during this waiting period Alan Kennedy and I passed the time with a game of cards.

By the time the decision was taken to play the game, on the premise that to cancel or postpone it would have been to invite further mayhem, I don't think anyone really cared about it. The memory of it, and the result – a 1–0 win for Juventus through a goal by Michel Platini – will always be overshadowed by the events that scarred the image of English football off the field.

For me personally, the nightmare of Heysel was prolonged by the experience of my in-laws, who had been seated above the area where the Italian fans lost their lives and saw everything that happened. For months afterwards my mother-in-law could not sleep. The experience was no less traumatic for the girlfriend of striker Paul Walsh, who was seized by a group of Italians and dragged off to look at the pile of dead bodies after the medical team had failed to revive them.

For most people, the reaction to Heysel was one of

shame as well as sadness. Inevitably, the reaction to Hillsborough, where both sets of supporters were well behaved, was even more emotive. Millions of words have been written about exactly why the disaster occurred and who was to blame, but the bottom line was that it all stemmed from a catalogue of mistakes in policing and stewarding. It had been a disaster waiting to happen.

It is widely acknowledged that the decision to put Liverpool's followers at the Leppings Lane end of the ground, rather than the much bigger Kop end, was one of the biggest mistakes that day. It was a ludicrous decision if only because of the difference in size of the two clubs' support. Liverpool's average home attendance that season was around 40,000, almost double Nottingham Forest's, yet Forest's fans were put in the section of the Hillsborough ground in which the capacity was twice as great as the area reserved for Liverpool's fans. This decision was made on the premise that the Leppings Lane end was the one that provided the easiest access to fans travelling to the game from Liverpool on the M62. It was overlooked that Liverpool had one of the widest fan bases in England, and that their supporters would be descending on Hillsborough from all directions.

There was a crush involving Liverpool supporters outside the ground before the kick-off, partly because many arrived late and partly because only one entrance gate was open. The sensible thing to do then would have been to delay the start of the game, as often happens nowadays when there is a dangerous build-up of fans trying to get into a ground. But, tragically, that did not happen.

This was followed by another error. When the other

access gates were opened, a breakdown in communication between the police officers monitoring the situation led to the fans being forced into the already packed central area of the terracing. The following Monday, a photograph in the *Liverpool Echo* showing the Leppings Lane end at 3.05 p.m., five minutes after the kick-off, told its own story. The central part was full to bursting point, but the two 'wings' were nearly empty. In those days, many leading English football stadiums had fenced in their terracing to stop fans going on to the pitch. At Hillsborough, the vast majority of fans fighting for breath – who had arrived early to ensure they had positions at the front – had no means of escape.

Of course, the same crowd arrangements were in operation at Hillsborough for the previous season's Liverpool–Forest FA Cup semi-final, and there was no trouble then – or, at least, no apparent trouble. However, I heard a number of complaints from supporters about the crowd-control methods at that tie, especially with regard to the build-up of fans trying to get into the ground.

Of all the hundreds of matches I'd had for Liverpool, the 1989 semi-final was the one that I least wanted to take part in. After being out of action for so long, I felt it was ridiculous to select me for my comeback in such an important match.

I had originally intended to spend the afternoon playing golf and when I was told that I would be travelling to Sheffield with the squad, I took it that the club just wanted me there to make me feel part of the first-team scene again. Not for one moment did I think I had a chance of playing, not even when it became known that there were fitness doubts about other players. At our hotel on the Friday night, Ian Rush had been told to share a room with me because his usual room-mate, Barry Venison, was suffering from a virus, and as Ian himself had been out of the team through injury, we discussed other players whom Kenny Dalglish might bring into the side. When Ian suggested that Kenny might bring me back, I said, 'You must be joking – no chance.'

However, having had the thought planted in my mind, I started to panic. So, too, did Ian, who was also unhappy about his level of match fitness.

At 12.30 p.m. on the Saturday, with both of us almost praying on our knees that we would not be picked, I told him, 'Look, if Kenny doesn't tell us we're playing before one o'clock [fifteen minutes before the squad were due to leave for the ground] we're in the clear.' By 1 p.m. we had still not heard anything – but at 1.05 there was a knock on our door from Liverpool's assistant manager, Roy Evans, to tell us that Kenny wanted to see us.

It was me who got the short straw by being included in the starting line-up. Ian was on the bench.

'I can't play – I don't want to play,' I told him.

'What do you mean you don't want to play?' he asked.

I tried to tell him that I lacked the necessary match fitness, but Kenny, supported by his backroom staff, would have none of it. 'You did well in the reserves on Tuesday night and you've looked good in training since then,' he pointed out.

In the end I had to say, 'All right, but I'm not happy about it.'

From then on, my mood could best be described as

distraught. By the time we got to the ground, my unease was so noticeable that some of the players were winding me up about it. However, nothing before kick-off gave us a clue that this was not going to be a normal game. Some might find it strange that we didn't notice anything untoward during the pre-match warm-up, but then players don't look at the crowd, and I was warming up on the edge of our penalty area. Even when the match started, and the crush behind our goal was beginning to take its toll, we were focused too much on the play to be able to take in what was happening.

The first I knew of the trouble was when two fans came on to the pitch. As they ran past me, I told them, 'Get off – you'll get us into trouble.'

One of them shouted, 'There are people dying back there, Al.' I could see some people trying to get over the terrace fence but, because I was concentrating so much on the game, his comment did not really register with me. Much as I hate to admit it, my reaction was one of cynicism. I remember thinking, Oh, yeah?

The next moment, the referee had stopped the game and the two teams were being taken back to the dressing rooms.

The scene in our dressing room was little different from what I had experienced at Heysel, in as much as nobody knew the extent of what was happening outside. There was just too much confusion about the situation for any of the players to address themselves to it. Professional footballers are conditioned to concentrate on a game, shutting out all distractions, and it can take time to step out of match mode. At Hillsborough, we were all aware that something terrible was happening on the terraces, but with the adrenalin pumping we were still half thinking of the jobs we had to do. Up to when we were told that the game had been abandoned, I found it difficult to stop thinking that we would be brought back on to the field and that I needed to be tuned in mentally to the game. To look back on it now is like viewing it through thick fog. We were so dazed that all I can remember about the rest of the time we spent at Hillsborough was the distress of our wives and girlfriends when we joined them in the lounge set aside for the guests of the two teams.

I think the catastrophe did not register with me until we went to Anfield the following day, and walked across the pitch to the countless flowers that were being put down at the Kop end. Those floral tributes remain my most vivid memory of Hillsborough. It was Hillsborough that brought home to me the effect that football can have on people's lives.

Previously, I never appreciated just how much the game means to fans because I'd never been committed to a team as a football-watcher, and I looked upon my involvement in the game as a job. I therefore found it extraordinary that after the initial period of mourning, so many fans – including the families and friends of the bereaved – were able to pick up from where they had left off in their support of the Liverpool team. I am convinced that, had I been in their position, football would no longer have meant anything to me. I would not have been in the least bit interested in watching Liverpool.

Indeed, in hindsight, I am not sure that it was right for Liverpool to continue that season, even though it was clear that the vast majority of the Liverpool public wanted us to do so. Many have argued that our win over Everton in the FA Cup final – just eight weeks after Hillsborough – was the best source of comfort that the grieving families and the public could have had from us. Yet, while there was a lot of evidence to support this view, I have never been at ease with it. When I was prancing around Wembley with the FA Cup, and letting my hair down at the celebration party afterwards, I couldn't help but feel guilty. I still do. I still think, Was it right for me to look so happy?

My first real insight into the horror of Hillsborough – and Liverpool FC's emotional links with the community – came on the following Monday, when the players visited the injured at Sheffield Infirmary. The first person we were asked to see was a 14-year-old boy, who was on a life-support machine. There was no hope for him, but his mother requested that he be kept on the machine until we arrived. Though he was not conscious, we sat there talking to him for a few minutes. Then someone announced that he was dead and started putting a screen around his bed.

At that point, I lost it completely. I cried my eyes out. I tried to say something to comfort the mother, but I almost felt that she was comforting me. She kept thanking me for coming to see him, and telling me how much he loved Liverpool – the strength she showed was incredible. Then I went into another ward, and reached a man's bed just as he was regaining consciousness. He recognized me instantly, and his first words to me were, 'If you reach the Cup final, can you get me a ticket?'

I did a lot of crying in the weeks ahead. I attended 12 funerals, but instead of becoming hardened to them, I found them increasingly difficult to handle. One of the problems for me was knowing what to say to the families and friends of the deceased. I thought I was supposed to be there to provide some form of counselling, but I tended to get as upset as they did.

Liverpool set up a system whereby the bereaved could visit the players at Anfield, but I struggled with that as well. I remember an elderly grey-haired gentleman who had lost his grandson coming up to me and saying, 'He was seventeen . . . How can you take somebody away at seventeen, with so much of his life in front of him?' I couldn't answer him. I don't think I could have been of any help to him because as the tears rolled down his cheeks I broke down, too.

Trevor Hicks, a London businessman, took his two daughters, Sarah, 19, and Victoria, 15, to the match. Also at the game was his wife, Jenny, who had a seat in the stand. His daughters had wanted to watch the match without his 'beady eyes' on them, so while they stood with the Liverpool fans on that central terrace, he stood directly under the police control box near by. At the judicial inquiry into the tragedy, Trevor said he saw people in that central pen showing signs of distress at 2.45 p.m. When a senior police officer stepped out of the control box and began to look at the crowd in the central area, Trevor shouted to him, 'For Christ's sake, can't you see what's going on? You've got [closed-circuit] cameras.' The officer did not respond. Then, as Trevor was becoming increasingly agitated about the safety of his daughters, another officer appeared. Trevor again tried to draw attention to what was happening, but claims he was told, 'Shut your ******* prattle.'

He made his way to the pitch just as one of his daughters, Victoria, was being lifted above the heads of the crowd. She was laid on the pitch beside her sister, who was being given the kiss of life. Both were dead.

Trevor is chairman of the Hillsborough Families Support Group (HFSG), which is still fighting for what it considers to be the proper action against the South Yorkshire police officers who were deemed at the inquiry into the disaster to be the more culpable, and for greater compensation than the small sums handed out by the Government. The inquest into the Hillsborough deaths recorded a verdict of misadventure, and the Crown Prosecution Service decided that there was insufficient evidence to prosecute any of the police involved.

In 1997, the HFSG's crusade for a new public inquiry gained new impetus as a result of a Granada TV programme about Hillsborough, which revealed new evidence to challenge the police's version of events. Though the Home Secretary, Jack Straw, did not see it that way, the HFSG's battle for justice has continued.

I have heard people say that they should now 'let it go' and 'get on with their lives', a view that stems partly from the massive changes that have taken place in English football as a result of Hillsborough. But for the tragedy, and the Taylor Report in January 1990, which enforced the transformation of British football grounds into all-seat stadiums, it is possible that the long history of stadium neglect, and spectators treated as turnstile fodder, would have continued. The new-style British club stadiums, which are among the most impressive in the world for safety standards and facilities, have made it easier for clubs to be better run, and therefore improve the quality of their football. However, though a great deal of water has passed under the bridge since Hillsborough, my attitude to those who feel that the HFSG should now forget its grievances is, 'It's easy for you to talk – you didn't lose anyone.'

Had I lost someone, I would never have let it go.

Not surprisingly, this was the only season in which being successful on the field did not mean much to me. In the aftermath of Hillsborough, I don't think it meant much to anyone at Liverpool. At the time of the disaster, Kenny Dalglish had said, 'Football is totally irrelevant.' To me, that was still so at the end of the season, when Liverpool were again poised to take major trophies.

Up to Hillsborough we had been on a roll, having achieved nine successive First Division wins, and though the sequence was broken when we started playing again on 3 May – with a goalless draw at Everton – we went on to put ourselves in a great position to achieve the double again. Indeed, it was the best position Liverpool have ever been in to land this honour. In addition to beating Forest 3–1 in the rearranged FA Cup semi-final on 7 May, we had another victory over them in the league three days later. This was followed by further First Division victories against Wimbledon and QPR and, after the FA Cup final, one over West Ham, which sealed the Hammers' relegation fate – and meant that all we had to do to win the Championship, at Arsenal's expense, was avoid defeat by two goals against them at home in our last match.

We had lost only three previous matches at Anfield that season (the last defeat was against Norwich in December) and had not been beaten by a two-goal margin there for three years. That Arsenal achieved their target, with a fifty-second-minute goal by Alan Smith and that famous last-minute strike by Michael Thomas, has gone down as one of the biggest surprises in the history of British football.

It is difficult for me to try to explain this without it coming across as sour grapes. Arsenal had an excellent team but I still feel Liverpool would have won the title but for the abnormal circumstances of Hillsborough. Both teams looked tired in the last 10 minutes, but this was particularly true of Liverpool, who had played two matches more than the Gunners in the previous month. From a psychological viewpoint, the pre-match position of the two teams in terms of their points and goal differences suited Arsenal better than us because Arsenal had no option but to go for victory.

The dilemma for Liverpool in how they should approach the match inevitably became bigger when Arsenal scored their first goal. Do you go all out for an equalizer, or do you concentrate on not conceding any more goals? As with a lot of teams who have been in this sort of situation, we were caught too much in the middle. Not that any of this really mattered. I can't say I wasn't bothered about the Arsenal defeat, but it didn't affect me as much as other Liverpool setbacks. I just felt flat, and I think it would have been this way for me even if we had been beaten in the FA Cup final.

To have gone through what we did would have finished a lot of teams, but nobody can have been surprised that it did not finish Liverpool. Being able to bounce back from disappointments was what this club was all about, so nobody can have been surprised that we won the Championship the season after Hillsborough. It was to prove my last season as an active Liverpool player.

I was fortunate in so far as the left-knee injury, which had put me out of the team for so long during the Hillsborough season, meant that I was able to protect my more troublesome right knee from further damage, and therefore prolong my career a little. There was no way I was going to get more than a year out of it, so my nine months out of action gave me an extra season. I was satisfied with that. Some players will push themselves through the pain barrier to continue playing, no matter what the consequences. Paul McGrath, the former Manchester United, Aston Villa, Derby and Irish Republic central defender, had knees in even worse shape than mine, yet he made himself a leading candidate for future artificial-knee surgery by playing at the top level – for Derby – until he was 38.

Perhaps I could have done likewise, with a less demanding club than Liverpool where the manager would have been happy to use me sparingly. But I wasn't in love with the game enough to allow it to affect my quality of life in later years. I was only able to play in the reserves or the A team in the opening months of the 1990/91 season, and towards the turn of the year my specialist said, 'Your knees are not as bad as those of other professional footballers I have seen, but you have to think long term.'

'From the day I retire to the day I die, I want to be able to walk properly and play golf,' I replied.

'Well, pack in football, then,' he said.

That was that.

Liverpool were fantastic to me. In May 1990 I had been given a new two-year contract, for which I received a signing-on fee of £90,000. When I told the club's chief executive, Peter Robinson, of my fears about continuing to play, he suggested that I went into coaching. We agreed that I would try it unofficially for three months, with a view to becoming a permanent member of the coaching staff.

After six or eight weeks, I knew it wasn't the road I wanted to go down. I found it difficult to adjust to the role, not least because it made me remote from the Liverpool players. I missed the dressing-room atmosphere. Then Liverpool amazed me. When I told Peter Robinson that I would prefer to make a clean break from the game, all they were obliged to give me was six months' salary. Instead, without any pressure from me, they settled my contract in full.

Not long afterwards, Kenny Dalglish's assessment of me as a 'lucky' person was borne out again, when I was given the opportunity of launching a new career as a TV pundit.

# 16 Poacher Turned Gamekeeper

John Fashanu, the former Wimbledon centre-forward, once made the most bizarre comment about me that I have ever seen. I had been working for the BBC for a couple of years, and Fashanu, in an article for a tabloid comparing me with BSkyB's Andy Gray, was quite complimentary about my analysis of matches. But, as far as my personality was concerned, he slaughtered me. He wrote that if your wife had just died the last person you would want to go for a drink with would be me.

The comment got to me more than it should have done – as a football journalist cynically pointed out when we discussed Fashanu's remark, 'Give some players a grand and they'll say anything.' But I still get a bit hot under the collar about it. Let me put it this way – when I hear people claim that Fashanu was one of the worst footballers ever to play for England, I am not inclined to leap to his defence.

I think Fashanu was trying to make the point that I came across on the small screen as too intense, and in fairness to him, he is not the only one to have said this. Whenever I meet Chelsea's chairman, Ken Bates, he's inclined to greet me with the words, 'Here is the un-smiling Alan Hansen.'

This is not the Alan Hansen who those close to me will recognize. They will confirm that I'm opinionated and argumentative – even abrasive occasionally. But I cannot believe that they would describe me as a person who takes football too seriously or doesn't have a sense of fun. At the same time, I can appreciate why people like Fashanu and Bates look upon me in the way that they do. I was a natural footballer, but whether I'm a natural TV person-ality is open to doubt.

My television role, in which I have put myself in the public spotlight more than I ever did when I was a player, was a big step to take for someone of my temperament. Graeme Souness, referring to my low profile off the field at Liverpool, recently remarked to me, 'Of all the players I worked with in the 1980s, you would have been one of the last people I expected to end up in a career in television.'

I never anticipated it myself. I made the telephone call that started the ball rolling to the BSkyB presenter Richard Keys because nothing was opening up for me in other fields and I was becoming increasingly concerned about the dangers of allowing my career to drift. Much as I loved playing golf, reading and spending time with Janet, Adam and Lucy, I realized that I needed something to keep me occupied professionally. Becoming a TV pundit is not something I would have picked, but as that TV ball gathered momentum for me I was forced to keep up with it. I just went where the work was.

Because of my aversion to pressure, having to talk in front of millions on TV was initially no less of an ordeal than stepping on to a football pitch to play for Liverpool. Though I get tremendous enjoyment out of my television work, thanks to the close rapport I have established with my colleagues at the BBC and their ability to help me get the best out of myself, it is still nerve-racking for me. It has taken me time to acquire the art of being relaxed in front of the cameras – or, at least, to give the impression that I am – and I like to think that the Alan Hansen whom viewers see now is a lot different from the one they saw when I started in the business. However, old images die hard, as Ken Bates still shows when he is unable to resist winding me up about it.

As it happens, there are one or two people in TV, too, who would be tempted to follow his lead. My broadcasting career started during the early part of the 1991/92 season, when I was given a six-month trial by BSkyB, and was also employed on a casual basis by BBC TV and Radio 5 Live. The arrangement with the satellite company was focused on their coverage of Serie A Italian league matches, with Trevor Francis and Ray Wilkins generally deployed as co-commentators at the games and me providing the analysis of the play from the studio in London. I was led to believe that BSkyB were happy with the job I was doing. Indeed, after about three months, the producer, Mark Schofield, said to me, 'Things are going really well. We're going to up your money.'

However, just a couple of weeks later, after I criticized the performance of the two sides in one of the most boring goalless draws I had seen, he had changed his mind.

When we were off air, he pulled me aside, and asked, 'Are you not enjoying yourself here?' He then explained that, before I was due to go on, he had seen me looking repeatedly at my watch. 'You looked as if you wanted to get away,' he said.

The comment amazed me. The reason I was looking at my watch was down to nerves more than anything, but when I told him this he did not seem convinced. So I then asked if he felt his observation had been reflected by my performance before the cameras, and he said, 'Well, I thought you looked a bit unhappy there as well.'

'I wasn't unhappy because I was here,' I stressed. 'I like working here. I was just unhappy with the match.'

From that point, it was downhill all the way with BSkyB. I continued to work for them, but as the BBC started employing me a lot more than they did, it was the BBC to whom I quickly became the most committed.

The only person at BSkyB who seemed concerned about this was Richard Keys. Towards the end of the season, when I was the BBC's co-commentator for the Southampton–Liverpool match and Richard was also there, he suggested that I had somehow let BSkyB down. 'What price loyalty?' he said to me.

However, after I had put my side of the story, Richard suggested that Mark Schofield had had reservations about me for that particular programme, because he felt I was not knowledgeable enough about Italian football. I had to concede that it was a reasonable point. I certainly did not know as much about Italian football as Trevor Francis and Ray Wilkins, both of whom had played in Italy. To Mark Schofield, my credibility problem through being the odd man out was exacerbated by my position 'at the top' of the programme. Whether that was all there was to BSkyB's doubts about me, I don't know. But I cannot help thinking that I was also considered too outspoken – or too honest, as I would prefer to put it.

If one goes into any pub after a match, almost everybody will have an opinion about the game and most of those opinions will be different. When people hear my views, it does not really matter whether they think I am talking rubbish or sense: I like to think that they respect me for not sitting on the fence and can relate to me.

In view of what I was like when I was a player, I suppose that most people would describe me as the epitome of a poacher turned gamekeeper. For example, I still wince over what the BBC TV commentator John Motson said about me during Liverpool's League Cup semi-final at Anfield. To this day, I have never spoken about it to John and I should imagine that he would be mortified if he felt he had offended me. In addition to being universally regarded as an outstanding TV professional, he is not noted for being a harsh critic. I think the closest he has ever been to saying something controversial was when he caused a media outcry by suggesting that it was sometimes difficult to distinguish individual black players on the field. The sense of surprise that the comment had come from him was almost as great as the outrage it generated.

That match against Walsall, who were then in the old Third Division, ended in a 2–2 draw – not the most impressive result for Liverpool, but there was nothing in our performance to be alarmed about (as we emphasized by going on to land that Championship–European Cup and League Cup treble) and I felt I had played quite well. But the fans who saw the highlights of the match later that evening on *Sportsnight* were led by John to think otherwise.

There were two instances towards the end of the game that John described as mistakes by me. On the first occasion, I think he used the phrase 'nightmare blunder', but I would argue until I am blue in the face that he made a totally wrong call. The incident came as a result of a Walsall cross from the right, which took a deflection and looked like going over my head. It was an exceptionally difficult ball to defend against because it was falling into the space between me and the goalkeeper, Bruce Grobbelaar, and Bruce never gave me a shout to let me know whether he was coming for it. At that moment, it was me against Walsall – I was actually backpedalling to try to get to the ball and I could see a Walsall forward moving to latch on to it. I remember thinking that if I could get a touch to the ball to divert it from the danger area, it would be all that anyone could possibly expect. That's what I did. Alan Hansen at his elegant best it wasn't, but the ball went wide of our goal and was cleared, and I thought, Sensational.

Needless to say, I was not amused when, while watching the incident on TV, John informed an audience of millions that I had blundered. He thought I had misjudged the flight of the ball.

It got worse. In the last minute, after I had cut out a Walsall through ball, I hit a back-pass from which they might easily have made it 3–2. As I turned towards Bruce and played the ball back to him, I did not see the Walsall player for whom the initial pass had been intended continuing his run on my blind side, and Bruce was forced into making a save that should have been unnecessary. At the time, I convinced myself it had not really been an error, on the premise that a First Division forward would not have made that run and that I had been caught out by the Walsall player's naïvety. I reasoned that even if John had been right to spotlight this as an error by me, it was given added significance by what he had said about my earlier header. I remember that I became even more irritated when the cameras panned on me as I was walking up the pitch after Bruce's save, and John remarked, 'Well, haven't they [Walsall] worked him hard tonight?'

I thought, What's he talking about? That wasn't working me hard – I hardly broke sweat all night.

The only way I can explain this oversensitive reaction is that the previous season, I had gone through a three-month bad spell and sensed that the Liverpool supporters had become disenchanted with my performances. Now, when I felt I was beginning to win them back, the last thing I needed was to be regarded as playing poorly again. It just goes to show how much television can influence people's thoughts that almost everyone I spoke to who had watched the recording seemed to want to throw an arm around my shoulder and commiserate with me. Even my mother-in-law, who has no interest in football, was caught up in the fuss. The following day, the women she worked with asked, 'What's gone wrong with Alan?' It also goes to show how players – me in particular – can make mountains out of molehills.

At the ground the following morning Graeme Souness inadvertently wound me up even more when he remarked, 'He [John Motson] was out of order. You played well.' I said: 'Right – and I'm going to tell him myself when I next see him.'

At this point, Joe Fagan, then Liverpool's manager, stepped in. 'No, you won't say anything to him, lad,' Joe told me. 'You'll do your talking through your performances on the pitch.'

The next Liverpool match covered by John was a European Cup tie against Benfica. I caught sight of him before the match in the dressing-room corridor and had half made up my mind to approach him when I saw Joe Fagan glaring at me. So that was the end of the matter. But the longer I played for Liverpool, the more such comments bugged me ... and the more I yearned for praise.

Perhaps the harshest criticism came from Emlyn Hughes, the former Liverpool and England captain, whose claims to fame after his retirement included a highly outspoken tabloid newspaper column. We had played together at Liverpool, of course, and I think the first thing that needs to be said was that he was a great player, a better player than he was often given credit for. His enthusiasm for the game, and Liverpool, was boundless. Sometimes, that enthusiasm was liable to run away with him – hence his nickname, 'Crazy Horse' – but there is no doubt that his will to win, and his underrated technical qualities, provided an essential ingredient to the blend of his team.

He was definitely one of the all-time Liverpool greats, although whether he was also among those held in the highest affection among his colleagues is another matter. Emlyn did not strike me as being a particularly popular figure in the Liverpool dressing room. I think he tended to come across as being a bit too full of himself, and he could be insensitive. Nevertheless, I got on OK with him. Indeed, at the start of my Liverpool career I spent a fair bit of time in his company because he and Terry McDermott were great horse-racing fans and I occasionally went to meetings with them. They were both very good company. I liked to think that we had a lot of professional respect for each other, especially as we shared the distinction of being Liverpool captain. Therefore, I feel I had every justification for being angry with Emlyn when he wrote in his column, in May 1988, two days after our shock FA Cup defeat by Wimbledon, that my knees had 'gone' and that I was finished as a top-class player. He was right about my knees, but I did not retire until two years later, and in the intervening years I helped Liverpool win the FA Cup and, in my last season, the Championship. But what really angered me was that his article appeared on the day of my Liverpool testimonial match.

He had retired as a player by then – he was a director of Hull City – and it was my wife, Janet, who drew my attention to the article on the morning of the match. I was still in bed when she came up the stairs with the paper shouting, 'Look at this.'

I have to give Emlyn full marks for nerve, because when Liverpool played at Hull in the FA Cup fifth round the following season, most of which I missed because of injury, he came up to me and started talking as if nothing had happened. 'How's it going?' he asked. 'How's the injury?'

'Oh, I'm finished,' I said, straight-faced.

He started to tell me that I should be optimistic. I then reminded him, 'No, Emlyn, you said I was finished. You were the one who said it, not me.' The penny dropped, Emlyn gave an embarrassed laugh and drifted away to talk to someone else.

I would love to be able to say that if I bumped into him tomorrow I would be happy to have a chat with him and buy him a drink. But I can't. While I can maybe forgive him for what he said, and when he said it, I cannot forget it.

There is no unwritten law that one Liverpool player, or ex-Liverpool player, should not criticize another. However, I would not dream of criticizing anyone in the way that he criticized me. I always try to be constructive, and my views are influenced by what I genuinely believe rather than what I feel I have to say to make an impact. I do not look at a match or an individual performance with an eye to finding something negative to say about it. I would much rather pick up something good. But the bottom line, as far as I am concerned, is that any assessment, either carried out by one person or a group, has to be balanced.

Hence the *Match of the Day* debates between Des Lynam and me over Tottenham's David Ginola. Des, in common with most football followers, takes an idealistic view of the game and, therefore, it is only to be expected that he has become captivated by Ginola's brilliant creative skills during the Frenchman's career in England. I admire Ginola too – he was far and away the best attacking player in Britain during the 1998/99 season. However, before George Graham's appointment as Tottenham manager, I felt that Ginola, while great on the ball, did not do enough off it in helping his team defensively. At Newcastle especially, he was too much of an individualist. In fact I felt that he played for himself. So while Des waxed lyrical about Ginola, I gave the other side of the picture.

I also came into conflict – albeit in a friendly way – with Leicester's manager Martin O'Neill over the performance of his England forward Emile Heskey in a match against Arsenal. Heskey, with his pace, power and willingness to attack the space behind the Arsenal defence, had an excellent game – as I acknowledged. However, as part of my analysis of his performance, I chose to compare him with Arsenal's Dennis Bergkamp, and the differences between the two in their first touch.

Afterwards, Martin suggested that, because of Bergkamp's stature, the comparison was not altogether fair on Heskey. However, I felt: 'That is the standard he has to aspire to.' My job is to make points like that. Moreover, the debates I have had with Des and other *Match of the Day* pundits are exactly the sort of arguments you will find taking place among groups of fans in their local, and I would suggest that this is an important part of the programme's appeal.

In the early days, there were times when I probably did go over the top, but the line between honesty and diplomacy has long been a difficult one to tread for TV football pundits. I would say that this has been particularly true for those on BSkyB during the company's emergence as the most dominant force in the battle for the exclusive television rights of major sports events. In football, BSkyB have obtained those rights not just because of the huge amounts of money they have been prepared to pay, but because they have been able to convince the selling parties of their ability to enhance the general appeal of the matches and the game. Of course, it is very much in BSkyB's interests to do that – to maximize their own income through their viewing figures and the advertising revenue that football attracts. There is nothing wrong in this, but it has created a dilemma at BSkyB over the extent to which the hype should be allowed to cloud its pundits sense of objectivity. I have to stress that I will always be grateful to BSkyB for the grounding they gave me in the business, and nobody has greater respect and admiration for Andy Gray than I do. Quite apart from the problems that his determination and aggression caused me on the occasions I played against him, I have always agreed with most of the points he has made in his analysis of matches. He is an extremely talented and versatile TV performer. At one time, though, it did seem to me that when Andy had to comment on a match that fell below expectations, he was in something of a verbal straitjacket. When I was working for BSkyB, I sensed that they would have liked me to be in one, too.

It has been tempting for the media to describe Andy and me as rivals – hence that article by John Fashanu. But I don't really see us like that. To me, we're just two former professional footballers who have found their ideal broadcasting niches and are having a good time. My own enjoyment has stemmed from working with a presenter of the calibre of Des Lynam – the best of the best – and with fellow pundits like Trevor Brooking, Mark Lawrenson and Jimmy Hill.

Jimmy, now with BSkyB, is a remarkable character. He has worn countless different hats in football and the last observation you could make about him is that he has been an under-achiever. One of his greatest claims to fame is that, as chairman of the Professional Footballers' Association, he organized and ran the successful fight to rid the game of the £20 a week maximum-wage restriction. As Coventry's manager, from 1961 to 1968, he steered the club from the old Third Division to the First. He is a qualified FA coach and referee, and he has been chairman of Coventry and Fulham and a director of Charlton. His CV in television is similarly impressive. Quite apart from his appearances as a pundit, which date back to the 1960s, he was head of sport at London Weekend Television from 1968 to 1972. He is nothing if not self-confident.

I love the story of a conversation involving Jimmy, Terry Venables and Des Lynam after England's 1990 World Cup semi-final defeat by West Germany. It was Bobby Robson's last match as England manager, and while the trio were having a drink with other members of the BBC team at a local hotel, Des asked Terry what he felt the criteria for a new England manager might be.

Before Terry could answer, Jimmy reeled off something like 10 qualities.

'Jimmy,' Des said, 'who in the world has all that going for him?'

'Me,' Jimmy replied. And, according to Des, he wasn't joking.

During another social gathering of our football troops, immediately after the 1994 World Cup final between Italy and Brazil, we were joined by John Birt, the BBC's director-general, who had popped into the hotel to congratulate us on our coverage of the competition. The final had been decided on a penalty shoot-out and when Birt asked me whether I had ever been involved in such a tiebreaker, and what it was like, I started telling him about the one in which Liverpool beat Roma in the 1984 European Cup final. While I was in full flow, however, Jimmy interrupted me to tell Birt about his own penalty shoot-out experience. It was very funny because, believe it or not, the game he was referring to was one of the staff friendly matches he used to play in when he was a member of the London Weekend Television side.

The number of stories told about Jimmy Hill could keep you amused for hours. My own favourite concerns the days when Jimmy had the job of closing the *Match of the Day* programme by giving viewers the address where they had to send their nominations for the Goal of the Month competition. He had to give them the address twice, and rather than writing the whole sentence twice, the person who had prepared his cue card had just added an appropriate instruction. Jimmy said: 'Goal of the Month, BBC Television, Wood Lane, Shepherds Bush, London, W12 – read twice.'

He can laugh at himself too. A couple of years ago, when Fulham and Gillingham were due to face an FA inquiry following a fracas between the players during a league match between the two clubs, Jimmy set out to back his claim that Fulham should not be held responsible with a video presentation of the game's flashpoints. He was clearly delighted with the job he had done. On the

Sunday before the FA probe, which was scheduled for the Friday, he said, 'I tell you what, they [the FA] should be selling tickets for this.'

When I saw him after the inquiry, he said, 'You'll never guess what happened on Friday.' He explained that midway through his presentation, when his case was going so smoothly that he even winked at a member of the disciplinary committee he knew well, everyone started laughing. Jimmy's wife had used the rest of the video to tape a Delia Smith cookery programme.

Jimmy is 70 now, and a few years ago he was suffering from cancer, but his continued energy never ceases to amaze me. He does more work for charity than anybody I know. While Jimmy, Des and I were sitting together in the studio before a recent England match, Jimmy got out his diary and challenged us to guess how many golf charity days he had agreed to attend over the next four months.

Des reckoned it was 28.

'No way,' I said. 'I would put it at fifteen.'

It was 49.

His energy was also apparent to me when we were in France for the 1998 World Cup finals. He thought nothing of getting up at seven to play a round of golf, taking part in the live broadcast of the match in the late afternoon and also the highlights programme at 12.50 at night. I could not have done that.

As a pundit, Jimmy provokes sharply contrasting reactions from fans and people in the game. Because of the age gap between him and many *Match of the Day* viewers, some perceive him as a bit out of touch. Compared to ex-professionals like Mark Lawrenson, Trevor Brooking and me, who concern ourselves with the technical aspects of the game, his views are certainly different: he asserted that Romania's success in the 1998 World Cup group matches could be attributed partly to their players having dyed their hair blond. According to Jimmy, it made it easier for them to see their passing options.

The fact is, though, that Jimmy makes a lot of interesting, valid points on the game. Where he suffers in terms of the public perception of him is that the positions he takes can be quite extreme. Thus, when he gets something wrong, it stands out. There are few grey areas. If he does not hit the bullseye, he is liable to miss by a mile. Yet that is his greatest television strength. Irrespective of what you might think of his opinions, he is always entertaining. I would love to think that I will be in as good shape at 70 as he is.

I have added other strings to my television bow since signing my first contract as a *Match of the Day* and *Sportsnight* analyst at the end of the 1991/92 season, notably with my two documentaries on football and one on the history of the Masters championship in golf. The latter, *The Magic of the Masters*, was one of the greatest experiences of my life because it brought me face to face with my true sporting heroes – Jack Nicklaus, Arnold Palmer, Gary Player *et al*. The fact that the BBC paid a golf nut like me to present it was great – I would gladly have paid *them* to be involved in a programme like that.

However, despite my enjoyment of such diversions from my basic BBC commitments, I have no ambition to take them much further. My philosophy has always been,

'Stick to what you're good at.' I think my main strengths are my knowledge of football and my ability to reveal aspects of it that the average supporters do not see. For *Match of the Day*, I watch the game from the studio in London on a Saturday afternoon, then decide on the theme of my analysis and spend maybe an hour with members of the technical staff organizing the parts of the recording that I want to use to illustrate my points. I usually go back to my hotel for a meal and to get changed, then return to the studio at about 9.15 p.m., an hour before our 'kick-off'. My stint when the cameras are rolling is not as easy as it might appear. However, the terms of reference of my role are very straightforward, and that suits me perfectly. I know that the more I try to stretch myself professionally, the more I would worry about it, and that just isn't for me.

The fact that I feel comfortable with the BBC partly explains why I turned down the chance to follow Des Lynam to ITV in the summer of 1999. Des's departure did worry me, as did the fact that the BBC had been left with no live matches in the major competitions following BSkyB's success in gaining the rights for all the Uefa Cup ties involving English teams. It was difficult to avoid feeling that the BBC, with their opportunities to use me becoming increasingly limited, might look upon me as surplus to requirements when my contract expired in 2001. This is when the BBC's agreement to screen Premiership and FA Cup highlights is due to end and the way things had been going, it seemed problematic to me that even these commitments would be renewed.

However, my concern about my future was lifted

when, shortly after Des's move, the BBC gave me a new five-year contract.

The BBC has a fantastic tradition for its coverage of major sporting events, but, as is emphasized by Manchester United's decision to pull out of this season's FA Cup, tradition does not talk anywhere near as loud as money these days.

The amount of dosh offered by BSkyB has been particularly impressive. It was at the time of my decision to sign an exclusive contract with the Beeb, at the end of the 1991/92 season, that BSkyB hit the football jackpot by securing the rights to screen Premiership matches live, at ITV's expense. BSkyB, who paid £380 million for a five-year deal, which was to be followed by £670 million for a four-year contract from the 1997/98 season, already had the rights to the live transmissions of FA Cup and England matches. They have since made it a clean domestic sweep by adding Football League and League Cup games to their portfolio – a fantastic situation for someone like Andy Gray.

ITV have bought the next biggest slice of the cake, and in terms of live games, the BBC has ended up at the bottom of the table.

One aspect of this, which is seen as a disadvantage for people like me, concerns the amount of 'space' that BSkyB are able to devote to football. While I get only four minutes' talking time on *Match of the Day* – three minutes for my analysis and one minute for my overview – the BSkyB sages inevitably get oceans of it. However, I feel that having too little time to discuss a match is better than having too much. More frustrating for the BBC team, perhaps, is that BSkyB have a considerably higher number of cameras at a live match than those used on *Match of the Day*. Not only this, but BSkyB's technology is more sophisticated.

Yet I have never felt that I would be better off elsewhere, partly because of my employer's attitude to me. The person who initially signed me for the BBC was Brian Barwick, then the *Match of the Day* producer. When he left to join ITV as their head of sport, it was felt that he might attempt to take me with him. Although it was only a rumour, the BBC responded by improving the terms of my contract – unprompted by me. For someone as neurotic about his ability as I am, that gesture meant a great deal to me.

The other reason I've been glad to be with the BBC is that the average number of viewers for a Premiership match on BSkyB is around 1 million, while the audience for *Match of the Day* is some 6 million. Moreover, BSkyB, unlike the terrestrial companies, has not been able to provide live coverage of the World Cup and European Championship finals. In France '98, England's matches attracted a BBC audience that ranged from 11 million to 24 million – figures that BSkyB can only dream about.

Of course, one of the drawbacks in such a wide exposure is that there are few places to hide when you make a mistake. People still have a go at me over my clanger about Manchester United, when I said that they had too many youngsters in their team to win the Championship. Viewers also delight in reminding me of my howlers in phraseology, as well as football judgement. Early in my TV career, I remember being embarrassed at having described

Liverpool's defending as 'criminal', but unquestionably my major *faux pas* came in my half-time analysis of the Argentina–Nigeria match in the 1994 World Cup finals, when I drew attention to the poor positioning of a defender by stating: 'He wants shooting for being in that position.' It was a phrase Phil Thompson had often used when we played together at Liverpool, and I had used it then as well, but it was the first time that it had sprung from my lips on television – and I could hardly have picked a worse time for it to happen.

Just a few days earlier, a shadow had been cast over the competition when the Colombian central defender, Andres Escobar – the scorer of an own goal in Colombia's 2–1 defeat by the United States – was shot dead in his home town of Medellín. Strangely, even after I made the comment, the folly of it did not immediately register with me. I only realized what I had done when, towards the end of half-time, Bob Wilson gave an update on the Escobar situation.

I remember thinking, Oh, my God, what have I said? and feeling a shiver go up my spine. Nobody on the programme said anything to me about it. In fact, when I tried to apologize to Brian Barwick, he admitted that he hadn't noticed it. When I told him what I'd said, his reaction was: 'Are you sure?'

The antennae of managers, coaches and players are more sensitive. Alex Ferguson of Manchester United seems particularly touchy about media criticism. He fired on all cylinders at Jimmy Hill and me a few years ago, after Jimmy condemned Eric Cantona's conduct. Alex described Jimmy as a 'prat', and suggested that Jimmy and

I were pro-Liverpool and anti-Manchester United. I got a fair bit of pleasure out of reminding Alex – through an article in the *Observer* – that he himself could have been accused of prejudice when he left me out of the Mexico squad in favour of selecting players with whom he was more familiar, and that TV pundits, like football managers, cannot please everybody.

I incurred the displeasure of Glenn Hoddle when he was Chelsea's manager: I claimed that Chelsea should have taken off their defender Terry Phelan earlier than they did in their 2–1 FA Cup semi-final defeat against Manchester United in 1996. Phelan sustained a hamstring injury in that match, and I felt that the extent to which his mobility was affected was a major factor in Chelsea conceding the second goal.

Hoddle, however, countered by suggesting that, as I had never been a manager myself – at the 'sharp end', as he called it – my opinion did not count. I found it ironic when Hoddle appeared twice on television shortly afterwards to discuss the teams with the best chance of winning the Championship and the European Champions League. By his logic, he should not have been involved in either programme. As far as his own English Championship record was concerned, it was tempting for me to point out: 'All he can talk about is what it's like to finish in the middle of the table.' Also, he had competed in the European Cup only once, when he was with Monaco, and they did not win the trophy.

Like Ferguson, Joe Kinnear has also accused *Match of the Day* pundits of prejudice. During the series of matches between his Wimbledon team and Tottenham in the opening months of 1999, when they faced each other five times in three weeks, Kinnear described us as 'Muppets' on the grounds of our so-called bias towards David Ginola, our star 1998 World Cup panellist.

I was on holiday for the opening two matches, the first of which – a 0–0 draw in the league – produced controversy over the claim that David was a 'diver'. David was involved in four incidents where he went down when being challenged in or around the penalty area. While George Graham insisted that the referee had been wrong not to give Spurs at least one penalty, Kinnear claimed that Ginola tried to con the official. The replays of the incidents on *Match of the Day* that night proved that the referee had been right, and Trevor Brooking had no compunction about saying so.

The following weekend Kinnear seemed to have forgotten this, when David scored a great goal to give Tottenham a 1–1 draw against Wimbledon in the FA Cup fourth round. He was upset that the *Match of the Day* team made David's performance the focal point of their assessment of the game, and ignored the work of the Wimbledon defender, Kenny Cunningham, in limiting him to only a handful of opportunities. But, in view of the arguments surrounding David's sense of sportsmanship and his ability, the BBC were justified in spotlighting him. For most footballer followers, his display was the major talking-point.

Anyone who knows anything about the dressing-room culture at Wimbledon will have appreciated that there was more to Kinnear's outburst than met the eye. Wimbledon are brilliant at motivating players through making them feel that their ability is not appreciated by outsiders. They have an 'everybody is against us' mentality and, when Kinnear was manager, he didn't miss a trick in ensuring that this chip-on-the-shoulder element is maintained.

The glamorous image of superstars like David Ginola is the very antithesis of what a club with Wimbledon's limited financial resources is all about. It pays Wimbledon to imbue their team with a feeling of resentment against such stars. Indeed, this aspect of Wimbledon was seen again in the third match against Tottenham, when Kinnear openly poured scorn on David as he limped off the field with a hamstring injury.

I do not like that sort of behaviour, but knowing what lies behind it – the development of Wimbledon's wonderful team spirit – I find it difficult to get on my high horse about it.

As I have said, I have mixed feelings about that word 'cheating' in connection with players who, like Ginola, are accused of bending the rules to gain penalties and free kicks. But I have to concede that it has got out of hand. In the past, this has not been ingrained in our football culture as deeply as it has been in other parts of Europe. That is why, when I played in the European Cup for Liverpool, the management always stressed the importance of keeping the opposition out of our penalty area. Now, as a result of the influx of so many foreign players into English football, this aspect of the game has been taken to the extreme.

The trend is reflected by the amount of time TV pundits spend in studying incidents on a video screen, to ascertain whether the apparent fouls really are fouls – and, of course, the ridiculously high number of bookings and sendings-off. The obvious difficulty for a referee and his two assistants in always making the right decisions has led to a campaign for a system whereby they could be helped by television technology while a match is in progress. This idea is already being investigated by the game's governing bodies who see much more value in it as a means of ending controversies on whether or not the ball has crossed the goal-line. It has yet to be streamlined, but I think that the introduction of television technology to help referees is inevitable.

For me, the play-acting that goes on reached a farcical level in the 1998 World Cup finals. At one time, forwards thought nothing of trying to make challenges by opposing defenders look like fouls, but in France '98, instead of defenders bumping into the forwards, a number of the forwards deliberately bumped into them.

Some strikers are better actors than others. In English football, there is little doubt that David Ginola attracts the most Oscar nominations. This is not entirely fair because when one is dribbling through a defence at the speed with which he does, it is only to be expected that the merest touch is liable to knock you off balance. Nonetheless, it's difficult to avoid the conclusion that David doesn't stay on his feet as much as he could.

From a defender's point of view, it's not easy to avoid physical contact; nor is it easy for a referee to differentiate between an accidental or premeditated clash. For instance, in the 1998/99 Coventry–Liverpool game at Highfield Road, Liverpool's defender Vegard Heggem conceded a free kick and was booked for apparently obstructing Darren Huckerby. The contact occurred because Heggem could not get out of the way. I did not think he ran into Huckerby.

In these situations, referees are inclined to give the attacking player the benefit of the doubt. Unfortunately for David Ginola, and his Tottenham team, his reputation for pulling the wool over referees' eyes has caused him to lose that advantage to a great extent. I have an enormous admiration for David – apart from his skills, I like him immensely as a person. He is warm and engaging. I have to admit, though, that when the BBC hired him as the top-of-the-bill act on their 1998 World Cup panel, following the defection of our Euro '96 star Ruud Gullit to ITV, I felt that it would prove a disaster.

While dazzling us with his Gallic charm and charisma, David hardly gave the impression of looking upon the job as something that was going to transform his life. Not surprisingly, he had all manner of public commitments to fulfil during France '98, and as far as his BBC role was concerned, he seemed laid-back to the point of being almost comatose, which was bound to prove disconcerting to someone as uptight about it as I was. This, together with the fact that he was often seen with an entourage of agents and assistants, prompted us to nickname him 'Diva David'.

My first meeting with him came a few months before the World Cup, when he and I were involved in filming the trailer for the BBC's coverage of the finals in Paris. We were told that we would be needed for two sessions over two days and the first one – on the studio roof – went smoothly enough. However, when we were reminded that we were required again at eight the next morning, David's expression and his body language clearly signalled that he was not happy.

'We can't do it,' his French agent remarked. 'David's got a press conference to attend.'

He turned up for the shoot, but not until eight forty-five. It took about 10 minutes, and then he was off.

Later, when Niall Sloane, the editor of the programme, Des Lynam and I were joking about what might happen with David during the World Cup, I said, 'Let me tell you something about professional footballers. If one of them is giving you trouble on day one, he will also be giving you trouble on day thirty-six.'

They became concerned when they tried to give him a pre-World Cup 'feel' for our football operation by arranging for him to be involved in our coverage of the Uefa Cup final. They sent a car to pick him up from his home at 5.30 p.m., only for David to relay a message that he could not make it.

As it turned out, David did well for us in the World Cup. Having him in the BBC fold proved successful, especially among female viewers. The number of e-mails he received from them via the studios was mind-boggling.

But the people who had the closest dealings with him – like Niall Sloane – did not emerge from the experience without a few grey hairs. The opening match of France '98 was Scotland against Brazil. When I arrived at the studios, I saw Niall in a heated discussion with David's French agent. 'No, no, it can't happen,' Niall was telling him. 'It won't happen. I will not allow it to happen.' David was also working for French TV, and his agent wanted him to leave us at half-time and go to the national stadium – on a motorbike – to comment on the game for them. Niall must have spent the entire World Cup living on his nerves, because while David never missed the programme, his list of other commitments, combined with his disarmingly casual nature, meant that you could never relax.

I have two especially fond memories of David. The first concerned the France–Paraguay match, when he came to the studio straight from a game of golf, wearing shorts and a T-shirt. Within a few minutes of the game starting, he had fallen asleep. He snoozed for about 20 minutes and only woke up as a result of his glasses sliding down his nose and hitting his chin. The second was my interview with him for my documentary *Football Millionaires*. That day, David had to attend two evening engagements in central London, a reception at the Foreign Office followed by the première of the film *Star Trek Insurrection*, and it was arranged that I would pick him up at his home, in a chauffeur-driven limousine, and conduct the interview with him during the journey back into London.

It was a nightmare. We were held up in heavy traffic *en route* to David's house and by the time we arrived, there was no way he was going to make his first appointment and the other seemed doubtful. In David's position, I would have been frantic. But when he opened the door to us he was in his pyjamas, and he said, 'Come in, let's have a drink.'

I thought, This man has style with a capital S.

Eventually we got going for the première, and David, for all those 'Diva' characteristics, was as cooperative and helpful to me as any of the figures who took part in that programme. Of all the players in Britain, he is arguably the easiest to envy. He has outstanding ability. He is good-looking, intelligent and articulate. He is wealthy. He is more like a film star than a football star.

But I would not relish being in his shoes. Because of the attention they attract I would not relish being in any of the leading players' shoes.

# **17** In the Spotlight

Since my retirement in 1991 English football has changed beyond recognition. Apart from the Hillsborough disaster in 1989, another factor in the metamorphosis was the public interest created by England's stirring performances in the 1990 World Cup finals in Italy and, more specific- ally, the extent to which Paul Gascoigne captured the emotions of millions with his tears after his booking in the epic semi-final battle with West Germany. It was on the back of this powerful new wave of support for the game that the First Division clubs broke away from the Football League to form an élite league of their own – the Premiership – under the auspices of the Football Association; and landed the BSkyB television deal which has brought them the biggest sums of money and the highest public profile in their histories.

Today football is far more of an industry than a game. Clubs have become multifaceted business empires. They represent a licence to print money. The players have benefited enormously, but not the ordinary fans, who have been frozen out by high admission prices and the emphasis of clubs on the corporate aspect of their customer base. The players are under greater pressure, though, not least because of the intense media focus on the game. They are living in a goldfish bowl. In some cases, I feel sorry for them.

The pressures of professional football at the highest level were chillingly documented in *Ronaldo*, a book that investigated the sensational background to the young Brazilian icon's disappointing performance in the 1998 World Cup final. Some passages in the book invite the view that Ronaldo, bearing the hopes and dreams of millions on his shoulders and being given prescribed drugs to ease the pain of thigh and knee injuries, was on the verge of a nervous breakdown. According to the author, Wensley Clarkson, a member of the Brazilian squad told him that 'Ronaldo was often shaking with fear' during the build-up to the final against France.

On the day of the game, eight hours before the 9 p.m. kick-off, Clarkson writes: 'Ronaldo was sleeping in his hotel room. His room-mate, Roberto Carlos, was listening to his Walkman when, he later claimed, he was disturbed by the muffled sound of Ronaldo apparently having some kind of fit. Ronaldo turned pale, began sweating profusely and then suffered convulsions, with his arms flexed and hands misshapen by the nervous tension.' I had not been remotely in his class as a player, and hadn't played in a match anywhere near as important as a World Cup final, so I was never in that state, but in my own small way, I can relate to the torment Ronaldo suffered. I can also under-stand Peter Schmeichel's decision to retire as a Manchester

United player at the relatively young age for a goalkeeper of 34. The mental and physical 'burn-out' factors in playing for such a high-profile club are enormous, as reflected by the problems experienced by players like Tony Adams, Paul Merson, Paul Gascoigne and Stan Collymore.

I cannot emphasize enough that 'pressure' is a word to which I have always been hyper-sensitive. I am a person whose life must be as straightforward as possible. When it gets complicated, I get jumpy – and for me there can be complications in all manner of apparently straightforward things. My brother still teases me about the time he took me to a Chinese restaurant, when I was about 15, and I did not want to try anything on the menu. All I wanted was sausages and chips, the food I was used to. Until I met Janet, I never ate vegetables. There are still some foods I shy away from, but she doesn't take no for an answer. She slices them up into tiny pieces so that I don't know what I'm eating.

It took her what seemed an eternity to persuade me to try a skiing holiday. Once she cracked it, she found that I wanted to spend more time on the piste than Jean-Claude Killy. It is a standing joke with Janet that, despite the amount of time we have lived in Southport, I might just as well be a total stranger to the town when it comes to finding my way around. I know exactly how to get around a football field, but Southport is another matter.

The biggest nightmare for her concerns my dread of instruction manuals. Most people might get stuck at step three or four, but I fall down at step one. In the circumstances, it has been great for me that Janet is a much more practical, methodical person than I am. It has also been great for me that she values our family life as much as I do.

I first met her when she was working as a part-time receptionist in the hotel that Liverpool used as their eve-of-match base, and we started going out together after bumping into each other at a nightclub. By then, she was working in a building society, and her main interest was art. She did not know anything about football and even when I became a successful player, my involvement in the game was where her interest in it began and ended. She would come to watch all the home matches in which I played, but for her the main attraction was the opportunity to talk to the wives and girlfriends of the other players. After one match in which I scored one of my rare goals, someone remarked, 'Your Alan did well to score that goal.' This puzzled Janet because she had been so engrossed in a conversation with the girl sitting next to her that she was unaware I had scored.

Being married to someone like that does much for one's sense of perspective. So, too, does having a son like Adam – the greatest mimic of me on TV I have heard – and a daughter like Lucy: they have remained unaffected by my fame. When I am with them and Janet, I can relax like any other family man. This means more to me than anything else. Indeed, the aspect of my life that I probably dislike most is being away from home.

It strikes me that being able to lead a normal family life is more difficult for the top players of today – particularly if your name is Alan Shearer, David Beckham or Michael Owen. I interviewed all three for *Football Millionaires* and, although I didn't spend a great deal of time with them, I couldn't help thinking that in some ways they should be pitied rather than envied.

This particularly applied to David and Michael, who are both younger than Alan and who are attracting more attention than is good for lads of their age. They are the equivalent of pop stars. There are few places where they can go in Britain without being mobbed. Pop stars, though, can hide themselves from the limelight by going away for a few months, but the scope for professional footballers to do that is much more limited. David has the added problem of having a Spice Girl as his wife.

One common theme running through my conversations with Alan, David and Michael – and, indeed, all the players featured in the programme – was their dislike of the fierce media spotlight on the game and themselves. The coverage of the game by newspapers, radio and television has become overbearing and intrusive. For today's professional footballers, cooperating with the media is recognized as a more important part of their jobs than it was when I was a player, but many mistrust it. Sensitive about the possibility of their comments being taken out of context and rebounding on them, they make talking to the press seem as stressful as walking across a minefield.

But the aspect of their lives that really caused me to wince was the energy they expend in personal appearances emanating from their lucrative endorsement, advertising and merchandising contracts. Alan, David and Michael earn much more off the field than they do on it, and although they take care to limit their commitments – or the time they have to spend fulfilling promotional obligations – I should imagine that their cut-off points can easily become blurred.

Contracts with kit manufacturers are a major source of outside income for the top players. Alan Shearer reportedly has a 14-year deal with Umbro worth £25 million, while David Beckham's contract with Adidas is said to bring him £1.3 million a year. I never earned more than £7,000 a season from my own links in this field with Puma. Though the contract was cancelled when injury forced me out of action for most of the 1988/89 season, I carried on wearing the boots until the end of the season without any payment – even in the FA Cup final – then fell out with Puma before the start of the following season when they offered me a new contract worth just £3,000. Between then and my retirement in 1991, I had no boot deal.

The first of my two interviews with David took place at the launch of his association with Adidas, a glitzy presentation that involved the Manchester United and England star being unveiled amid a cloud of dry ice like the new model of a top-of-the-range sports car. He did not look very comfortable but had it been me, I would have been hiding in the toilet.

The major downside to being in the boots of a David Beckham is that so much is expected of you, and a lot of those expectations are quite unreasonable. Also, there is a tendency in Britain for people to build up sportsmen and sportswomen and then, when they are at the top, try to knock them down. David is an obvious target because of his glamorous lifestyle and the stature of his club – hence the stick he took after his sending-off in the 1998 World

320

Cup quarter-final against Argentina. The offence that brought him a red card – a retaliatory flick of his foot at Diego Simeone after the Argentinian had knocked him to the ground – was silly and petulant, and arguably the biggest factor in England's defeat.

His rashness was seen again with the challenge that caused him to be sent off in the World Club Championship in Brazil.

However, I would say that 99 per cent of professional footballers have done things which they have regretted and when it comes to keeping their heads in the heat of battle, some inevitably find it easier to master this than others. While David has deserved to be criticized, the 'stick' he has taken has been well over the top. I have never known any player who has experienced as much abuse from spectators as he does. In the circumstances, his performance level has been remarkable.

He has found himself under a lot of pressure in the England team, too, with people expecting him to do what Paul Gascoigne did for the national team. Yet the truth is that David, a talented attacking player, does not have Gazza's skill on the ball – none of the present England players do. Beckham's greatest asset is the quality of his crosses and long, diagonal passes. He is the best crosser of a ball in the country – superior even to Ginola because, while the Frenchman can get the ball into the middle equally well with either foot, he does not put the same pace on it that Beckham does. When David Beckham fires the ball across, any striker must feel that Christmas has come early for him.

So, at this stage of his career, I believe that David is far better suited to playing on the right side of midfield than he is to operating in the central area.

Paul Gascoigne's decline has unquestionably been one of the disappointments of the 1990s. It seems perverse that his career started to go downhill so soon after the 1990 World Cup finals. The obvious turning-point for him was his rash tackle on Gary Charles in the 1991 Tottenham–Nottingham Forest FA Cup final, which put him out of action with a cruciate ligament injury for more than a year. Physically he was never the same after that. His loss of pace was obvious. Previously, when Gascoigne took the ball past an opponent, he would hold out his arms to keep the player away from him. When he started playing again after the Cup final, he was doing that before he had gone past him. For me, that told its own story, and it became even more pronounced when Gazza returned to the game after the further blow of his broken leg at Lazio.

It speaks volumes for his talent, his touch and his passing that he was still able to do well for England in Euro '96 and, more recently, for Middlesbrough in the Premiership. It is not for me to comment on the factors in his private life – the heavy drinking, the bouts of depression and the stormy marriage – that have clearly contributed to his decline. I do not know him personally but I have met a number of people who do, and not one has had a bad word to say about him. They all talked in glowing terms about his down-to-earth nature and willingness to contribute to the dressing-room spirit. Gascoigne is the sort of person who when driving down a road and seeing a bunch of schoolkids playing football is liable to stop his car and join them. How many other professional footballers of his class would do that?

Some have felt that one player with the potential to fill the Gazza role in the England team is Steve McManaman. In going past players with the ball, Steve fits the bill as well as anyone. But while he could take on three or four defenders in the Premiership, it is a different matter in international football – which was also borne out by John Barnes when he played for Liverpool and England. Unfortunately for Steve, and for England, he is not as good a passer of the ball as Gazza, and lacks Gazza's scoring ability. While it is possible that playing for his new club, Real Madrid, will make him even better, I would love to have seen Steve remain at Liverpool.

I cannot be hypocritical about this: had I been offered the sort of money that Steve had dangled before him, I would have gone to Real. I saw nothing wrong with his decision in financial terms. What did slightly irritate me, though, was his assertion that he wanted to leave in order to 'broaden' himself. He was 'ambitious', he said. This is the song that most players sing when they go abroad but my own view is that it has much more to do with the money. In my experience, only one player has come clean about this: Graeme Souness, when he moved from Liverpool to Sampdoria. I would have thought that the best way in which Steve could have shown his ambition would have been to stay at Liverpool and help them win the Championship. But, then, I would say that because of the depth of my Liverpool roots, wouldn't I?

Since my retirement the decline of Liverpool as a Championship-winning team has been a sore point. I try to be impartial on *Match of the Day*, but it is asking the impossible for me to be totally detached when I'm watching my old team. I'm not ashamed to admit that when Liverpool score I cheer. But that is not to say I can't appreciate the achievement of Manchester United in taking over from Liverpool in the 1990s as the top side in the country, not to mention the success of Arsenal, Leeds and Blackburn, the other title-winners during this period.

The irony of United's run under Alex Ferguson is that Liverpool were the team who set the standards in Britain when he was a manager in Scotland, and he has said that Liverpool's 5–0 European Cup win over his Aberdeen team in 1981 was one of the most defining experiences in his learning process. In order to build a successful team, it is essential to start from the back. Therefore, the turning-point for United was when they got Peter Schmeichel, Gary Pallister and Steve Bruce together. They'd had good goalkeepers before but Schmeichel, whose ability in one-against-one situations alone must have been worth 12 points a season to them, was in a class of his own.

The other pieces in the United jigsaw, of course, have included Eric Cantona and the talented home-produced players – Phil and Gary Neville, Nicky Butt, David Beckham, Paul Scholes and Ryan Giggs. I do not think there is any need for me to explain what made Cantona so special, although his ability in the air is worth highlighting. This tended to go unnoticed because of his ingenious passing and shooting skills, but Cantona, tall and powerfully built, was also a great person to have going for a cross at the back post.

That United were able to bring so many products of

their youth system into the first team was a massive bonus for them. Having come up through the ranks together at Old Trafford, the Neville brothers, Butt, Beckham, Scholes and Giggs – all internationals – have provided the sense of unity that I consider essential for any team with hopes of consistent success. United are quite different in style from my Liverpool teams: they defend deeper than we did and play more of a counter-attacking game. They are brilliant at it, and quite apart from being effective, they are also exciting to watch.

Not surprisingly, the most common questions fired at me since United's treble achievement are how I would rate them in comparison with the Liverpool teams I played for, and whether I would single them out as the best of all England's post-war teams. It's difficult to make such a judgement because there are so many different aspects to the debate. One can only go on the track records of teams – and, of course, even that criterion can be misleading. If one accepts that the true test of any team's stature is what they achieve in European competition, you have to say that the English teams were stronger when Liverpool was at the top than they are today. Liverpool stood out from the rest in the Championship at a time when English teams were riding the crest of a wave in Europe. In Liverpool's 1979/80 and 1981/82 title-winning seasons, Nottingham Forest and Aston Villa won the European Cup. Throughout the 1970s and 1980s, Liverpool also had to contend with a number of teams who had made their mark in the European Cup-winners Cup and Uefa Cup.

The Championship competition for Liverpool was

particularly strong in the season in which Villa qualified for the European Cup. We won the trophy that season – 1980/81 – and also got our hands on the League Cup, but finished fifth in the First Division. In addition to Villa, the other sides in front of us included Ipswich, who won the Uefa Cup, and Arsenal, who had reached the Cup-winners Cup final the previous season. In fourth place were West Bromwich Albion, Uefa Cup quarter-finalists with Manchester City in 1979. Nottingham Forest were seventh, and Tottenham, who were to get to the Uefa Cup semi-finals the following season, were tenth.

In the 1990s, the only successful European teams that Manchester United have had to contend with have been Arsenal and Chelsea, who, like them, have lifted the Cup-winners Cup – the easiest of the three European tournaments.

However, whatever one's views on this, nobody can deny that Manchester United's achievements last season were phenomenal.

I thought the way in which Alex Ferguson rotated his squad was brilliant. When I was a player, managers would be horrified if you suggested they might be better off not picking their best teams for the big matches. But, as United's results emphasized, Ferguson played the rotation game to perfection. Perhaps the most impressive examples were his decisions to leave both his outstanding strikers, Andy Cole and Dwight Yorke, out of the starting line-up for the FA Cup semi-final replay against Arsenal – they were replaced by Teddy Sheringham and Ole Gunnar Solksjaer – and, even more surprisingly, putting Yorke on the substitutes' bench for the FA Cup final against Newcastle.

Remember, this was the FA Cup final – the most glamorous match in the English football calendar – and that Yorke, bought from Aston Villa for a club record £12 million, had been one of United's most effective players. As if to underline Ferguson's superb management skills, Yorke didn't seem to make any fuss at all about the decision. It was the same with all the United players involved in Ferguson's rotation policy.

If there is anyone else who can be given special praise for United's success it is their captain, Roy Keane, whose leadership qualities did so much to lift them when they were going through their inevitable bad periods in matches. I particularly recall the 2–1 win over Tottenham with which United clinched the title on the last day of the season. United went a goal down in the 24th minute, and for most of the first half did not play well. But the example set by the indomitable Keane gradually took them to a different level. Andy Cole and David Beckham were the scorers of the 42nd- and 47th-minute goals that brought United their success. But the most influential figure was Keane.

Manchester United have evolved into a team with a bit of everything. I don't think that Arsenal, their closest Championship rivals, have yet acquired as many strings to their bow as United, especially in attack, but they certainly seem to be heading in the right direction. Arsenal's development under the management of Arsene Wenger emphasizes the importance of teams making defence their first priority.

Having a back four of the calibre of Lee Dixon, Tony Adams, Steve Bould or Martin Keown and Nigel

Winterburn has bought the Gunners time to fine-tune their play in other areas. It has meant that, even with men of average ability in front of them, Arsenal would have held their own at least at the top level. The result is that today's Arsenal, in addition to being effective, are also a joy to watch.

The Arsenal team who won the Championship–FA Cup double in 1998, with Frenchmen Emmanuel Petit and Patrick Vieira and Dutchmen Dennis Bergkamp and Marc Overmars, had greater attacking quality than the sides I used to play against. Petit and Vieira form the most complete midfield partnership I have seen in years. Since my retirement, the only other pair of central midfielders who have come close to matching them have been Roy Keane and Paul Ince when they were together at Manchester United. Like Keane and Ince, Petit and Vieira are both tenacious, hard-working players, who can be seen making a tackle in their own box one minute and creating a scoring chance at the other end the next. The difference is that Petit, a key member of France's 1998 World Cup-winning side (and a player who joined Arsenal as a centre-half), has the edge on all of them in technical ability. If I had to pick just one current Premiership player whom I would have liked to see in any of the Liverpool teams I played for it would be Petit. How they need players like him now. Last season they also needed to be stronger in defence and have a big centre-forward to take some of the weight off Michael Owen and Robbie Fowler. Of all the strikers in the Premiership, these two would be the first I would want in my side if I were a manager.

As England's manager, Glenn Hoddle attracted a lot of criticism when he suggested that Owen was not a natural goal-scorer. I think the comment rebounded on Hoddle because he did not explain it properly, but if my interpretation of what he was trying to say is right, then I agree with him. The way I look upon it is that some great goal-scorers are more natural exponents of the art than others. Therefore, while Owen is liable to end his career as one of the highest scorers in the game, I would suggest that Fowler's record will be better. I am hard-pressed to think of any striker I have seen who creates space for shooting chances as he does. If I had to select the outstanding piece of skill produced by a striker in the 1998/99 season, it would have to be the Fowler shot that almost brought him an astonishing goal against Sheffield Wednesday. When the ball broke to him, just inside the area, there seemed no way he could do anything with it. The ball had got stuck under his feet, and with Wednesday defenders bearing down on him I thought he would do well just to retain possession. Yet he managed to move his feet quickly enough to get in a shot, which went just over the bar. If that had gone in, it would have been the goal of the season, no question.

The problem in comparing Owen with Fowler is that Owen is at an earlier stage of his development. Every time I have seen him, he has produced something that I had felt was missing in his game. At one time, I felt that when he went forward with the ball he did not see his best passing options, but he quickly proved me wrong on that, just as he did when I thought that he did not vary his shots enough. Every question I have raised about him, he has answered.

The one part of his game that has never been in doubt has been his pace: it's frightening. In the 1998/99 season, though, this could also have been said to have been a handicap to Liverpool. Owen's pace meant that many teams defended deep against them, and Liverpool, denied the scope to get the ball behind them, compounded the problem by being too slow and deliberate in their build-up play. If Championship points had been awarded to the team who strung the most passes together, Liverpool would have won the title by a mile. Their football was pretty to watch, but it was not getting them anywhere in terms of results. That's why I was disappointed that they did not have a big striker who could have given them an aerial option and helped make them more direct.

I thought Dion Dublin, who moved from Coventry to Aston Villa for £5 million, would have been ideal for Liverpool. Some might argue that it was a lot of money to pay for a 30-year-old, but Dublin is a player who has looked after himself and I would be surprised if he does not continue to play in top-class football until he is in his mid-thirties. Bearing in mind that Liverpool also lacked height in defence at the time he became available from Coventry, the other advantage of having him at Anfield was that he could also play at centre-half.

Had I been Liverpool manager, I might even have tried to pip Newcastle for the £7 million signing of Duncan Ferguson from Everton. Given the injury problems that kept him out of Newcastle's team, he would not have been much use to Liverpool in the 1998/99 season, but a fit Ferguson – or someone like him – could do wonders for Liverpool. He has the reputation of being a headstrong, volatile figure, but I think I would have been influenced more by his ability: he is by far the best centre-forward in the air in Britain. Ferguson, with his determination and aggression, is a handful for any central defender, not least those who have the same approach to the game and temperament that I did when I was playing for Liverpool.

As English football has become more sophisticated, those traditional-type British centre-forwards who relish bruising physical contact and have giant-sized hearts have become quite rare. Today I am certainly hard-pressed to think of one like Billy Whitehurst. I was told recently that Whitehurst is now running a pub near Barnsley. When I'm next in that area, I must go there, buy him a drink and tell him what a good player he was.

# List of Illustrations

Eat your heart out, Shearer! *Liverpool Daily Post & Echo Plc.*
Dribbling my way out of trouble. *Observer/Eamonn McCabe*
Winning the Milk Cup replay final 1983/84 season. *Liverpool Daily Post & Echo Plc.*
Rush scores, 1984 European Cup final. *Colorsport*
The climax to my first season as Liverpool captain. *Author's collection*

*SECOND PLATE SECTION*

Gary Lineker made me look a mug. *Colorsport*
Ian Rush beats Everton defender Kevin Ratcliffe. *Colorsport*
A tussle with Everton's Graeme Sharp. *Colorsport*
Goodbye, Wembley. *Bob Thomas/Popperfoto*
Hogging the trophy in the dressing room. *Colorsport*
Me guarding the trophy. *Colorsport*
Graeme Souness does my job. *Colorsport*
My Scotland appearance against Argentina. *Colorsport*
Hillsborough tributes at Anfield. *PA News*
John Barnes and I at a Hillsborough memorial service. *Mercury Press Agency Ltd*
Arsenal's Tony Adams. *Colorsport*
Emmanuel Petit. *Colorsport*
Billy Whitehurst. *Colorsport*
Karl-Heinz Rummenigge. *Colorsport*
David Beckham. *Colorsport*
Roy Keane. *Colorsport*
Jaap Stam. *Colorsport*
The best of all my team-mates. *Author's collection*

# Index

342

Rush, Ian, 87, 129, 143, 201, 220–2, 229, 232, 233, 236, 240, 267, 277

Russia, 242–3, 264–6. *See also* Union of Soviet Socialist Republics

Ryan, John, 171

Sacchi, Arrigo, 209

*Sack Race, The, see* television

St Mirren, 52

Salako, John, 152

Sammer, Mathias, 212, 214

Sampdoria, 203–4, 233, 258, 323

Sauchie, 14, 45, 48, 121, 123

Sauchie Athletic, 43, 52, 55, 56, 57–8, 69, 75, 83, 110

Sauchie Juniors, 56, 62, 78

Saunders, Tom, 29–30, 160

Savage, Robbie, 128

Schawpark, 55–60

Schmeichel, Peter, 134, 316–17, 324

Schofield, Mark, 289–90

Scholes, Paul, 119, 128, 324

school, *see* education

Scotland
AH plays for, 15, 51, 144, 199, 215, 228, 242–3, 251–2, 257–68
European Championship (1968), 42; (1971), 53; (1980), 262; (1982), 215; (1983), 266–7; (1987), 255; (1988), 252
Under-15, 45
Under-18, 45
Under-21, 67, 75
Under-23, 53, 67, 75
World Cup (1968), 42; (1982), 259, 263–6; (1986), 34, 267; (1998), 312

Scottish Boys' Championship (golf), 58, 60

Scottish Cup, 52–3

Scottish Junior Cup, 51

Scottish League Cup (1971), 54

Scottish Stroke-play Championship, 58, 59

Serginho, 264

Shankly, Bill, 50, 95–6, 99, 136, 140, 253, 255

Sharp, Graeme, 150, 197–9, 201, 239

Shearer, Alan, 143, 167, 193–4, 195, 200, 318–20

Sheedy, Kevin, 198, 239

Sheffield United, 11, 172

Sheffield Wednesday, 68, 70, 180, 204, 232, 329

Shengelia, Ramaz, 265–6